Economic Thought and Modernization in Japan

Economic Thought and Modernization in Japan

Edited by

Shiro Sugihara

Professor Emeritus, Kansai University and Professor Emeritus, Konan University, Japan

and

Toshihiro Tanaka

Professor Emeritus, Kwansei Gakuin University, Japan

IN ASSOCIATION WITH THE SOCIETY FOR THE HISTORY OF ECONOMIC THOUGHT, JAPAN

Edward Elgar
Cheltenham, UK • Northampton, MA, USA

Published by
Edward Elgar Publishing Limited
Glensanda House
Montpellier Parade
Cheltenham
Glos GL50 1UA
UK

Edward Elgar Publishing, Inc.
6 Market Street
Northampton
Massachusetts 01060
USA

HB
126
J2
E25
1998

A catalogue record for this book
is available from the British Library

Library of Congress Cataloguing in Publication Data

Economic thought and modernization in Japan / edited by Shiro
    Sugihara, Toshihiro Tanaka : in association with the Society for the
    History of Economic Thought, Japan.
        Includes index.
        1. Economics—Japan—History. 2. Japan—Economic policy.
    I. Sugihara, Shiro, 1920– . II. Tanaka, Toshihiro, 1929– .
    III. Society for the Study of History of Economic Doctrines (Japan)
    HB126.J2E25   1998
    330'.0952—dc21   98–21062
                                                                     CIP

ISBN 1 85898 624 9

Typeset by Manton Typesetters, 5–7 Eastfield Road, Louth, Lincolnshire LN11 7AJ, UK.
Printed and bound in Great Britain by MPG Books Ltd, Bodmin, Cornwall

Contents

Contributors   vii
Preface   ix
Toshihiro Tanaka
Introduction   Modernization and the development of economic
                thought in Japan   xi
                Shiro Sugihara

1   Trends in economic thought in the Tokugawa period   1
     Masamichi Komuro
2   Enlightenment and economic thought in Meiji Japan: Yukichi
     Fukuzawa and Ukichi Taguchi   23
     Jiro Kumagai
3   The Japanese social policy school: its formation and breakup   44
     Takashi Fujii
4   Two inquirers on the divide: Tokuzo Fukuda and Hajime
     Kawakami   60
     Takutoshi Inoue and Kiichiro Yagi
5   The debate on Japanese capitalism: the *Koza* faction and its
     perception of society   78
     Takaho Ando
6   General equilibrium theory and beyond: Yasuma Takata and Kei
     Shibata   97
     Takashi Negishi
7   Modernization and the studies of Adam Smith in Japan during
     and after World War II: Kazuo Okouchi, Zenya Takashima and
     Yoshihiko Uchida   117
     Satoshi Niimura
8   Economic development and economic thought after World War II:
     non-Marxian economists on development, trade and industry   131
     Aiko Ikeo
9   Economic development and economic thought after World War II:
     economic development and Marxian political economy   152
     Toshio Yamada

General bibliography   171
Name index   175
Subject index   179

Contributors

Takaho Ando, Nagoya University, Nagoya.
Takashi Fujii, Niigata University, Niigata.
Aiko Ikeo, Kokugakuin University, Tokyo.
Takutoshi Inoue, Kwansei Gakuin University, Nishinomiya, Hyogo.
Masamichi Komuro, Keio Gijuku University, Tokyo.
Jiro Kumagai, St Andrew's University, Osaka.
Takashi Negishi, Aoyama Gakuin University, Tokyo and president, the
    Society for the History of Economic Thought, Japan.
Satoshi Niimura, Okayama University, Okayama.
Shiro Sugihara, Professor Emeritus, Kansai University, Osaka and Konan
    University, Kobe and ex-president, the Society for the History of
    Economic Thought, Japan.
Toshihiro Tanaka, Professor Emeritus, Kwansei Gakuin University,
    Nishinomiya, Hyogo and ex-president, the Society for the History of
    Economic Thought, Japan.
Kiichiro Yagi, Kyoto University, Kyoto.
Toshio Yamada, Nagoya University, Nagoya.

Preface

Toshihiro Tanaka

The present volume is the first one of essays written in English and edited at the request of the Society for the History of Economic Thought, Japan. The society was founded in April 1950 with 123 initial members, and it has since grown into a well-established organization with more than 800 members. It is scheduled to celebrate the fiftieth anniversary of its founding in 2000.

In addition to the *Annals of the Society for the History of Economic Thought* since 1963, the *Newsletter* since 1992 and the two booklets of its history, *The Study of the History of Economic Thought in Japan*: *Ten Years of the Society for the History of Economic Thought* (1961) and *Thirty Years of the Society of the History of Economic Thought* (1980), the society has edited and published the following four volumes:

1. (1967) *Shihonron no Seiritsu* (The Formation of Das Kapital: Essays in Commemoration of the Centenary of Volume One), Tokyo: Iwanami Shoten.
2. (1976) *Kokuhuron no Seiritsu* (The Formation of the Wealth of Nations: Essays in Commemoration of the Bicentenary of its Publication), Tokyo: Iwanami Shoten.
3. (1984) *Nihon no Keizaigaku* (Economics in Japan: The Track of the Economic Thinking of the Japanese), Tokyo: Toyo Keizai Shinpo-sha.
4. (1992) *Keizaigakushi no Kadai to Tenbo* (History of Economic Thought: Surveys and Problems) in commemoration of the fortieth anniversary of the society, Hukuoka: Kyushu University Press.

In spite of these important publications of the society, Japanese studies on the history of economic thought have not been formally available to foreign scholars, because these publications were all written in Japanese. Reconsidering this condition, we have decided to dispatch the results of our studies in Japan to foreign scholars in this field through editing and publishing essays written in English. After active discussion among the editorial committee, *Economic Thought and Modernization in Japan* was selected as the subject of the first volume. Needless to say, we think this is a very important subject not only for the Japanese but also for those in developing and developed countries who are interested in the relationship between the modernization process and the development of economic thought in Japan.

As suggested above, the present collection is the first volume of the series of essays on the history of economic thought edited by the society. We hope the second volume will be published in a few years. We sincerely hope that the studies on the history of economic thought in Japan will be better understood in the world through this project and may contribute to the world academic community.

I would like to extend my sincere thanks especially to Professor Shiro Sugihara, one of the most distinguished scholars in the field of the history of Japanese economic thought, for his excellent leadership and advice to the contributors in the editorial process. In the introduction of this volume, written by Professor Sugihara, I hope every reader will find our methodology and the intention of these essays. I am also grateful not only to all of the contributors but also to Professors Chuhei Sugiyama, Saiichi Miyazaki, and Takuya Sakamoto for their editorial advice and generous cooperation. Especially I owe thanks to Professor Jiro Kumagai for his thoughtful editorial help. Lastly I would like to thank Barbara Slater, editor at Edward Elgar, for her assistance and efforts in the production of these essays.

Introduction   Modernization and the development of economic thought in Japan

Shiro Sugihara

INTRODUCTION

While no one disputes Japan's impressive record of economic development over the last 150 years, there is less agreement about the degree and ingenuity of the intellectual modernization which accompanied it. Economic thought is no exception. Part of the assessment problem has to do with the difficulties inherent in any intellectual history. But it is particularly difficult in the Japanese case, as almost all the main figures concerned were Japanese who were primarily educated in Japan and expressed their ideas in Japanese, that is, there was an accumulation of knowledge with relatively few face-to-face contacts with Western academia. On the face of it, Japan's history looks like a process of their absorption of, reaction to and articulation of Western thought. Of course, this is not a straightforward story of the diffusion of Western ideas. A range of Japanese thoughts which had existed prior to the Western impact exerted a strong influence, by adapting to new circumstances and mixing with Western thought throughout the period of the modernization drive. This introduction seeks to present the general historical context in which such intellectual endeavours took place.

Although its origins can be traced back to the seventeenth century, Japan's modernization process undoubtedly gathered pace after the middle of the nineteenth century. Two major institutional changes made a powerful impact on Japanese society and accelerated its pace of modernization. They also coined its patterns of thought. The first of these was the Meiji Restoration of 1867, which ended 265 years of peace and stability enjoyed under the Tokugawa regime. The arrival of Commodore Perry in 1853 and the subsequent opening of Japanese ports to foreign trade exposed the regime's inability to deal with national crisis. The Tokugawa Shogunate thus accepted the restoration of imperial rule. After a short period of internal warfare, the new government carried out a series of institutional changes, abolishing the samurai class and the caste-like occupational division, monetizing the land tax and freeing the peasant farmers from the land, and introducing Western technology and organizations in government-sponsored model factories. Looking at the whole process leading to the enactment of the Constitution in 1889, scholars debated whether it should be understood as a revolution or a change with qualified acceptance of modern ideas, and placed varied emphases on elements of continuity and change.[1]

The other major change came with the Japanese surrender at the end of World War II in August 1945. The occupation by allied forces lasted until 1951 when the peace treaty was signed, during which time, as with during the Meiji Restoration, a series of important institutional changes were carried out without causing severe political disruption. While democratization was undoubtedly attempted and largely realized, scholars also found room to argue, on the one hand, that part of the change was an extension of the institutional reform which had begun during the war and that, on the other, due to the change in the occupation policy (the so-called reverse course) some of the reforms were watered down and ended up as reorganization that lacked substance.[2] Nevertheless, there is no doubt that surrender and occupation marked the start of Japan's recovery from the ashes, which eventually led to the 'Japanese miracle', just as the Meiji Restoration marked the beginning of Japan's emergence as Asia's first modern nation.

Yet there was another turning point in modern Japanese history, which chronologically separates these two changes, and it is this second turning point that makes the study of Japan's modernization truly important from a comparative perspective. While the two other changes were induced by pressures from Western Europe and the United States, this one occurred in the period from the latter half of the 1920s to the early 1930s, in response to interwar depression and the growing influence of Marxism. While advanced Western countries suffered from the Great Depression and the collapse of world trade, Asia, following the Bolshevik revolution in Russia in 1917, saw the increasing penetration of the Third International, especially into China. If the two other changes were both successful in bringing about the enhancement of national economic strength, the course of action taken in response to this pressure was confrontation with the outside world through the use of force, denying the liberalist hope of the successful 'cooperation diplomacy' pursued during the period of 'Taisho Democracy'. It resulted in defeat and occupation. An important feature of Japan's modernization lies in the fact that the two successful modernization drives were interrupted by this unhappy turn of events.[3] In placing the history of Japanese economic thought in the general context of Japan's modernization, we need to take all three changes into account, and trace how Japanese intellectuals perceived, reacted to or responded to these changes.

This volume presents a collection of nine chapters, each illuminating aspects of the development of Japanese economic thought from the perspective broadly outlined above. They are all concerned with how economists and other thinkers perceived economic and social issues of the time, some theoretically, others in relation to policy and history. Some are similar in their thought processes to Western thinkers, while others are so different that it is difficult to identify Western equivalents. But all of them were concerned with the reality of contemporary Japanese society. Even when they were tackling issues that were purely theoretical, their thought processes were affected by that reality.

Chapter 1 traces the development of several currents of economic thought during the Tokugawa period: how economic activity came to be recognized by the government as a phenomenon independent from political and other purposes; how economic policy developed in response to the expansion of the market economy; how the non-samurai population, having got themselves involved in the market, came to learn the nature of economic activities; and how the issues of the relations between private and public interests, and between the economy and morality, came to be raised. Clearly, the perceptions and policy tools developed in this period prepared Japan for development in the Meiji era. They represent the intellectual 'prerequisites' of modern economic growth.

Chapters 2 and 3 relate the development of economic thought in the Meiji period (1868–1912), Chapters 4 to 6 deal with the interwar period, and Chapters 7 to 9 are concerned with the period during and after World War II. In the next three sections I shall deal with these three periods respectively, and try to relate some of the contents of these chapters to the general picture which will be summarized in the final section.

THE IMPACT OF THE MEIJI RESTORATION

In 1893 a short article entitled 'The study of political economy in Japan' appeared in *The Economic Journal*. The author was Juichi Soeda[4] (Soyeda in contemporary spelling) (1864–1929), a corresponding member of the British Economic Association whose main task was to write on the relevent aspects of the economy and economists of his country for the Association's journal. It is useful here to examine how he introduced the state of political economy in Japan to the British reader in this article. Soeda was perhaps best suited to the task among his contemporaries as, after graduating from the Imperial University of Tokyo, he studied at Cambridge and attended the lectures given by A. Marshall. He also visited Germany and France, and, upon his return to Japan, on the recommendation of Inejiro Tajiri[5] (1850–1924), assumed office in the Ministry of Finance. By the time of publication, the Constitution having been enacted and the parliament opened, the Meiji political system looked firmly set in train. This time was also the eve of the outbreak of the Sino–Japanese War.

Soeda stated that in Japanese universities, colleges and schools the works of Western economists such as J.S. Mill, M.G. Fawcett, W.S. Jevons, A. Marshall, F.A. Walker[6] and W.G.F. Roscher were lectured upon, and that, because books were reasonably priced in Japan, both lecture notes and books were widely read outside these institutions. In describing the development of economic thought before the Meiji Restoration, he listed eleven Tokugawa thinkers, and classified them into the categories of physiocrat (the majority belonged to this category), cameralist, mercantilist and state socialist.[7] Since the study of English became prevalent after the opening of the ports, however, the introduction of English and American political economy became the main feature. Economists were then roughly divided into schools of free trade and protectionism, and four associations connected to the study of political economy, as well as the major newspapers and periodicals concerned with economic affairs, were all inclined to express their stance in terms of this division. That some associations explicitly declared their 'neutrality' in the matter proves this tendency. Again, listing 26 Meiji economists, Soeda classified them into the categories of free trader (8), protectionist (6), state socialist (6) (this corresponds to the members of the Japanese Association for the Study of Social Policy, see below) and neutral (6). His observation was that while the university professors' views – which exerted great influence in government, parliament, the press, and colleges and schools – tended towards free trade, the lack of tariff autonomy stipulated under the unequal treaties which Japan was forced to sign with Western powers was presently fuelling the fire of the protectionist agitation. The labour question was also gaining importance. Thus he stated that 'We also are gradually paving the way for Socialists to come and reproach us in some future days.' He concluded that

> To harmonise, therefore, hostile elements, preserve the good part of the old while checking the evils incident to the new social institutions, and to set up an original school of economists, are the tasks awaiting the hands of Japanese economists. If the present zeal in economic study be maintained there is no reason to fear that they will collapse before this responsibility, however weighty it may be.

Chapter 2 of this volume deals with the first twenty years of the Meiji period, focusing on Yukichi Fukuzawa (1835–1901) and Ukichi Taguchi (1855–1905). The two men had much in common. Both were committed to enlightenment and interested not just in economic thought but in a wide range of subjects relating to the humanities, social sciences and history. Neither of them was content to be a mere observer of events, and both of them were heavily involved in the actual evolution of politics, economic affairs, education and publication in Japan. Furthermore, both acquired a basic education during the Tokugawa period, and tried hard to absorb modern western culture when they were exposed to its powerful impact. As for economic thought, they were both classified by Soeda as free traders. While their stance was liberal and individualistic overall, Fukuzawa tended to be receptive to nationalist and protectionist causes when it came to actual policy implementation, while Taguchi believed in the universal applicability of the principle of free trade, and retained a more fundamentalist approach. He argued that the study of political economy must be confined to the study of principles, and confronted sharply the historical school which emphasized historical and policy oriented research. Taguchi's stance is worth noting, because Japanese political economy was generally inclined to leave theoretical study aside and concentrate on historical and policy oriented research, a tendency common to late-developer countries.[8]

Soeda noted the overall numerical superiority of protectionists and state socialists combined, as against free traders, and included Noboru Kanai (1865–1933) and Kuranosuke Matsuzaki (1865–1919) of the Imperial University of Tokyo, and Sadamasu Oshima[9] (1845–1914) and Tsuyoshi Inukai (1855–1932) among independent economists in the former categories. They were responsible for the introduction of German historical and social policy schools to Japan in the early Meiji period. They contributed to the diffusion of German thought by learning the thought themselves from the lectures of invited German employees of the Japanese government, from studying abroad, and also by translating German books into Japanese. *Doitsugaku Kyokai* (the German Studies Association: founded 1881), *Kokka Gakkai* (the Nation Studies Association: founded 1887) and *Kokka Keizaikai* (the National Economy Society: founded 1890) were active in the 1880s and 1890s, serving researchers interested in German-style studies seeking the legal, political and economic basis of the state.

As a result of these activities, interest in German-style economic policy which was based on historicism and nationalism grew into a strong enough force to counter the influence of the liberal economic thought of Britain and France. In the second half of the Meiji period the state promoted the policy of 'enriching the nation' through rapid industrialization and 'strengthening the military' for external expansion, without much concern for their effects on the lives of ordinary people. In order to deal with the resultant *shakai mondai* (social problems) which appeared both in cities and the countryside, the government attempted to enact various pieces of social legislation, modelled on German practices. It was out of this environment that a group of social scientists, consisting of bureaucrats, academics and independent intellectuals, emerged. Thus the Japanese Association for the Study of Social Policy, the subject of Chapter 3, was founded in 1896, with the hope of providing a viable intellectual framework for solving such social problems.

The Association started with something like a reading group led by those university professors who returned from Germany. By 1899 when the 'Purposes of the Association' were published, however, it looked much more like a nationwide academic association. The 'Purposes' stated that the Association aimed at preserving the existing 'economic system based on private property rights', in opposition to the socialism led by Isoo Abe (1865–1949), while at the same time seeking social reform, in opposition to the idea of *laissez-faire* represented by Ukichi Taguchi. Having formally become a full academic organization in 1907, the Association held its first meeting at the Imperial University of Tokyo at the end of that year. Heated debates took place between conservatives and progressives on the question of the legislation of the Factory Law, making it felt to the public that the Association was rapidly becoming the core of social science circles in Japan. The 'opening speech' by Noburu Kanai, which appealed for a clear distinction between socialism and social policy in favour of the latter, gave a vivid impression of its political stance.

As for the main constituent forces of the Association, the standard perception put Noburu Kanai as leader of the right or reformist 'from above', Kumazo Kuwata (1868–1932) as leader of the centre or reformist both 'from above' and 'from below', and Tokuzo Fukuda (1874–1930) as leader of the left or reformist 'from below'. By 1913 when the seventh meeting was held, taking up the theme of 'labour dispute', the difference of opinion between the right and the left had become so large that the discussion had to be made confidential to avoid open confrontation. With the advent of the Bolshevik Revolution, the Association came to a crisis point as to whether it could justify its existence as a unified force. In 1919 the right wing of the Association joined *Kyochokai* (The Society for the Harmony and Cooperation [between Capital and Labour]), headed by Eiichi Shibusawa[10] (1841–1931), which published *Shakai Seisaku Jiho* (Journal of Social Policy). The left wing, on the other hand, came to base itself in the Ohara Institute for Social Research which was also established in 1919 and headed by Iwasaburo Takano[11] (1871–1949). Among the members of this group were Hajime Kawakami and Tatsuo Morito (1888–1984). Thus the Association, with nearly 300 members at its peak and a reasonable record of promoting social reform including the implementation of legislation (in this sense it did respond to the hope Soeda expressed in 1893), was no longer able to hold a cohesive platform by the end of the Taisho period (1912–25), and disappeared in the midst of the second major turning point described above.[12]

Chapter 4 takes up the thought of Tokuzo Fukuda and Hajime Kawakami who both represent the new generation of scholars after Noburu Kanai and Kenzo Wadagaki[13] (1860–1919) during the Japanese Association for the Study of Social Policy era. Liberally inclined Fukuda expressed his appreciation of the works of Baien Miura (1723–89), particularly his price theory, among the Tokugawa thinkers, while nationalistic Kawakami had a serious interest in Nobuhiro Sato (1769–1850) who was termed socialist in Soeda's list. Within the Japanese Association for the Study of Social Policy, Fukuda represented a liberal (left-wing) camp, and Kawakami gradually joined forces with him. During the period of Taisho Democracy both men advocated the new liberalism from Britain and other reformist ideas, before receiving the full impact of Marxist–Leninist ideas. Yet their responses to the Bolshevik Revolution showed a stark contrast: Fukuda tried to observe the new development as calmly as he could and to understand the fate of the new regime and the ideology behind it, while Kawakami accepted it completely. This difference anticipated the development of two conflicting economic thoughts after World War II.[14]

THE IMPACT OF THE INTERWAR DEPRESSION AND MARXISM

During the period between the Sino–Japanese War of 1894–95 and the Russo–Japanese War of 1904–5, rapid industrialization took place, as a result of which labour disputes became frequent and socialist movements developed in the cities, while tenancy disputes became widespread in the countryside. During the 1920s there was agricultural depression, due partly to the imports of cheap rice from Korea, and also to the falling exports of raw silk to the United States. The government responded by enacting the Factory Law and creating the rural improvement movement. With the Wall Street Crash of 1929 and the collapse of world trade, an acute crisis hit the Japanese countryside, which culminated in strong state intervention in the economy, the rise of military expenditure, and increased external aggression represented by the Mukden Incident of 1931 and the establishment of the puppet state in Manchuria. Japan left the League of Nations in 1934, went to war with China in 1937, founded an alliance with Germany and Italy in 1940, and attacked Pearl Harbour in 1941, triggering war with the United States.

The same period saw the institutionalization of economic studies. In 1919 the economics section was separated from the Faculty of Law at the Imperial Universities, and the faculties of economics were formed in Tokyo and Kyoto. Takano and Kawakami led this independence movement in each university respectively. In the meantime, the Tokyo Higher Commercial School became the Tokyo University of Commerce in 1920, and Fukuda, himself a graduate of this School, returned from Keio University to teach the principles of political economy there. Thereafter, these three universities became the centre of the study of political economy within Japanese academia. The mainstream view of the time was social reformist, based on British liberal ideas, which all of the three professors mentioned above shared. Their academic interest is reflected, for example, in the fact that in 1923 the three universities all held bicentennial events for the commemoration of the birth of Adam Smith. In that year the Ohara Institute for Social Research, headed by Takano, started a journal, the first issue of which was also devoted to the commemoration.

Around this time there was a growing interest in modern British economic thought. In particular the works of J.S. Mill were vigorously translated and studied. The translations of not only his *Principles of Political Economy* (1848) but also *On Liberty* (1859), *Utilitarianism* (1863) and *Autobiography* (1873) were widely read. Among the studies of Mill, those by Hajime Kawakami of the Kyoto Imperial University and Eijiro Kawai of the Imperial University of Tokyo are the most important. Kawakami paid special attention to the humanitarian aspects of Mill's economic thought, and discussed his concept of stationary state and his views on socialism.[15]

Far more noteworthy, however, was the strong impact of Marxism after the end of the 1920s. During the period of Taisho Democracy[16] various types of socialism blossomed, ranging from Marxism, 'anarcho-syndicalism' and Fabian socialism to state socialism, and they competed with each another for influence in the labour and peasant movements. After the establishment of the Japanese Communist Party in 1923, however, Marxist–Leninist ideas became the dominant ideology among the left-wing activists. Their influence also penetrated deeply into the liberal–left-wing circles of academics, artists and critics.

This is reflected in the split of social reformers as well as in the development of Marxism. The three professors mentioned above, Takano, Kawakami and Fukuda, were also leading public figures outside academia. If they had reorganized the Japanese Association for the Study of Social Policy into an academic association, an 'academism' across the universities and schools of thought, capable of fighting against political pressures, might have taken root in the field of Japanese political economy. As was already touched upon, however, the responses of these three men to the Bolshevik Revolution and the penetration of Marxist–Leninist ideas differed substantially. In particular, Kawakami's complete acceptance of Bolshevism was unacceptable to Takano and Fukuda, and led to heated debates between Fukuda and Kawakami, and between Kawakami and Tamizo Kushida (1885–1934) who was a student of Kawakami. Thus, by virtue of its great influence on the whole of Japanese academia, the rapid diffusion of Marxist–Leninist ideas brought unfortunate factional division among influential economists.

As far as the Marxist camp was concerned, the need to formulate the revolutionary strategy requested by the Comintern made it imperative for them to undertake a scientific investigation of the history of the development of Japanese capitalism. Yet there were few academic posts for Japanese economic historians in the university at this time, and those devoted to the study of the modern and contemporary period were virtually non-existent. In the non-governmental sector, research had just begun in a few places like the Ohara Institute for Social Research mentioned above and the Industry and Labour Research Institute (founded 1924). The task was thus left to a few individuals such as Eitaro Noro (1900–1934) and Kamekichi Takahashi[17] (1891–1977). Between 1927 and 1932 the discussion was largely focused on the revolutionary strategy itself, but with the publication of the *Lectures on the History of the Development of Japanese Capitalism* in 1932–33, it developed into a full-scale debate on the nature of Japanese capitalism.

Between 1933 and 1937 the *Koza-ha* (the Lecture School: so termed as it represented the views of those who participated in the above publication) and the *Rono-ha* (the Worker-Farmer School: so termed as it published a journal under this name) debated on a variety of topics such as the 'structural characteristics' of Japanese capitalism, the nature of the Meiji Restoration, the nature of Japanese agriculture (especially the reasons for the high ground-rent extracted from tenant farmers), and the existence and degree of development of 'manufacture' (handicraft or commodity production that was managed 'capitalistically' on the basis of hired labour) before the Meiji Restoration in order to determine the initial conditions for Japanese development. Chapter 5 details some aspects of this debate. Looking back, it is clear that the strong ideological and political orientations of both camps severely hampered the development of theoretical and empirical investigations. The debate ended abruptly with the arrests of the participants as the government tightened its control over their political activities.

The introduction of modern economics after the Marginal Revolution began in the early Meiji period. Tokuzo Fukuda was among the pioneers, and encouraged his students, including Shinzo Koizumi[18] (1888–1966), Kinnosuke Otsuka[19] (1892–1977) and Ichiro Nakayama (1898–1980), to pursue this line of study. As a result, a number of young researchers had obtained posts in universities by the early Showa period (1925–1989). In the western part of Japan, Yasuma Takata[20] (1883–1972: Kyushu Imperial University and later Kyoto Imperial University) led the study. His *Keizaigaku Shinko* (New Lectures in Economics: 1929–32) is the first major publication derived from these efforts. Kei Shibata (1902–86: Kyoto Imperial University), while having learnt *Das Kapital* from Kawakami, studied the general equilibrium theory under the guidance of Takata, and attempted a theoretical synthesis of modern economics and Marxian economics.[21] There were very few attempts to introduce Japanese economics in foreign languages at this time, one of the exceptions of which was the *Kyoto University Economic Review*, a quarterly journal published in Western languages by Kyoto Imperial University. Some of Shibata's articles published in the *Review* caught the attention of O. Lange and M.H. Dobb, and circulated among Western academia in the 1930s. Sadly, however, this is one of the rare examples of international intellectual contacts in the prewar years.[22]

THE IMPACT OF WORLD WAR II

By 1939 when World War II began, a quasi-wartime regime was already in place in Japan. Various committees had been established in and outside the government, involving academics and intellectuals, to prepare for the management of the wartime economy. This trend accelerated after the war started in the Pacific. By this time participation in wartime management was not confined to ultra-nationalists sympathetic to the government, but included liberal and even Marxist thinkers. After the War, many of them continued to be heavily involved in the economic management of the country.[23] The contributions of Hiromi Arisawa (1896–1988) and Nakayama to the implementation of the postwar rehabilitation programme are good examples of this. The understanding of the nature of their activities gives an important clue to the significance of postwar reforms for Japan's modernization. Here, however, we shall first look at the question of continuity and change from a different angle, that is, at the level of economic thought. Chapter 7 thus takes up the study of Adam Smith in Japan during World War II.

The persistence of serious academic interest in the study of Adam Smith in Japan since the early Meiji period is evident from the following few instances. Firstly, the first complete Japanese translation of the *Wealth of Nations* was published before the Chinese translation came out. Secondly, as was mentioned above, bicentennial events commemorating the birth of Adam Smith were held nationwide. Thirdly, as the study of Marxian economics became popular, a number of researchers studied the works of Adam Smith from the perspective of the development of the theories of value and surplus value. Fourthly, a number of works of and relating to Adam Smith were systematically translated and published in the postwar period by the Adam Smith Society. Finally, an international symposium was held in Japan to commemorate the bicentennial of the publication of *The Wealth of Nations*.[24] The question here is why the study of Smith reached a new height during the wartime period when strong political pressure was applied to liberal thinkers as well as to Marxists.

In the 1940s Japan, perhaps for the first time, faced a situation where the concentration of all its social energy into productivity increases became a matter of the nation's life and death. Japanese economists, in search of the most important factor in the enhancement of productive power and the best system of mobilization of productive forces, turned to the study of Smith, which after all seemed to be the starting point of political economy. They turned to Smith rather than Marx, not just because the freedom to study Marx was denied them. In the Marxist studies of Japanese capitalism, led by the *Koza-ha*, objective and systematic analyses of Japanese society were attempted, but it was soon realized that such approaches would not provide the understanding of the relation between economics and ethics which determined human behaviour at a deeper level. In this respect, Japanese study of Smith during the war was not just a matter of going back to Smith as the father of economics. It also implied that Japanese scholars sought a clue to rethink the political economy of civil society, by going back to Taguchi as the father of Japanese economics.

Chapters 8 and 9 deal with the development of Japanese economic thought in the postwar period. Chapter 8 on non-Marxian economics, Chapter 9 on Marxian economics. Those interested in the latter regained the freedom to conduct research, and both the *Koza-ha* and the *Rono-ha* began their research as soon as the war was over, while those interested in non-Marxian economics gained reasonable access to Western academia, and the study of Keynesian and neoclassical economics began to take firm root in Japan for the first time. Attempts were made to develop a dialogue between the two types of economics, but the two camps soon proceeded to form different academic associations. Not until the 1970s did they try to reopen an intellectual dialogue.

Chapter 8 focuses on the five non-Marxian economists who made influential observations on the development of trade and industry in the postwar Japanese economy: Kaname Akamatsu (1896–1973), Ichiro Nakayama, Hiromi Arisawa, Miyohei Shinohara (1919–) and Osamu Shimomura (1910–89). In particular the chapter discusses Nakayama's argument for the vital significance of free trade in the development of the postwar Japanese economy, in contrast to Arisawa's emphasis on fostering domestic industries. In section 6, '"Central planning" and the economic council', it argues that it was important for the Japanese economy to grow while keeping a 'harmonious balance' within it, and that harmony remained a 'lofty Japanese value'. Although the chapter does not refer to it, it was the case that, after the 1970s when the Japanese economy faced new kinds of serious problems, national harmony was indeed sought, and a more active dialogue between Marxian and non-Marxian economists took place.

Chapter 9 identifies three currents in Marxian economics in postwar Japan. The first followed the prewar tradition of orthodox Marxism. In line with the theory of state monopoly capitalism, this group argued for the coming of general crises or the stagnation and eventual decline of capitalism. It failed to appreciate the development of postwar capitalism, including the strong recovery and growth of the Japanese economy and the spectacular productivity growth in the United States. The second current also sprang from the *Koza-ha*, but attempted to broaden its perspective, by acknowledging the reality of postwar democratization in Japan, and also by responding to various currents of thought developed in Euro-Marxism, especially in Italy, and the 'New Left' movement in Western Europe. Associated with the 'theory of civil society', this group tried to go beyond the intellectual scope of socialism realized in the Soviet Union and Eastern European countries. The third group, originating from the *Rono-ha* and led by Kozo Uno (1897–1977), attempted to sort out the methodological issues inherent in Marxian economics, by separating it into three levels of analysis (Uno called them pure theory, stage theory and analysis respectively). Some of the main claims of the Uno School, such as a thorough distinction of the scientific elements of economics from its ideology, and the methodological clarification of the relation between the system of pure theory modelled on *Das Kapital,* and country-specific and historical stage-specific analyses, attracted international attention. This may be the most significant achievement of postwar Japanese Marxian economics. Chapter 9 discusses the works of the more recent writers of the Uno School, such as Makoto Itoh (1936–) and Hiroji Baba (1933–), which offers varied perspectives of the future of the society.

CONCLUDING REMARKS

The 1970s saw the growth of worldwide scepticism about economic growth as the unqualified goal of society or economic policy. The 'limits to growth', published by the Club of Rome in 1972, in particular helped the realization of the negative effects of industrialization and urbanization on a global scale which made rapid progress over the last 200 years. In Japan a series of disclosures of the effects of industrial pollution made the people aware of the seriousness of this issue. On a wider scale, the need to supply food and energy to keep pace with the growth of population, without causing serious damage to the environment, became a major international concern.

Some Japanese economists such as Shigeto Tsuru (1912–), Kenichi Miyamoto (1930–), Yoshiro Tamanoi (1918–85) and Hirofumi Uzawa (1928–) took the pollution issue seriously. During the period of high-speed growth Japan went through industrialization and urbanization at an unprecedented speed, and it was no coincidence that those economists found it disturbing. In order to achieve coexistence between man and nature, they felt it was necessary to secure individual freedom and a sense of responsibility. And, to achieve this end, the realization of a democratic social system was needed. In other words, there was something more fundamental here than the simple choice between capitalism and socialism was offering to man that needed to be taken into account. The collapse of socialist regimes in the Soviet Union and Eastern Europe partly proved the validity of this view. That is to say, the need for coexistence between man and nature suggested the need for creating a new kind of economics by combining economics with a new kind of social philosophy.

It was J.S. Mill who first addressed this question as an economist over 150 years ago. In his *Principles of Political Economy* (Book 2 on distribution), he discussed systematically the question of the transition from capitalism to socialism for the first time. At the same time, in Book 4, Mill questioned the premise behind modern ideas that economic development was the permanent policy goal, and argued that it would be under the stationary state that true human progress would be realized. While his vision anticipated that of the Club of Rome, his version of socialism has also attracted attention in recent years, especially after the collapse of socialist regimes, as one which antici-pated the change in socialism towards a more decentralized, democratic and peace-oriented system. There are signs in Japan too that the study of J.S. Mill from such a perspective has taken off.[25]

As was outlined above, the core of modern Japanese economic thought has been the persistent absorption and articulation of Western liberalism. Japan was more anxious than any other Asian country to introduce Adam Smith and British liberal economic thought to its soil. Furthermore, the Japanese will to absorb Western economic thought survived the second and third turning points described above. In this process the centre of gravity of Japanese interest has arguably shifted gradually from Adam Smith to J.S. Mill. In the Meiji era Fukuzawa had already learnt a great deal from Mill's utilitarianism, while during the period of Taisho Democracy the study of Mill, centring around Kawakami, extended from political economy to his entire thought system. The revival of Japanese interest in Mill in the most recent period, is a natural extension of this long-standing tradition.[26]

Chapters 8 and 9 point out that both schools of thought are anxious to open up new perspectives in the light of recent developments. What kind of mes-sage would they offer us as we approach the next century? This volume would suggest that, underneath the process of Japan's economic development as a late-developer nation, a tradition of economic liberalism was formed which was expressed in persistent scholarly interest in Smith and Mill. This enabled a country which had belonged to the civilization with Confucian values to acquire an essentially democratic political and legal system and promote education and culture, thereby succeeding in economic moderniza-tion. It is hoped that a full understanding of this heritage would help us participate in the development of economic thought which would guide a mature economic society such as Japan into the twenty-first century.[27]

NOTES

1. For recent discussion, see Chapter 1 of Nakamura (1985) and the introductory chapter by Odaka in Odaka and Yamamoto (eds) (1988).
2. For recent discussion, see Teranishi and Kosai (eds) (1993) and Nakamura (1995).
3. It may be instructive to compare the contents of this volume with those of Morris-Suzuki (1989). Chapter 1 of the latter deals with Tokugawa economic thought, Chapter 2 the Meiji period, Chapter 3 the interwar years and Chapters 4 to 6 the postwar period The periodization coincides well with the one suggested here, although this volume places considerably more emphasis on the interwar period, while Morris-Suzuki details postwar developments. Yet she too clearly recognizes the significance of the impact of Marxism. Around the time of World War I Japanese economists began to engage in the systematic analysis of the country's economic structure, in response to and under the influence of Marxism. Pointing out that this invited the enactment of the Peace Preservation Law, which was designed to suppress labour and socialist movements, Morris-Suzuki devotes most of Chapter 3 to the discussion of the rapid penetration of Marxism in Japan.
4. See Soeda (1893).
5. An eminent bureaucrat at the Ministry of Finance. Having studied at Yale University, Tajiri also taught at the Imperial University of Tokyo with E.F. Fenollosa.
6. Introductory textbooks by Fawcett (1870/1889) and Walker (1892) played an important role in the process of familiarization with Western political economy.
7. Soeda classified Nobuhiro Sato in this category. Sato regarded a bureaucratic state under an absolutist monarchy as ideal.
8. Taguchi did not follow the labour value theory developed by Smith and Ricardo, but rather appreciated the value theory of H.D. Macleod, and was sympathetic to the subjective value theory of the Austrian School. He believed that political economy should essentially be a science of psychology.
9. Oshima translated the main work of F. List from its English translation, and published it in 1889. He was the editor of *Kokka Keizaikai Hokoku* (Journal for the National Economy Society).
10. Shibusawa left the Ministry of Finance in 1873 to pursue his career as an entrepreneur. He was involved in the establishment of modern enterprises in Japan in a number of fields such as finance, industry and commerce. Following the traditional Confucian thought, he tried to absorb the idea of modern management and advocated *roshi kyocho* (harmony and cooperation between capital and labour).
11. Iwasaburo Takano came into contact with the labour question through his brother Fusataro Takano who had received the guidance of Samuel Gompers, leader of the labour movement in the United States. While engaged in the research and teaching of social statistics at the Imperial University of Tokyo, Iwasaburo helped his brother in organizing the labour movement in Japan.
12. As is pointed out in Chapter 3, the Japanese Association for the Study of Social Policy failed to make a major contribution towards the study of economic history, which its German counterpart famously succeeded in under the leadership of G. Schmoller. Even so, Eijiro Honjo (1888–1973), who was a student of Ginzo Uchida (1872–1919) and was also taught by Kawakami, later taught economic history, Japanese economic history and the history of Japanese economic thought at the Faculty of Economics of Kyoto Imperial University. He also headed the Institute of Japanese Economic History and helped the development of the study of economic history in Japan. Kawakami and Fukuda too studied economic history as well as economic theory and the history of economic thought, and nurtured a number of economic historians.
13. Wadagaki studied in Europe, and, upon his return, taught finance and the history of political economy in German style at the Imperial University of Tokyo.
14. For Fukuda's reaction to the Bolshevik Revolution, see Fukuda (1922). For Kawakami's stance, see Sugihara (1996), especially Chapter 7 'The Impact of the Bolshevik Revolution'.

15. See Kawakami (1923), Kawai (1923) and Hirai (1986).

16. In a paper published in 1916 political scientist Sakuzo Yoshino (1878–1933) argued that the fundamental objective of politics lay in the improvement of the welfare of the people, and accused aristocrats and the *Zaibatsu* groups of tyrannical behaviour. In his *Binbo Monogatari* (A Tale of Poverty) (1917), the economist Kawakami pointed out that poverty remained a serious issue even in advanced Western countries, and argued that the concentration of wealth among a small number of people was its cause. In 1916 the statistician Takano conducted a household survey of factory workers in Tokyo, and provided evidence on the degree of poverty in Japanese society. Under the intellectual influence of these people Japanese society went through a period where democracy surged for about ten years after World War I.

17. Graduating from Waseda University, Takahashi joined Toyo Keizai Shinposha (the Oriental Economist) where he began the study of Japanese capitalism. Although he was involved in the socialist movement at one point, he spent most of his career as an independent economist. During the war he was involved in the policy implementation of the controlled economy. After the war he continued to be an influential market analyst, while writing books on Japanese economic history at the same time.

18. Under the supervision of Tokuzo Fukuda Koizumi translated the main works of W.S. Jevons and David Ricardo. He made a critical study of the political economy and social thought of Karl Marx, and engaged in the debate with Kawakami and Kushida.

19. Under the supervision of Tokuzo Fukuda Otsuka translated the main works of A. Marshall. On his return from studying abroad, however, he concentrated on the study of Marxian economics, and contributed a chapter on the history of Japanese economic thought in the *Lectures on the History of the Development of Japanese Capitalism*.

20. Some of the main works of Takata, including parts of *Seiryoku-ron* (A Theory of Power), have recently been made available to the English reader (Takata, 1995). Edited by Michio Morishima and others, this volume also contains Takata's critique of the work of Eugen von Böhm-Bawerk and a debate on it with Ichiro Nakayama.

21. To some extent, this was a result of an accidental chain of events. Originally a student of sociology at the Faculty of Arts, Kyoto Imperial University, Takata came into contact with Kawakami around 1912, at an informal meeting among the economists. Shibata studied *Das Kapital* when he attended Kawakami's seminar as a student in 1927. When Kawakami resigned in 1928 as a result of his indirect involvement in politics, Takata replaced him to teach the principles of economics. Thus Shibata was taught the general equilibrium theory by Takata.

22. See Shibata (1933, 1934), Lange (1935), Dobb (1937) and Sugihara (1987).

23. For the activities of those scholars, including Arisawa, who belonged to the Akimaru Kikan, a special intelligence unit of the Japanese Army during the war, see Wakimura (1993).

24. Adamu Sumisu no Kai (Adam Smith Society) (1955/1979) provides useful information, not only for those interested in the development of the study of Adam Smith since the Meiji period, but for the general understanding of the nature of the history of Japanese economic thought. For a recent symposium, see Mizuta and Sugiyama (eds) (1993).

25. Mawatari (1997) argues that the socialism which Mill sought consisted of a decentralized market economy composed of a group of communities which were left to the hands of the workers' autonomous control, a gradualist and reformist approach in political processes and the democratic system which would disallow bureaucratic control. In his conclusion Mawatari describes with much sympathy Mill's vision of the future in which such socialism would allow a variety of systems, ranging from the producer cooperative to the joint stock company with profit sharing between capitalists and workers, to compete for its respective advantage under the market system. For Mill this was the best way forward for humanity.

26. See Sugihara and Yamashita (1977).

27. The way in which Morris-Suzuki (1989) deals with liberal economic thought since the Meiji period is insufficient and unsatisfactory. As a result, it fails to distinguish the history of Japanese economic thought from those in Russia and other Asian countries. It seems to

me to be extremely difficult to account for the great development of economic thought in postwar Japan which she stresses so much, if one assumes that liberal economic thought had been of minor significance in the earlier period. The persistence of 'the contrast between faith in the free market and belief in the need for state planning' (Ibid., p. 195) throughout the modern period suggests the significance of the weight of this tradition for postwar development.

REFERENCES

Adamu Sumisu no Kai (ed.) (1955/1979), *Honpo Adamu Sumisu Bunken* (Works relating to Adam Smith in Japan), Tokyo: Kobundo, 1955, Enlarged edition, Tokyo: Tokyo Daigaku Shuppan-kai, 1979.

Dobb, Maurice Herbert (1937), *Political Economy and Capitalism*, London: Routledge and Kegan Paul.

Fawcett, M.G. (1870/1889), *Political Economy for Beginners*, London: Macmillan, 1870, 7th edition, 1889.

Fukuda, Tokuzo (1922), *Borushevizumu Kenkyu* (A Study of Bolshevism), Tokyo: Kaizo-sha.

Hirai, Atsuko (1986), *Individualism and Socialism: Kawai Eijiro's Life and Thought (1891–1944)*, Cambridge, Mass., and London: Harvard University Press.

Kawai, Eijiro (1923), *Shakai Shisoshi Kenkyu* (A Study in the History of Social Thought), Tokyo: Iwanami Shoten.

Kawakami, Hajime (1923), *Shihonshugi Keizaigaku no Shiteki Hatten* (The Historical Development of the Political Economy of Capitalism), Kyoto: Kobundo.

Lange, Oskar (1935), 'Marxian economics and modern economic theory', *Review of Economic Studies*, **2**(3), 189–201.

Mawatari, Shoken (1997), *Jei Esu Miru no Keizaigaku* (The Political Economy of J.S. Mill), Tokyo: Ochanomizu Shobo.

Mizuta, Hiroshi and Chuhei Sugiyama (eds) (1993), *Adam Smith: International Perspectives*, Basingstoke: Macmillan and New York: St Martin's Press.

Morris-Suzuki, T. (1989), *A History of Japanese Economic Thought*, London: Routledge.

Nakamura, Takafusa (1981), *Meiji, Taisho-ki no Keizai* (The Economy of the Meiji and Taisho Periods), Tokyo: Tokyo Daigaku Shuppan-kai.

Nakamura, Takafusa (1995), *The Postwar Japanese Economy: Its Development and Structure*, Tokyo: University of Tokyo Press, 2nd edition, 1995.

Odaka, Konosuke and Yuzo Yamamoto (eds) (1988), *Bakumatsu, Meiji no Nihon Keizai* (The Japanese Economy of the Bakumatsu and the Meiji Periods), Tokyo: Nihon Keizai Shimbunsha.

Shibata, Kei (1933), 'Analysis of capitalism and the general equilibrium theory of the Lausanne School', *Kyoto University Economic Review*, **8**(1), 107–36.

Shibata, Kei (1934), 'On the law of decline in the rate of profit', *Kyoto University Economic Review*, **9**(1), 61–77.

Soyeda, Juichi (1893), 'The study of political economy in Japan', *Economic Journal*, **3**, 334–9 (For the Japanese version, see Juichi Soeda, 'Nihon ni oite Keizaigaku Kenkyu no Jokyo', *Kokka Gakkai Zasshi*, **6**(79), 1573–83).

Sugihara, Shiro (1987), 'Shibata Kei', *The New Palgrave: A Dictionary of Economics*, Vol. 4, London: Macmillan, p. 325.

Sugihara, Shiro (1996), *Tabibito Kawakami Hajime* (The Intellectual Journey of Hajime Kawakami), Tokyo: Iwanami Shoten.

Sugihara, Shiro and Shigekazu Yamashita (1977), 'J.S. Mill and modern Japan', *The Mill News Letter* (the University of Toronto Press), **12**(2), 2–6.

Takata, Yasuma (1995), *Power Theory of Economics* (Michio Morishima et al. comp.), Basingstoke: Macmillan and New York: St Martin's Press.

Teranishi, Juro and Yutaka Kosai (eds) (1993), *The Japanese Experience of Economic Reforms*, Basingstoke: Macmillan and New York: St Martin's Press.

Wakimura, Yoshitaro (1993), *21–seiki o Nozonde* (Looking into the Twenty-first Century), Tokyo: Iwanami Shoten.

Walker, F.A. (1892), *Political Economy, Briefer Course*, London: Macmillan.

1. Trends in economic thought in the Tokugawa period

Masamichi Komuro

1. WHY BEGIN WITH THE TOKUGAWA PERIOD?

There are people who might wonder why the analysis of the history of economic thought in Japan should begin with the Tokugawa period. Presumably these people assume that the appropriate point to start such a study is the Meiji Restoration, because the political and economic systems of Japan underwent tremendous changes at that time, and the actual industrialization and modernization of Japan dates from that time. It was also around this time that the ideas of the Western world were introduced widely into Japan, and completely new approaches were introduced into the study of the economy.

Then why were the thinkers of the early Meiji period open to economic thought from the Western world and why were they often drawn to such ideas? Of course they also felt some of those ideas were foreign to them and sometimes they even tried to change them. The reason why they could do these things then is that, in the Tokugawa period, Japanese people already possessed the ability to form certain views on society and economy.

Before moving to the main theme, let us briefly consider why the ground was able to be prepared in the 'feudal' Tokugawa era for the development of economic thought in Meiji Japan. One aspect that can be identified as a reason is that in those days people became gradually interested in the study of real society, and the language and logic used in such studies became generally known. During the period of civil war (Sengoku era) preceding the Tokugawa period, thinkers were more interested in the afterlife than in the events in this world, and many people were drawn to the teachings of Buddhism. However, during the prolonged peace that was realized under the rule of the Tokugawas, people came to be more interested in the actual society where they resided. The tendency of the Shogun government (Bakufu) and the feudal lords' governments (Han) from the middle of the seventeenth century onward to put more emphasis on the importance of learning also greatly contributed to the people's increased interest in various ideas. Confucianism, in particular Chu Hsi philosophy, was one of the philosophies that were widely disseminated amongst Japanese people in those days.

Confucianism advocates natural economy. It promotes the rationality of the hereditary status system and a spiritualistic approach to nature and society. Thus, Confucianism tended to deny the objective cognition of nature and society. In the early Meiji period Yukichi Fukuzawa harshly criticized the mentality of Japanese people by saying that they lacked a 'mechanistic view of nature' and 'independent spirit' (Fukuzawa [1899] 1978, p. 206). According to Fukuzawa, it was the influence of Confucianism that had brought about such a mentality among the Japanese people. However, since Confucianism addressed the issue of people's real society and economy, it contributed to the development of the language and the methodology used for logical thinking of societies, and this point should not be overlooked.

It is also necessary to note that the philosophies studied by the Japanese people during the Tokugawa period were not limited to Confucianism. Stimulated by the diffusion of Confucianism, the philosophy of 'National Learning' came to have great influence over the thinking of Japanese people in the latter half of the Tokugawa period. Also, with the introduction of 'Dutch Learning', the natural scientific spirit of the Western world was introduced, and people came to increase their knowledge on matters outside of Japan. Consequently, various ideas originating from different sources came to address the issue of society, conflicting with and influencing each other. This situation delivered a framework where the social and economic issues could be studied from various different angles.

A second aspect that contributed to the later development of economic thought was the fact that the economy and the society of the Tokugawa period were by no means static entities, though of course there were various retrograde pre-modern steps in the Tokugawa period. According to certain calculations, during the 270 years of the Tokugawa period the population increased by 2.8 times, the cultivated area by 1.6 and food production by 2.4 (Hayami and Miyamoto, 1988, p. 44). In the seventeenth century Japan was importing raw silk from abroad, but in the 1850s when Japan opened its ports to the outside world, Japan's raw silk production became the major export industry. At the end of the Tokogawa period, about 80 per cent of the people were engaged in agriculture, and Japan might be considered as an agrarian nation. However even in those days many peasants were also involved in non-agricultural production activities. For example, it is estimated that in the Choshu domain, 48 per cent of all the products from the domain were non-agricultural products (Nishikawa, 1979, p. 27). These facts are often regarded as evidence of so-called proto-industrialization that took place during the Tokugawa period. Also, it is necessary to note that in Edo, Osaka and other major cities, commercial capitals emerged. Though such capitals were often privileged, there appeared various rational management techniques such as credit systems, double-entry book-keeping and the separation of management and capital. These movements point to gradual changes in society in the Tokugawa period. Society in those days had come to acquire a more market-oriented nature. It is no wonder that the thinkers in such a world started to study economic affairs seriously.

A third aspect influencing the emergence of economic thought was the social structure of the Tokugawa period. The Tokugawa era started after the period of the civil war (Sengoku era) that was characterized by large scale social change. According to Kunio Yanagita, two-thirds or three-fourths of the villages that existed in the Meiji period were formed from the mid-fifteenth century to the seventeenth century. What constituted these new villages were households from various different places, so the villages were not the traditional kinship-based communities (Yanagita [1926] 1969). Similarly most cities were also formed after the civil war, and the people populating these cities were from different places (Nakai, 1975). After all, in the society of the Tokugawa period cities and villages were not simple groups of households based on traditional relations by blood or territory, but communities based on certain cooperative functions. They were neither the developed *Gesellschaft* nor the simple *Gemeinschaft*. In this chapter the society of such communities is referred to as 'Tokugawa community'. In this community the members were encouraged to study their social relationships and their meaning.

Another point that needs to be studied is the legitimacy of the authorities. There is no doubt about the fact that the military power of the Bakufu and Hans helped create the social order of the Tokugawa period. However it was not military power alone that sustained the reign over 250 years. According to studies of the last couple of decades, the period of civil war was not only the time of strife among civil war barons (Sengoku Daimyo), but also a time of confrontation between popular rebellions (ikki) and civil war barons (Fujiki, 1975). The end of the civil war period marks the unification through the military power of warriors, but one needs to note that this unified society came into being also through the compromises between the warrior class and various other social groups that had stood together under the banner of rebellion. During the Tokugawa period people's occupations were fixed as hereditary and peasants were forced to pay heavy taxes, but at the same time, as a result of the compromise, the pursuit of one's occupation in the agrarian villages, manufacturing and trading groups was guaranteed and the rights of self-management within such groups were given to the people as inalienable inherited rights (soho). On condition of these guarantees, the notion that authority was legitimate emerged. In this society certain social roles or rewarding jobs, accompanied by necessary rights, were given to every group, and the sphere for self-decision was clearly given. Thus this society can be called the 'social roles system' (Bito, 1992). It was because of this characteristic that the people of ruled classes gradually came to study their role, their rights and the mechanisms of society, which then became the driving force of their own philosophy on economics.

In short, though there was much backwardness in the Tokugawa era, it was also the period of transition in which new social views might be generated. The stagnant nature of this period that was harshly criticized by Fukuzawa was also often evident even in the Meiji period, but we have to remember that Fukuzawa, who grasped the essence of Western culture, was born and educated in the very Tokugawa era. This is why we need to start the analysis of economic thought in Japan from the period of Tokugawa. Below I discuss the philosophical tendencies in the economic thoughts that emerged during this transient Tokugawa period through five different themes.

2. THE INFLUENCE OF CHU HSI PHILOSOPHY

Over the last several decades, doubts have been raised about whether Chu Hsi philosophy had already spread in Japan by the middle of seventeenth century (Bito, 1961, Watanabe, 1985). However in fact at the beginning of the eighteenth century, this philosophy began to be introduced not only to highly intelligent people but also to the leaders of peasants and merchants. In those days in East Asia Chu Hsi philosophy was one of the most systematic and powerful socio-political philosophies. According to this philosophy, the universe was created by the mysterious activity of the Moralistic Principle called '*li*', and this principle was inherent in all beings and all social systems. Also a ruler should become in accord with this principle through his own moralistic endeavour. This moralistic ruler then invokes morality in those who surround him, first in vassals, then from vassals to domains, and then all over the country, according to the most popular text of the Chu Hsi school, 'Daigaku' (Great Learning) (Hattori, 1921). Thus, what was important for politics was morality and educational influence rather than empirical and positivistic cognition of society and economy. Furthermore, this moralistic principle of Chu Hsi philosophy was derived from the hereditary order and family moralities based on the agricultural society of ancient China, and this philosophy was accepted as natural law a priori (Maruyama, 1952).

Because of the influence of Chu Hsi philosophy, there existed three tendencies in the philosophical world of the Tokugwa period. First, social and economic issues were associated with morality. This remained one of the characteristics of Japanese economic thought even in modern times. Second, this philosophy of the Tokugawa period had led to the idea that the moralistic ruler should control economic activities, because these activities were thought to be frequently controlled by immoral desires. Third, in spite of its pre-modern moralistic character, this philosophy urged people to think of the principle of things. Thus the desire to obtain rational interpretations in order to understand social and economic phenomena increased gradually among the people (Minamoto, 1972).

3. THE DEVELOPMENT OF EMPIRICAL AND POSITIVISTIC APPROACHES

We cannot talk about the Japanese interpretation of economics during the Tokugawa period without recognizing the presence of Sorai Ogyu (1666–1728), because he was the Confucianist who had established the empirical and positivistic methodologies that could be applied to society and the economy. However this does not mean that other Japanese people in those days were not capable of empirical observation. For example, the merchants depicted in *Nihon Eitai Gura* (The Japanese Family Storehouse) written by Saikaku Ihara (1642–93) had a keen sense of profit-making and these people observed the commercial society around them realistically (Ihara [1688] 1959). Also the author of *Nogyo Zensho* (A Complete Book of Agriculture), Yasusada Miyazaki (1623–97), had established scientific approaches to agriculture by conducting information collection, experiments and observations (Miyazaki [1697] 1978). Therefore Sorai does not stand out so much when we compare him to other people with respect to their ability to see things objectively. What made Sorai unique is his achievement in establishing the methodology of objectivity within the framework of Confucianism. His studies led to the development of a socio-political philosophy that was a good match for Chu Hsi philosophy in its well-polished logic. In short his contribution to the philosophy of those days is important in the sense that he combined the systematic approach of Confucianism (which regards the society as a whole body) and the methodology of empirical and positivistic philosophy.

Sorai revealed this new Confucianism in his works, *Bendo* (On Distinguishing the Way) and *Benmei* (On Distinguishing Terms). He began his epoch-making philosophy by raising doubt against and negating the existence of '*li*' in Chu Hsi philosophy. Because of this doubt, he tried to interpret correctly 'The Six Classics', the classic or the oldest texts of Confucianism before the emergence of Chu Hsi philosophy. Through this process he established a thoroughly inductive method to analyse the ancient Chinese used in 'The Six Classics'. He concluded that in 'The Six Classics' there was no reference to '*li*'. He said that what was explained in 'The Six Classics' were various institutions and civilizations invented and created by the competent

Early Kings of ancient China. Therefore he claimed that the ideal or 'The Way' of Confucianism was not something determined by the natural order, but rather by the institution artificially created by the Early Kings, and thus the task of rulers was to recreate institutions of their days by consulting the examples depicted in 'The Six Classics' (Ogyu [1717] 1973).

His unique view that 'The Way' was something man-made completely overturned the traditional Eastern Asian view of Confucianism where 'The Way' was considered as some kind of natural order. Sorai thought that the world depicted in 'The Six Classics' was the ideal society. Therefore in this sense he was a Confucianist. But he made it clear that his acceptance of the philosophy of this ideal society was only his own opinion.

Sorai's approach greatly influenced the way people viewed society and the economy. First, priority came to be placed on politics by his successors. This grew from his idea that the task of administrators was not to present the norms to the people but to create and establish social and economic systems that suited the situation of each time, as had been done by the Early Kings of ancient China. Second, he also claimed that since society was something created by men, there did not exist any universal social order and, therefore, society had to be studied and accepted objectively according to its own characteristics. To this end, he said that the society depicted in 'The Six Classics' needed to be used only as a standard in understanding each society. As mentioned above, Sorai had already adopted an empirical, positivistic approach to the study of society and history.

In his *Seidan* (Political Discourses) which describes the society of his time in detail, Sorai commented on the lack of solid institutions that needed to be established by the rulers for society (Ogyu [c.1727] 1973). According to his interpretation, the rulers or samurais who left rural villages and lived in castle-towns were like 'a traveller staying at an inn', and these samurais were living in the world of the money economy. This kind of life would nurture the money economy still more, which would then result in the weakening of the samurai's power to rule over the people. Sorai then thought that the solution to this problem was the reversal of the process, that is, the return of the samurais to their rural villages. In this he was one of the thinkers who correctly recognized the potential harm of the money economy to the ruling structure of the Bakufu and Hans. He was also considered to be an advocate of revisionism because he thought it would be ideal to return to the rural economy. However we should not summarize his economic thought as revisionist, because, just as in several sections of his *Seidan*, he also supported realistic approaches to the problems of society. For example, in times of economic distress in the early part of the eighteenth century, to restore the weakening economy, he proposed to double the amount of circulating copper coins (Ogyu [c.1727] 1973, p. 333). This kind of approach to the money economy was contrary to what he had advocated as his ideal. In the end Sorai was torn between the philosophy of the ideal world depicted in 'The Six Classics' and the realistic recognition of actual society.

Shundai Dazai (1680–1747) and other thinkers who followed Sorai took over his empirical and positivistic method and at the same time emphasized the objective recognition of the power of the money economy. Thus, Sorai's philosophy guided the objective understanding of the economy during the Tokugawa period. However the philosophies of the Sorai school sometimes became Machiavellian, and their tendency to treat ethics lightly came to be criticized. Because of such critical views of the Sorai school, the philosophy of Chu Hsi also continued throughout the Tokugawa period without losing its power, and the economy was studied from the viewpoints of both Sorai and Chu Hsi philosophy. There also emerged another school of philosophy, the so-called eclectic school, which was effectively a combination of these two schools.

4. EMPIRICAL AND RATIONAL COGNITION OF THE ECONOMY

Sorai did not accept Chu Hsi's mysterious and moralistic principle called '*li*' as something based on natural law. He also did not acknowledge all the universality of entities. In other words, though he tried hard to understand the historical characteristics of each society, Sorai did not pay much attention to the principals or natural order underpinning society and the economy. However in the late eighteenth century, there appeared several thinkers who tried to understand the laws and order that existed behind various social and economic phenomena that they recognized empirically and positivistically. Baien Miura (1723–89), another thinker whom I shall mention later, is one philosopher who was interested in immanent laws and order. But here I would like to focus on other two thinkers, Seiryo Kaiho (1755–1817) and Banto Yamagata (1748–1821), whom I think are representative of the philosophers of this category. These two people were of different status and of different educational backgrounds, but they both believed that behind the objectively recognizable economic phenomena, there existed certain fixed laws and order.

Seiryo was the eldest son of a chief retainer of a Han in Tango province. After giving the status which he should inherit to his younger brother, he spent the rest of his life touring around the country as a lecturer of political economy and giving financial advice to the Hans or patrons resident there. In Seiryo's days, that is, from the late eighteenth century to the early nineteenth century, commercial capital grew still more and handicraft manufacturing was also increasing. These two components played indispensable roles in the economy. Bakufu and Hans which had been treating agrarian production as the basis of their financial resources began to have an interest in acquiring commercial capital. Especially during the reign of Tanuma (1767–86), there was a strong tendency in the Bakufu to lean towards commercial capital. In such an environment Seiryo came to view the principles, in his book *Keikodan* (Preliminary Discourses), that controlled commercial capital and the activity of 'buying and selling' for profit-making as natural phenomena. He said, 'All things in this world are commodities for exchange, and it is in the nature of the commodities that they should produce other commodities. There is no difference between fields that produce rice and money that produces interest' (Kaiho [1813] 1970, p. 222). He then expanded this principle beyond the economic field and came up with the idea that the same principle governs all over the society. For example, he said as follows.

> Feudal lords are the rich who have commodities called domains. They loaned their domain as merchandise to the people under their rule and earned interest from it. What they do is the same as the activity of vassals who sell their knowledge and power to their lord, or sedan-chair carriers who earn their food and liquor by providing service to other people (Kaiho [1813] 1970, p. 223).

In this way his interpretation of this social relationship was applied to the lord–vassal relationship, one of the most sacred moralistic relationships in Confucianism. Seiryo attempted to explain the whole social systems of society by introducing the principle of selling and buying merchandise.

As for the finance of Hans, Seiryo regarded the activities of commercial capitalists as natural and necessary. He thought that wealth was generated in the process of commercial transactions, and the size of each Han's wealth should be measured by the difference between the amount of gold and silver that moved out from the Han and that which entered the Han. Therefore he denounced the lord's decision to increase land-taxes within the Han as a means to improve their financial situation, because this would simply stir conflict between the ruler and the ruled and no change would occur in the actual wealth of the Han. What he proposed was a strategy to acquire the wealth of other Hans through the cooperation of the ruler and the ruled. He advocated a trade protection policy, a strategy undertaken by the ruler to increase the amount of products sold to the people outside the Han (Kaiho [1813] 1970, pp. 323–4). This approach, which was to some extent similar to mercantilisms, could be called 'Han-Mercantilism'.

This philosophy of Seiryo, which was not bound by the moralistic view of Chu Hsi, seemed to be influenced by the philosophy of Sorai. It is said that in his youth, Seiryo was deeply impressed by the thinking of Sorai. However his view differed slightly from that of Sorai. Unlike Sorai, Seiryo showed a strong interest in the rational law and order that existed behind all objects and phenomena. He said, 'The "*li*" rules all matters in the Universe. There are no irrational matters outside reason. We regard something as irrational because we don't have enough ability to pursue and recognize the reason' (Kaiho [c.1810s] 1935, p. 624). For him '*li*' was a cause and effect relationship that man had no control over. In this sense, his '*li*' is somewhat similar to the philosophy of natural law, and it clearly differed from Chu Hsi's '*li*'. For Seiryo, '*li*' was something that man could come to recognize gradually through the accumulation of objective recognition processes.

On the other hand, Banto was the top manager of a privileged rice-wholesaler and financier for feudal lords in Osaka, the centre of economy in Japan. The above-mentioned Seiryo recognized the excellent management skill of Banto, who succeeded in restoring the finances of Sendai Han by issuing exchange rice bonds. There were similarities between these two people in that they both placed importance on the role of commerce, though they had different educational backgrounds. While Seiryo mainly followed the teaching of the Sorai school, Banto studied at Kaitokudo, a school for Osaka merchants. The education at Kaitokudo was based on the philosophy of Chu Hsi, and the existence of '*li*' was acknowledged by the people at this school. However in understanding the '*li*' the empirical and objective recognition was emphasized. As is expressed in the slogan of the school that said, 'In this world there is nothing that man cannot understand. Simply due to lack of knowledge, man tends to think that there exists things that man cannot understand.' (Goi [c.1740] 1913). Thus, the academic principle of Kaitokudo was said to be based on intellectualism. Banto also strengthened his rational view by accepting and recognizing the importance of the knowledge of astronomy and other information obtained from natural science of the Western world through studies called 'Dutch Learning'.

Banto's theory of economy is explained in his work, *Yume no shiro* (Instead of Dreaming). What he tried to do was to clarify the relationship between the agrarian villages which constituted the base of production activity in his view and the market economy of the central city where he worked as the manager of a business. Overall he applied the empirical rational approach in this process. Contrary to Seiryo, he basically had a physiocratic view. He thought that wealth was generated in the agrarian village, therefore society becomes wealthier if the number of peasants increases and the number of the city dwellers or consumers decreases. Therefore he claimed that benevolent and moralistic politics starts if the policy of revering agriculture and suppressing commerce is followed. However he also acknowledged the importance of the function of a central market. He thought that contemporary society was no longer based on a self-sufficient economy. He knew that the agrarian villages, as well as the finance of the lord who had to rule the people benevolently and moralistically, were supported by the proper prices of rice and other products sold in the central market. Then what was the proper price determined in the central market? Banto, who did a considerably objective analysis of the function of the rice market and other markets in Osaka, saw that '*li*' existed in the automatic and fair demand–supply adjustment mechanism or in the pricing mechanism of the market. He then concluded, 'Now in this world there is nothing so efficient and rational as the function of the rice market' (Yamagata [c.1807] 1973, p. 398). To the Bakufu, he said, 'The selling and buying is a natural transaction' (Yamagata [c.1807] 1973, p. 378). Therefore 'the government should not interfere with this mechanism intending to manipulate the demand–supply relationship and the price of products' (Yamagata [c.1807] 1973, p. 378). His idea was based on a free economy in the central market of Japan, and he observed that the very activities of merchants for profit-making supported this free market economy.

From the ideas and concepts advocated by these two people, we can see in the late Tokugawa period the emergence of attempts to seek out the rational order or laws that are hidden behind empirically recognizable phenomena, and that the focus, at the same point, shifted to economic phenomena.

5.　'NAIYU GAIKAN' (TROUBLES AT HOME AND ABROAD) AND NOTIONS OF A NEW STATE SYSTEM

From the third quarter of the eighteenth century onwards, intelligent and informed people began to discuss coastal defence problems ('gaikan'), because of the increasing menace of Russian and British ships during those years. On the other hand the commercialization of the rural economy sometimes destroyed the livelihood of small peasants and increased the trend of peasants deserting their villages. The finances of the feudal domains, which were inflexible in the face of these transformations, were seriously affected. Some rulers and intellectuals therefore began to consider that unless these domestic problems ('naiyu') were resolved, they could not build up the nation against 'gaikan'. Toshiaki Honda (1744–1821) and Nobuhiro Sato (1769–1850) were the thinkers who set out to address both troubles at home and from abroad at the same time by a drastic reform of the economy and policy. It is noteworthy that their plans had some characteristics of a prototype for the Meiji Government's policies that aimed to transform Japan into 'a rich and strong nation'.

Both scholars were masterless samurais with similar careers. They grew up in comparatively backward rural districts and then came out to Edo to pursue their studies in their youth. During their lives they could not get into regular samurai service but rather made their living as freelance intellectuals. They both also travelled throughout Japan and were well informed about the economic and geographical circumstances in various districts. They were strongly affected by their experience of witnessing the misery of the Tenmei famine in their travels around the Tohoku district in their youth. They were also influenced by the Dutch learning as well as by the Sorai school, because they had access to the scholars of Dutch learning and Western books translated into Chinese, though they themselves didn't understand Dutch well. They were both well grounded in the natural science of those days. Toshiaki was a mathematician of the Seki school and Nobuhiro was particularly at home with mining and agricultural science amongst the encyclopaedic range of his intellectual interests.

Toshiaki attributed the poverty of the backward rural districts not only to a decline in productivity due to heavy taxes but also to the undeveloped state of domestic transportation. It was typical of him to attach much importance to transportation. But much more attention is devoted to a population theory, similar to that of Malthus, which was one of the bases of his thinking. This theory is found in his book *Saiiki Monogatari* (A Story about the Western World) (Honda [1798a] 1970) which was published in the same year as the first edition of Malthus' *The Principle of Population*. In this book he estimated that increases in the productivity of the land would not match population growth, whatever the rate of development; he believed that this principle lay at the root of poverty. In another book in the same year, *Keisei Hisaku* (Secret Plans to Manage the State) (Honda [1798b] 1970), he emphasized that there was no choice but to obtain gold and silver as the balance of trade in order to solve the population problem and poverty. To make this possible, it was necessary to develop marine transportation. Simultaneously the government, he advocated, should develop the islands around Japan including Hokkaido, Saghalien and Kamchatka and then create settlements in and around these foreign trading posts. Though Toshiaki planned to carry out these settlements peacefully through trading activities, of course he also had a strategic purpose: to head off the Russian menace through active Japanese overseas expansion. Toshiaki also regarded it as necessary to establish public schools to spread industrial education, because Japan had to have the ability to produce exportable manufactured goods to support the above mentioned policies.

In this way Toshiaki considered the development of transportation and foreign trade as important components of the national interest. But he looked upon private commercial activities with deep distrust. In his view merchants 'make crafty and avaricious designs without shame' (Honda [1798b] 1970, p. 18), exploit the wealth of samurais and peasants and ignore national losses for the sake of their own profit making. Therefore he asserted that control of commerce and such important businesses as 'overseas shipping and trade' should be 'the calling of the national ruler' (Honda [1798b] 1970, p. 18) or the task performed by 'the great men of talent and virtue' (Honda [1798b] 1970, p. 61). On this point he despised the people, believing instead in the hereditary status system. In so far as he conceived of a newly unified state as the axis of an industrial trading nation, he was the first intellectual to transcend the barrier of the closed country.

Toshiaki considered that his plans were 'the natural way of administration' which is consistent with the scientific theories of meteorology, geography and so on (Honda [1798b] 1970, p. 22). It is said that at the root of this notion was his respect for the Western natural sciences which he encountered through Dutch learning.

Unlike Toshiaki, Nobuhiro Sato based his arguments on mystical and religious beliefs. That is, 'the divine will of the gods of productivity' which Nobuhiro learned from Atsutane Hirata's philosophy. In Atsutane's philosophy, which was itself a school of national learning strengthened through the influence of Christianity, the gods of productivity were the creators and simultaneously lurked in all beings as potentially infinite productivity. Nobuhiro argued that it was the mission of the political authorities to develop this infinite productivity according to the divine will so that human beings could multiply themselves.

In Nobuhiro's book *Keizai Yoryaku* (An Outline of Economic Policy), he argued that rulers who could not relieve the people from misery such as the desolation of rural villages, abortion, infanticide and famine betrayed 'the divine will of the gods of productivity' (Sato [1822] 1977). To solve such 'Naiyu', Nobuhiro, like Toshiaki, considered it necessary to develop internal and external transportation and trade. But it was typical of Nobuhiro that he was interested in the production methods of various primary and secondary industries and wrote many books about them. For the development of such productive powers, he judged, it was indispensable for government to take the lead systematically, because he despised the people's abilities just as much as Toshiaki. He had such a deep distrust of merchants that he also planned that commerce and foreign trade would be exclusively managed by the government. For this purpose in his book *Suito Hiroku* (A Secret Book for the Everlasting Administration), which described his ideal nation, he concretely proposed a bureaucratic network of offices all over the country (Sato [c.1833] 1977).

Nobuhiro also regarded the growing separation of the peasantry into rich and poor as a serious problem for society. And he thought the rich farmers and merchants were very dangerous because they exploited the peasants and plundered their lands and professions. In *Suito Hiroku*, therefore, he gave full play to his fanciful idea of a national-socialistic nation whose government nationalized industries and prohibited all private businesses. This government, he envisaged, would establish and maintain schools, orphanages, poorhouses, old people's homes, nursery schools, hospitals and so on in every small part of Japan to carry out education, particularly industrial education, and social policies. It is particularly notable that he did not take into consideration any hereditary status system in this book. There was no reference to the rule of the samurai class but only a detailed explanation that all people were divided into eight occupational groups each of which was controlled by the appropriate government offices (Sato [c.1833] 1977).

This nation outlined by Nobuhiro was a centralized nation state which clearly went beyond the limits of the administration performed by Bakufu and Hans. Also it possessed strong military power on the basis of economic power attained through the development-oriented policies. Through this military power, in his other book *Kondo Hisaku* (A Secret Policy to Unify the World) (Sato [1823] 1977), he foresaw Japan would invade the Asian countries from Korea and China to India, and 'develop their products' to relieve the people in these countries from poverty. This argument is seen to be an aggressive over-reaction to the expansion of the western powers around Japan. But he regarded it as the divine mission of Japan as 'the first country created by the gods of productivity in the world'.

Both Toshiaki and Nobuhiro advocated a domestic market integrated by the government, with policies to lead and develop the industries, make inroads into foreign trade, implement social policies and so on under the control of a strong centralized nation. Though their plans were somewhat Utopian, it is undeniable that they participated in some of the policies of the Meiji government, that is, the policies involving 'increasing production and developing industries' and for 'a rich and strong nation'.

6.   POPULAR AWARENESS OF ECONOMIC AUTONOMY

Traditionally, it has been clear that the major proponents of economic thought in the Tokugawa period were mainly ruling-class thinkers. Of course some personalities from the ruled classes such as Baigan Ishida (1685–1744) and Sontoku Ninomiya (1787–1856) are also widely studied. But these people dealt with practical ethics for private economic life, and they mostly focused on attitudes of abstinence, diligence and economic rationality. On the other hand, not much attention has been paid to the thinkers amongst the common people who observed economic society systematically and, on the basis of this observation, affirmed the economic activities of the common people in this intellectual context. In the Tokugawa period, such ideas were just beginning to emerge.

One of the people who influenced these new ideas was Jinsai Ito (1627–1705), one of the greatest Confucianists of the Tokugawa period. Jinsai came from an upper class merchant family in the old capital of Kyoto where the power of the merchants had been rather strong in the middle ages. His experience living in such a tradition and his study of positivistic philosophy made him a critic of Chu Hsi philosophy. 'The Way' of Chu Hsi philosophy was a metaphysical concept which was far too difficult for the common people to comprehend. Also the ideal world of Chu Hsi philosophy was a society where the ruler or the virtuous person 'chun tzu', who had grasped the truth of 'The Way' by overcoming their own desires, led people to understand the norms of society. Jinsai, on the other hand, thought that 'The Way' was not so hard to reach. He believed that 'The Way' was a human relationship which even men and women of humble origin could enter daily through normal social and economic life (Ito [1705] 1971, p. 28). He thought that it was not necessary for the people to be taught this human relationship by the rulers, and this relationship rather was based on the emotions of people who had various common desires. For him, this emotion was not wild and bare but proper human nature which had been awakened and polished through daily existence in society, and, in other words, it was natural feeling that people commonly share in this world (Ito [1705] 1971, pp. 56–8). Therefore, the ideal way to rule the society 'Ohdo' was not through the moralistic education of people by the ruler but through the ruler's effort to learn and follow 'the common ways of his society' and 'to share the good and the bad of the time with the people' (Ito [1707] 1966, p. 109). Thus, according to his view, the entity responsible for establishing society was not the ruler but rather the common people. Jinsai, though he did not develop his own economic thought in detail, entrusted the formation of morality to the autonomy of 'the Tokugawa community', and as a result he opened the way to a new logic which acknowledged economy created by the common people as an independent entity.

Kyugu Tanaka (1662–1729) was a head of the Kawasaki village near Edo. He was an intelligent farmer but his name was not well known at all in his day. What made him famous later was his work entitled *Minkan Seiyo* (An Outline of Matters among Common People) (Tanaka [c.1722] 1996), which he wrote in his last years. This book was about rural administration and was based on his experiences. In the early eighteenth century the peasants around him in the suburban village were beginning to work in the money economy. How the upper class peasants in such circumstances viewed the function of economy in those days was depicted in this book. The first point that captures our attention in this book is Kyugu's view of the money economy. He realistically grasped the mechanism of the money economy and accepted its progress. For example he studied the effect of the Bakufu's policies on reissuing coinage that had been undertaken several times over the period of the last 30 years. He saw the effect of this policy on the demand and supply of labourers in each industry, the distribution of wealth among the people and the fluctuations in the economy as a whole. He concluded that the policy of economic expansion, or the strategy to increase the issue of money by devaluation, had helped the poor peasants. He called this kind of policy 'the honour of the Shogunate world' (Tanaka [c.1722] 1996, p. 107). Another point that we need to note is that Kyugu had some positive views on freedom in people's economic activities. He advocated the practice of 'free trade for land and forest', which was a well-known view advocated by him. It was partly because of his position as a landowner that he came to have such a view, but at the same time he tended to believe in the general idea that equilibrium existed in the market in the long term.

What supported his belief? First, he recognized that the economy was driven by the common aspiration in Japan 'to leave as many assets as possible to offspring' (Tanaka [c.1722] 1996, p. 31). In other words, the economy needed a certain motive such as the private pursuit of profit to facilitate development. Second, he felt that the changes in the money economy might be the natural course of historical progress. He said, 'There are both bright and dark sides in this ongoing change, and there is nobody who can determine whether we should move on or stop' (Tanaka [c.1722] 1996, p. 503). Thus, he was not sure about the direction of the changes taking place in the economy, but he was leaning towards the view that change means progress. He said, 'Wealth generates more available time, and if people have more time, better methods can be invented for each occupation. People can increase their knowledge and become smarter. Compared with the people in the past, we can produce better tools and undertake larger scale construction works' (Tanaka [c.1722] 1996, p. 400). This way of thinking was obviously different from the philosophy of Confucianism which claimed that people's life and morality, if unrestricted, would eventually degrade itself.

Late in his life, Kyugu joined the school of Sorai. What made Kyugu feel close to Sorai, who advocated strong political and economic policy on the part of the ruler? It is obvious that Kyugu and Sorai both recognized society and its economy objectively without the moralistic view of the Chu Hsi school. But it deserves more attention that Kyugu might have been affected by the Sorai's view about the personal domain in human life. Sorai was the first Confucian who claimed that there should exist a certain personal domain in human life. Kyugu must have identified with this view. In Sorai's case, this personal domain was only the human inner world, that is, poems, literature and so on, where people's feelings could be expressed. But Kyugu expanded Sorai's notion of a personal domain and included the economy in it, on the basis of the idea that there was a strong relationship between personal motive and active economy. In this way, the economic thoughts of the ruled class often developed by replacing parts of the existing philosophy of the ruling class.

Baien Miura (1723–89) came from a prestigious landowner's family in the rural area of Kyushu. He was both a doctor and a philosopher. He was influenced by both the empirical and positivistic views of the Sorai school and the studies of 'the Yi-King', one of 'the Six Classics', a book on the mystical and mathematical order that existed in the universe and in all beings. Through his friend who was an astronomer, he was also informed about Western astronomy and scientific thinking. Referring to these different ways of thinking, he considered his own philosophy. His book about economy, *Kagen* (The Origin of Value), was written on the basis of this unique philosophy (Miura [1773] 1953).

He wrote this book after he was asked by his feudal lord to address the relationship between changes in magistrates' wages and the harvest of agricultural products. In the book, he used the example of an imaginary island to simplify the explanation of economic phenomena. He described the changing economic situation of the island which was first supplied with resources and labour, and then by money in increasing amounts. In the course of this explanation he illustrated a typical quantity theory of money. And using this island model, he tried logically to explain the cycle of reproduction in agrarian villages which was being transformed into a society based on the money economy. He recognized the status of agrarian villages where money lenders were controlling the producers, and tried to find ways to change this situation. Unlike other contemporary thinkers, he did not think that the dominant power of money lenders was an unavoidable result of a growing money economy. Baien thought that gold and silver simply provided people with a convenient means of exchange. He said, 'gold and silver do no harm to the people. It is people who make gold and silver harm others' (Miura [1773] 1953 p. 67). Thus, he did not try to interfere with the progress of the money economy. He thought the effort to increase the surplus of products left in the hands of peasants was important. Therefore, he proposed the reduction of tax and an increase in production because, if the peasants possessed enough surplus, they could control the economy. He thought that whether peasants could increase the disposable surplus depended especially on the degree of tax reduction achieved under a benevolent lord. His analysis stopped there, so there are people who say that his thought is insufficient. However that would be a harsh criticism. His clear theory to affirm 'the wealth among producers' based on a rational understanding of the law of the economy was an innovative idea in his days. His conclusion anticipating the benevolence of feudal lords was optimistic, to be sure, but his idea that there would be healthy equilibrium brought about in the economy if surplus were secured for the people is also something that needs to be pointed out.

Norinaga Motoori (1730–1801), whose family were cotton merchants in Ise province, was one of the best known scholars of National Learning in the

Tokugawa period. He summarized his basic philosophy in *Tamakushige* (Precious Comb Box) (Motoori [c.1785] 1974). In this book he romantically idealized the society of ancient Japan where, in his view, people led their lives according to their frank emotion and gentle feeling, being watched over by various gods. On the other hand, he did not accept the conceptual normative standards of Confucianism, calling it 'the Chinese Mind'. In this judgment of value he accepted all historical events and happenings of society as 'intention of the gods' whether they were good or bad. This approach made him look like a conservative advocate who approved of the contemporary feudal system too. But if the situation of those days is taken into consideration, another interpretation may appear.

In Norinaga's day, in the late eighteenth century, Confucianists and political authorities were worried because the money economy was spreading further into the villages, the landowner–tenant relationship was expanding, the number of landless peasants was increasing, and the financial situation of the feudal lord was worsening. As a countermeasure, many Hans planned to reform their policies. The reform measures included the equal allotment of fields, which was for the protection of landless peasants, restrictive measures for the money economy and interference in it, for example via a monopoly system, approval of privileged trade groups and so on. Most of these actions derived from the concept of benevolent and moralistic policies found in Confucianism, for example, concepts such as the control of the money economy, maintenance of a sound society and the protection of landless peasants.

Observing these situations, Norinaga claimed in *Hihon Tamakushige* (A Secret Book of the Precious Comb Box) (Motoori [1787], 1974), that all the events and happenings of this world are controlled by the gods, so it was beyond the power of man to understand them. Therefore he said,

> The rulers should not try to undertake new policies based on shallow human considerations. If the ruler follows the path of his predecessors and never tries to counter the changes that occur over time, the lives of the people will be stabilized, even though people might face problems temporarily. (Motoori [1787] 1974, pp. 331–2)

This book was written in response to a request from his feudal lord who wanted to know the appropriate action that needed to be taken from time to time. However he simply answered that rulers should not launch any new policy. On the other hand, he affirmed common people's efforts in the economic world to make their family prosperous because such endeavours were prompted by spontaneous human nature. He also supported social change that was brought about as a result of the accumulation of people's economic efforts because it was driven by 'natural forces' and was considered to be 'the gods' will'. In short, Norinaga rejected deliberate interference by political

authorities into societies and the economy, but he tried to encourage economic activities by the common people. It was because of this notion of non-
interference in economic activity that the philosophy of Norinaga was so well
accepted by merchants and upper-class farmers and spread all over the country (Komuro, 1992).

Banto Yamagata, whom I referred to in Section 4, may be categorized also
in the same group. Banto's thoughts on an independent economy supported
by merchants' activities were limited to the central market, but his achievement was important in that he combined the moralistic view of Chu Hsi
philosophy with the theory of a free economy.

7. CONCLUSION

The above-mentioned five trends of philosophical thinking in the Tokugawa
period formed a foundation for the thinkers who followed. This legacy from
the Tokugawa period was used as the starting point of economic thinking by
the people in the Meiji period. What I have mentioned in this chapter might
lead readers to assume that there was a smooth process of transition from the
early philosophical thinking to the modern thought on the economy. However
we need to be aware of the fact that various differences existed between the
thought of the Tokugawa period and the modern thought of the Western
world. For example, during the Tokugawa period, the idea of individualism
was almost non-existent in economic thought. Though there were conflicts
and exchanges of views among the major schools of philosophy such as Chu
Hsi, Jinsai, Sorai and National Learning, each idea of economic thought was
rather isolated, and there was little dialectical development among them.

One of the major characteristics seen in economic thought during the
Tokugawa period was the emphasis on the relationship between the economy
and morality. Based on the moralistic viewpoint, there was a tendency to
regard economic activity as something harmful to the people. For example
the Chu Hsi school warned against involvement in profit making because
such activities were based on people's desires which were thought to be
immoral in themselves. But the devotees of such metaphysical norms of the
Chu Hsi school were few in number. What was much more usual in the
Tokugawa period was the 'Tokugawa community' itself which was established as 'the social roles system'. In short, if something seemed to destroy
this system, it was regarded as immoral. Even Sorai and Nobuhiro who were
looked upon as Machiavellian supported cooperation among the people and
the distribution of responsibility, and they claimed economic and profit-
making activities were immoral if they destroyed this cooperative relationship among the people. Ultimately their views supported the idea that for the

harmonious co-existence of people, the political authorities had to have control over the economy. This idea then served as the root of new thinking after the Meiji period that the government had to guide the economy.

However, as already discussed, in the Tokugawa period, there was a group of people who claimed that the guiding power of the economy should be left to the common people. The ruler's control over the economy could easily be supported by the moralistic teachings of Confucianism, but the advocates of prioritizing self-management on the part of the common people had much more difficulty in legitimizing their idea. They were also aware that economic and profit-making activities would have some harmful effects on the 'Tokugawa community', when they only paid attention to the dark side of these activities. Therefore they were considering with much effort how to relate their claim to the moralities. One example of the results of these considerations was the introduction of the notion of 'self learning'. The thinkers such as Baigan Ishida who were involved in the pursuit of new practical ethics thought that, through 'self learning' on the part of the common people, they became aware of the moralities in economic activities. In this way the co-existence of 'the Tokugawa community' and profit-making spirit would be realized.

On the other hand, there arose the desire to explore another idea that, even if the power to control economic activity were left to the common people, the co-existence of economic activity and morality, which was often the equivalent of cooperation, could be realized through the natural adjustments that took place in society. Jinsai thought that even when the common people became the guiding power of society and the economy, the spirit of cooperation would be maintained because the people would naturally learn the rules of their lives in society. On the other hand, Baien thought that as long as the feudal lord successfully found ways to leave a surplus of products in the hands of the people, the equilibrium of the economy would be realized and the process of sound reproduction would continue. He seemed to consider that in such a society there would be no destruction of the spirit of cooperation among the people.

There was also another idea that, even if a temporary destruction of cooperation among the people occurred, there might arise a better harmony in society afterwards. For example, Kyugu had a vague idea of progress. He thought that, as the number of chess pieces increased, the chances for successful problem solving would expand. In Norinaga's case, he thought that if left to the natural trend of the times, or to the intention of the gods, the best result would be obtained in the end.

However all those thinkers who said that the power to control economic activity should be left to the common people could not clearly show the ideal society that could be achieved through their free economic activities. What countered the value of the ruling class that had been upheld by Confucianism was only conveyed through mystical ideas, the intention of the gods, or uncertain emotions in common at large. Though there was a certain awareness that the guiding power should be left to an autonomous society for the proper functioning of the economy, they did not come up with a theory that could connect this view to a powerful idea of value. This period may emerge as the bottleneck for the further growth of philosophical thinking of this kind. However it is important to note that in those days some of the ideas of the economy were based on the common people's activities. At the beginning of the Meiji era, liberal theories of politics and the economy were accepted rapidly by the people, as was the policy of encouraging and promoting various industrial activities by the government. This rapid response to new ideas indicated that the people of the Tokugawa period set the stage for the subsequent appearance of the ideas of not only the control by the government but also the economic autonomy of the common people.

REFERENCES AND FURTHER READING

Bellah, Robert N. (1957), *Tokugawa Religion,* New York: Free Press.
Bito, Masahide (1961), *Nihon Hoken Shisoshi Kenkyu* (Study of the History of Japanese Feudal Thought), Tokyo: Aoki Shoten.
Bito, Masahide (1992), *Edojidai towa nanika* (What was the Edo Period?), Tokyo: Iwanami Shoten.
Dore, Ronald P. (1965), *Education in Tokugawa Japan,* Berkeley: University of California Press.
Fujiki, Hisashi (1975), 'Toituseiken no Seiritu' (Emergence of the Authority to Unify Japan), in *Iwanami Koza Nihon Rekisi,* vol. 9, Tokyo: Iwanami Shoten.
Fukuzawa, Yukichi (1899), *Fukuo Jiden,* reprinted in S. Tomita (ed.) (1978), Iwanami Bunko, Tokyo: Iwanami Shoten, translated by E. Kiyooka (1966) as *The Autobiography of Yukichi Fukuzawa,* New York and London: Columbia University Press.
Goi, Ranshuu (c.1740), 'Ranshuu Meiwa' *Kaitokudou Isho* (The Selected Lectures by Ranshuu), reprinted in T. Nishimura (ed.) (1913), Oosaka: Matsumura Bunkaido.
Hattori, Unokichi (ed.) (1921), *Shi Sho* (The Four Great Books), Tokyo: Yuhodo Shoten.
Hayami, Akira and Matao Miyamoto (1988), *Keizai Shakai no Seiritu* (Development into the Economical Society), Tokyo: Iwanami Shoten.
Honda, Tosiaki (1798a), *Saiiki Monogatari* (A Story about the Western World), reprinted in A.Tsukatani (ed.) (1970), *Nihon Shiso Taikei,* vol. 44, Tokyo: Iwanami Shoten.
Honda, Tosiaki (1798b), *Keisei Hisaku* (Secret Plans to Manage the State), reprinted in A. Tsukatani (ed.) (1970), *Nihon Shiso Taikei,* vol. 44, Tokyo: Iwanami Shoten.
Honjo, Eijiro (1965), *Economic Theory and History of Japan in the Tokugawa Period,* New York: Russell and Russell.
Ihara, Saikaku (1688), *Nihon Eitai Gura,* translated by G.W. Sargent (1959) as *The Japanese Family Storehouse,* Cambridge: Cambridge University Press.

Ito, Jinsai (1705), *Gomo Jigi* (Meaning of the Words in the Analects of Confucius and Mencius), reprinted in S. Shimizu (ed.) (1971), *Nihon Shiso* Taikei, vol. 33, Tokyo: Iwanami Shoten.

Ito, Jinsai (1707), *Doji Mon* (Boy's Questions), reprinted in S. Shimizu (ed.) (1966), *Nihon Koten Bungaku Taikei*, vol. 97, Tokyo: Iwanami Shoten.

Kaiho, Seiryo (c.1810s), *Tennodan* (Discourses of Supreme Administration), reprinted in K. Nomura (ed.) (1935), *Nihon Keizai Gakusetusi Shiryo*, Tokyo: Keio University Press.

Kaiho, Seiryo (1813), *Keikodan* (Preliminary Discourses), reprinted in S. Kuranami (ed.) (1970), *Nihon Shiso Taikei*, vol. 44, Tokyo: Iwanami Shoten.

Komuro, Masamichi (1992), 'Motoori Norinaga ni okeru shinpo to senki' (New and traditional policies in Norinaga's thought), *Rikkyo Keizaigaku Kenkyu*, vol. 45, no. 3, 35–54.

Maruyama, Masao (1952), *Nihon Seiji Shisoshi Kenkyu*, Tokyo: University of Tokyo Press, translated by M. Hane (1974) as *Studies in The Intellectual History of Tokugawa Japan*, Tokyo: University of Tokyo Press.

Minamoto, Ryoen (1972), *Tokugawa Gori Shiso no Keifu* (History of Tokugawa Rationalism), Tokyo: Chuokoronsha.

Miura, Baien (1773), *Kagen* (The Origin of Value), reprinted in H. Saegusa (ed.) (1953), Iwanami Bunko, Tokyo: Iwanami Shoten.

Miyazaki, Yasusada (1697), *Nogyo Zensho* (A Complete Book of Agriculture), reprinted in T. Ymada and T. Iura (eds) (1978), *Nihon Nosho Zenshu*, vols 12–13, Tokyo: Nosangyoson Bunka Kyoukai.

Morris-Suzuki, Tessa (1989), *A History of Japanese Economic Thought*, London and New York: Routledge.

Motoori, Norinaga (c.1785), *Tamakushige* (Precious Comb Box), reprinted in S. Ono and T. Ookubo (eds) (1974), *Motoori Norinaga Zenshyu*. vol. 8, Tokyo: Chikuma Shobo.

Motoori, Norinaga (1787), *Hihon Tamakushige* (A Secret Book of the Precious Comb Box) (1974), reprinted in S. Ono and T. Ookubo (eds), *Motoori Norinaga Zenshyu*, vol. 8, Tokyo: Chikuma Shobo.

Najita, Tetsuo and Irwin Scheiner (eds) (1978), *Japanese Thought in the Tokugawa Period*, Chicago and London: The University of Chicago Press.

Najita, Tetsuo (1987), *Vision of Virtue in Tokugawa Japan*, Chicago: The University of Chicago Press.

Nakai, Nobuhiko (1975), *Chonin* (Town Dwellers), Tokyo: Shogakukan.

Nishikawa, Shunsaku (1979), *Edojidai no Political Economy* (Political Economy in the Edo Period), Tokyo: Nihon Hyoron-sha.

Ogyu, Sorai (1717), *Bendo* (On Distinguishing the Way), reprinted in T. Nishida (ed.) (1973), *Nihon Shiso Taikei*, vol. 36, Tokyo: Iwanami Shoten.

Ogyu, Sorai (c.1717), *Benmei* (On Distinguishing Terms), reprinted in T. Nishida (ed.) (1973), *Nihon Shiso Taikei*, vol. 36, Tokyo: Iwanami Shoten.

Ogyu, Sorai (1727), *Gakusoku* (The Academy's Regulation), reprinted in T. Nishida (ed.) (1973), *Nihon Shiso Taikei*, vol. 36, Tokyo: Iwanami Shoten.

Ogyu, Sorai (c.1727), *Seidan* (Political Discourses), reprinted in T. Tsuji (ed.) (1973), *Nihon Shiso Taikei*, vol. 36, Tokyo: Iwanami Shoten.

Sato, Nobuhiro (1822), *Keizai Yoryaku* (An Outline of the Political Economy), reprinted in T. Shimazaki (ed.) (1977), *Nihon Shiso Taikei*, vol. 45, Tokyo: Iwanami Shoten.

Sato, Nobuhiro (1823), *Kondo Hisaku* (A Secret Policy to Unify the World), reprinted in T. Shimazaki (ed.) (1977), *Nihon Shiso Taikei,* vol. 45, Tokyo: Iwanami Shoten.

Sato, Nobuhiro (c.1833), *Suito Hiroku* (A Secret Book for the Everlasting Administration), reprinted in T. Shimazaki (ed.) (1977), *Nihon Shiso Taikei*, vol. 45, Tokyo: Iwanami Shoten.

Shimazaki, Takao (1968), 'Introduction to the economic thought of Japan', *Keio Economic Studies*, vol. 5, 11–34.

Sugihara, T., T. Sakasai, A. Fujiwara and T. Fujii (eds) (1990), *Nihon no Keizai Shiso 400 nen* (A History of Japanese Economic Thought Last 400 Years), Tokyo: Nihon Keizai Hyoron-sha.

Tanaka, Kyugu (c.1722), *Minkan Seiyo* (An Outline of Matters among Common People), reprinted in T. Murakami (ed.) (1996), Tokyo: Yuurindo.

Watanabe, Hiroshi (1985), *Kinsei Nihon Shakai to Sougaku* (Society of Early Tokugawa Era and Sung Philosophies), Tokyo: University of Tokyo Press.

Yamagata, Banto (c.1807), *Yume no Shiro* (Instead of Dreaming), reprinted in T.Arisaka (ed.) (1973), *Nihon Shiso Taikei.* vol. 44, Tokyo: Iwanami Shoten.

Yanagita, Kunio (1926), *Nihon Noumin Shi* (A History of Japanese Peasants), reprinted (1969) in, *Teihon Yanagita Kunio Shu*, vol. 16, Tokyo: Chikuma Shobo.

2. Enlightenment and economic thought in Meiji Japan: Yukichi Fukuzawa and Ukichi Taguchi

Jiro Kumagai

INTRODUCTION

Both Yukichi Fukuzawa (1835–1901) and Ukichi Taguchi (1855–1905), like many other thinkers of Meiji enlightenment, were greatly influenced by the ideas of F.P.G. Guizot, H.T. Buckle, Herbert Spencer, J.S. Mill, Samuel Smiles, as well as liberal political economists mainly originating from the British classical school.

However the evaluation of their thoughts by scholars has been striking in their contrast. Fukuzawa, one of the most distinguished and influential thinkers in the Meiji era, has been discussed from various viewpoints. At one end of the spectrum is a view that regards Fukuzawa as an advocate of autocratic enlightenment, and at the other as a civic liberal. Even where appraisal is confined to Fukuzawa's economic thought, it has been called 'a system of miserable contradictions'.[1] On the other hand, Taguchi has gained quite a unanimous evaluation in the respect that he was a consistent advocate of free competition, free trade, and *laissez-faire* doctrine.

The diversity of estimations regarding Fukuzawa can be better understood when one realizes the fact that his writings fundamentally lay in proposing prescriptions for dealing with the problems surrounding Japan in the late nineteenth century. Confronted with the imperialistic encroachment of Western nations into Asia, the foremost objective for Fukuzawa was how to preserve Japan's independence. In order to accomplish this objective, Fukuzawa had to tackle two main tasks: first, the destruction of feudalism and Confucianism, both of which hinder the spirit of individual independence that assuredly constitutes the basis of national independence; and second, accepting Western civilization as a means of retaining the independence of the country whilst making Japan develop as a strong and wealthy nation.

These two tasks contain contradictions such as individuals filled with independent spirit vs. a strong nation, the people's rights vs. the state's rights, and the idealized Western civilization vs. the factual one. Thus Fukuzawa's arguments are inevitably characterized by realistic responses to situations in the light of his fundamental mission to conserve national independence and cope with the Western nations. As specific situations prescribe Fukuzawa's particular responses, he often expresses alternative views on the similar problems in different situations.[2] The diversity of interpretations of Fukuzawa's view undoubtedly springs from this complexity of his ideas.

Taguchi, though not so well known as Fukuzawa, was yet a remarkable figure in carrying forward the banner of *laissez-faire* doctrine in Meiji Japan, mainly with his journal the *Tokyo Keizai Zasshi* (the Tokyo Economist).

Taguchi was firmly convinced of the harmonious natural law in the economic world. This conviction enabled him to remain a staunch non-interventionist as far as economic policy was concerned, although not being entirely free from imperialistic traits in the days after the Sino–Japanese War (1894–95) and during the Russo–Japanese War (1904–5).

This chapter will elucidate the sources of the contrasting evaluations of Fukuzawa and Taguchi and in doing so demonstrate the significance of their thoughts in modern Japan.

FUKUZAWA AND CRITICISM OF CONFUCIANISM

Although opportunities to visit Western countries were rarely available in the Tokugawa era due to Japan's national isolation policy, Fukuzawa was given the chance to make three voyages as a member of the missions despatched by the Shogunate government in the mid-nineteenth century.[3] Following his experiences abroad, Fukuzawa became possessed with a solid conviction that national independence would be impossible without the spirit of individual independence. Fukuzawa's conviction was reinforced when he saw the servile attitudes of the Chinese towards the English in Hong Kong on his way to Europe in 1862. The scene unquestionably implanted in his mind that people who had no spirit of independence and self-reliance could not embrace any patriotic mind and felt no shame in obeying foreigners (FYZ, 8/65–6; 19/6).[4]

The lack of independent spirit was found not only in Hong Kong, but also in Oriental countries by and large under the control of the Western powers. The main cause of this spiritual weakness, Fukuzawa felt, lay in feudalism and Confucian learning which ideologically bolstered up the feudalistic social order. It was Confucianism that stood in the way of cultivating the spirit of individual independence which was prerequisite to the establishment of a strong and wealthy nation. Fukuzawa says in his autobiography:

The Confucian civilization of the East seems to me to lack two things possessed by Western civilization: sciences in the material sphere and a sense of independence in the spiritual sphere (FYZ, 7/167) ... I must try to change the whole people's way of thinking from its very foundations. Thereby I cannot fail to make Japan into a great new civilized nation in the East, comparable with Britain in the West (FYZ, 7/259).

Confucian learning that identifies hierarchical social order as a reflection of the immutable natural order of the heavenly body, says Fukuzawa, imbeds a dependent and servile spirit in Japanese people. They are bound by a misconception that social hierarchy is as natural as heaven is higher than the earth. Consequently they show a docile and obedient attitude to power. Thus Fukuzawa characterizes Japanese civilization as a 'preponderance of power' (FYZ, 4/146–7).

Preponderance of power exists in almost all social relations in Japan; between teacher and pupil, master and servant, rich and poor, high and low. The Japanese spirit of dependence and deplorable irresponsibility both derive from this preponderance of power, and the resulting lack of independent spirit generates apathy among most Japanese towards nationwide affairs like national independence. Preponderance of power also curbs the rise of commerce and manufacturing by creating disdain for the pursuit of individual benefit.

In contrast with the Japanese civilization, Fukuzawa contends, the Western one is characterized by its tendency of political and economic powers moving towards an average condition, helped by the rise of the bourgeoisie with its free and independent spirit (FYZ, 4/142, 145–6). From his comparison of these two civilizations, Fukuzawa intentionally stresses the necessity of separation from the Confucian ideas. In this regard, Fukuzawa is a great stalwart in the struggle against feudalism and its ideology, and deserves to receive the honour of the champion of Meiji enlightenment.

The tendency of Western civilization to head for an average social condition or the realization of equal rights among people must also be discernible in international relations; all nations have equal rights like all men do. Western civilization must be based on these sort of natural and rational principles. Based on this understanding of Western civilization, Fukuzawa declares in section one (1872) of his unprecedented best-seller, *Gakumon no Susume* (An Encouragement of Learning, 1872–74):

Both Japan and Western countries lie between the same heaven and the same earth. They enjoy the same sunshine, look at same moon, share the same oceans, and possess the same human affections... We should promote each other's interests and pray for each other's welfare. We should associate with each other in accordance with *tenli-jindo* (the real principles of life and nature). We must respect even black African slaves if they have *li* (the natural reason, or principle) on their side. ... Both individuals and countries possess freedom and independence based on *ten no doli* (the natural reason ordained by heaven). (FYZ, 3/31)

Notably Fukuzawa uses here key Confucian words in expressing the real principles of life and nature in spite of his stern criticism of Confucianism. As many current scholars of Meiji enlightenment have pointed out, Confucian words or concepts helped to facilitate the absorption of Western ideas and served as an effective bridge towards their understanding. Such facilitation seems to be applicable even to Fukuzawa's case. Considering this, we should take notice of the distinction between Fukuzawa's criticism of Confucianism as a feudalistic ideology and Confucian learning as an academic study. For Fukuzawa, it is one thing to evaluate Confucius and other Confucians as scholars, and another to criticize the social and ideological function of their ideas, which are conducive to upholding hierarchical social order.[5] His way of criticizing Confucianism, which attaches importance to its functional role rather than its academic substance, is also utilized in his accepting Western civilization.

WESTERN CIVILIZATION AS A MEANS

Fukuzawa accepts those universal features of Western civilization which bolster the natural principles of equal rights among men and nations, together with the encouragement of an independent spirit. However, he simultaneously recognizes the factual aspects of Western civilization by saying that wars are incessantly repeated among the Western countries, their ordinary measures for intercourse are deceitful trickery, and not a day passes without hearing news about robbery and murders (FYZ, 4/18). Actual Western civilization is inflicted with diseases in its social institutions, manners and customs, and distribution of wealth and power. Therefore it is 'neither absolute nor perfect' (FYZ, 4/628).

Additionally, real relations in the contemporary world did not consist of equal rights among various nations. As early as 1875 Fukuzawa wrote in his most important work, *Bunmeiron no Gairyaku* (An Outline of a Theory of Civilization):

> To whom did the present America originally belong? The white men drove out the Indians, original masters of the country, and the position of host and guest has entirely changed. Hence the civilization of the present America is really that of the white men and cannot be called the civilization of America. ... In all places touched by the Europeans, are there any that have developed their powers, attained benefits, and preserved their independence? (FYZ, 4/202)

After referring to countries which lost independence by contact with Western countries such as Persia, India, Siam, Luzon, Java, the Sandwich Islands and Hawaii, Fukuzawa continued:

> In the case of a vast country like China, the white men have not yet penetrated into the interior land and their traces have been left only along the coast, but it is very likely that the Chinese Empire will become nothing but a garden for the Europeans in the future. Wherever the Europeans come, the land ceases to be productive, and trees and plants cease to grow. ... When people realise that Japan is also a country in the East, they must inevitably fear for the future, even though up till now Japan has suffered no great harm from foreign intercourse. (FYZ, 4/202–3)

Through these sentences, one understands that Fukuzawa does not believe that Western civilization is an ideal state. This being the case, should Japan then discard Western civilization, and yet preserve her independence with her traditional civilization? If Japan chose this path, she would have to stay at the stage of a semi-civilized nation like China or Turkey, superior to Africa and most of the rest of Asia, but inferior to the West (FYZ, 4/16). Therefore Fukuzawa insists that there is no other way but to accept Western civilization at the level it is, even though it is far from perfect.

Thus it follows that the adoption of Western civilization is a means to preserve national independence. Fukuzawa emphasized that the Japanese acceptance of Western civilization would enable her to escape the disastrous fate which India and other countries under Western dominance were suffering. 'Western civilization', he writes, 'is an incomparable means for both strengthening our national polity and increasing the prestige of our imperial line' (FYZ, 4/33). 'To fear strong opponents and at the same time to admire their civilization' is his attitude towards Western civilization (FYZ, 3/107).

In 1881 Fukuzawa published another important essay, *Jiji Shogen* (Current Affairs Briefly Discussed) which is considered to mark a decisive turning point in his thinking. The essay was written at the time when 'contemporary civilization is extraordinary filled with wars' (FYZ, 5/98), and the domestic government, which Fukuzawa supported as contributors to the reforms of the Meiji Restoration and promoters of Westernization, was exposed to crisis from an upsurge of the movement for freedom and people's rights. Against these intensive situations, he urges that Japan should rely on the power of arms in order to compete with Western nations: 'when others [Western nations] use violence, we must be violent too. When others use deceitful trickery, we must do likewise' (FYZ, 5/108).

In the same vein he stressed the necessity to reverse the order of priority of the leading motto in modern Japan, that is, 'wealth and strength' into 'strength and wealth' which meant the strengthening of arms first and the enrichment of the country next. According to Fukuzawa, only when we can succeed in strengthening the government's power and expanding national rights will we enjoy a glorious reputation as a wealthy and strong nation. Hence he created the well-known catchword: 'Peace inside and emulate outside' (FYZ, 5/118) which means the pursuit of domestic tranquillity (restraining the movement for freedom and people's rights) whilst expressing a national unified power outwards in order to compete with more advanced countries.

Fukuzawa says further in *Jiji Shogen* that 'the people of Western nations call themselves "Christian nations" in order to demonstrate a clear distinction between themselves and everyone else'. The British way of ruling the Indians is one example of this distinction, since 'the British relations with the Indians could hardly be described as human intercourse' (FYZ, 5/184).

He was very anxious that the spread of Christianity in Japan was exerting harmful effects on the spirit of people in regard to the conservation of national rights. 'The Westerners were our teachers of tangible things, that is, external form of civilization but not of mind, whereas nowadays Western Christians are attempting to be the teachers of our mind and some Japanese really admire foreigners' minds' (FYZ, 5/212). Worried about this tendency, he even insisted on inspiring the 'spirit of *shizoku*' (the descendant of *samurai*) to emulate and counter this foreign influence (FYZ, 5/221).[6]

Taguchi could not overlook these arguments of Fukuzawa and rose to criticize him, saying that a strong government and the reinforcement of military power had nothing to do with the welfare of the people and that the government should restrict its role to the protection of the people's rights (TUZ, 6/128–9).[7] And then Taguchi sarcastically refutes Fukuzawa's view of Christianity and the Western mind: Where has the Western spirit Fukuzawa had so admired gone? How does Fukuzawa justify his own devotion to Western learning in his youth, if he declares the mind of Western learning destroys the country? After this denunciation, Taguchi maintains that 'Western learning has facilitated the national rights rather than has done harm on them' (TUZ, 8/450). It is far more harmful to interfere with religion than to let it go freely. Taguchi believed that the best way to secure national rights was to adopt a *laissez-faire* attitude towards religion (TUZ, 8/450–51). The feature of Taguchi's ideas, in contrast to Fukuzawa, seems to be expressed in this debate.

In spite of his emphasis on the spirit of *shizoku*, Fukuzawa, in an article entitled 'Gaiko-ron' (On Diplomacy, 1883), claims that there is no alternative for Japan but to 'eat up uncivilized countries on the side of civilized countries'. And if we do not take this option, the only way left for us is to join together with Asian countries with old manners and customs, and 'lay ourselves before civilized countries to be eaten up by them' (FYZ, 9/195–6). Hereby he joined the camp of imperialism and in a famous article entitled 'Datsua-ron' (Going out of Asia, 1885) declared:

We cannot wait for our neighbour countries to become so civilized that all may combine together to make Asia progress. We must rather break out of the companion and behave in the same way as the civilized countries of the West are doing. We would do better to treat China and Korea in the same way, as do the Western nations. (FYZ, 10/240)

According to Fukuzawa, Asian countries were still captured by Confucian bonds and not able to progress towards the path of Westernization. Japan's intervention in Korean domestic affairs, therefore, could be justified under the plea of promoting civilization. The same argument can be applied to China. Fukuzawa states that 'to destroy the [Chinese] government is the only way to direct the people towards civilization' (FYZ, 7/214). Thereby the Sino–Japanese War is classified as 'the war between civilization and barbarism' (FYZ, 14/491).

POLITICAL ECONOMY AND TRADE

In a speech made at the Keio Gijuku school in 1889, Fukuzawa recollected the days when he first encountered political economy: 'political economy is really fascinating and its refined argument often takes us by surprise. It overturned our inbred Confucian mind' (FYZ, 12/131).

It was over 20 years before this that Fukuzawa first published his writing on political economy, *Seiyo Jijo Gaihen* (External volume of Conditions in the West, 1868), in which he introduced classical political economy based substantially on *Chambers's Educational Course: Political Economy* (1852) and partly on Francis Wayland's *The Elements of Political Economy* (1837).

What we can see by reading *Seiyo Jijo Gaihen* is that Fukuzawa learnt through the writings of Chambers and Wayland that there are economic laws in social life beyond the control of human beings just as there are natural laws in physical phenomena. By referring to daily life in London, he describes how enormous amounts of food come from various countries and are exchanged in the market without confusion in accord with the law of supply and demand (FYZ, 1/240). For Fukuzawa 'this is really an amazing thing' (FYZ, 1/459) and the market mechanism based on economic laws is conceived by him as 'a huge machine with exquisite structure' (FYZ, 1/461). He was undoubtedly impressed with market mechanism as seen in his statement: 'Social order shines most brilliantly amidst confusion' (FYZ, 8/666).

In Fukuzawa's mind, market mechanism is sustained by the principle that self-interest is the foundation of public interest, and public interest is in turn fulfilled by the act of people who pursue their individual profit. 'Human beings', says Fukuzawa, 'have a sort of natural propensity to act' which is mistakenly regarded as 'narrow-minded self-interest', but 'works just like a gift from heaven by which welfare and happiness are increased and the best virtue is realised' (FYZ, 1/458). It follows from this that 'fighting for profit is nothing but fighting for *li*' (the natural reason, or principle) (FYZ, 4/97). By resorting to the fundamental concept of Confucian learning, *li*, Fukuzawa attempts here to convert negatively perceived ideas of self-interest and profit into positive ones.

Fukuzawa's harmonious understanding of self-interest and public benefit leads him to limit the economic role of the government to the field of providing public utilities, constructing infrastructure and in the fulfilment of social capital: 'Generally speaking, government should not interfere with the affairs of agriculture, manufacturing, and commerce' (FYZ, 1/437). He stresses that free competition must be predominant in domestic economic policy.

Fukuwaza apparently applies his comprehension of market mechanism to international trade. He contends in *Seiyo Jijo Gaihen* that every country can gain mutual profit by the utilization of its own natural resources and in specializing in specific products suitable to its own country. Therefore setting national boundaries is equivalent to disturbing the expected profit through mutual intercourse of trade. There is no advantage in dividing each country into a sovereign state from an economic stance. So it is the best policy to pursue free trade in order to extirpate the causes of wars (FYZ, 1/414, 460–61). Fukuzawa thus seems to acknowledge the general adaptability of market order both domestically and internationally.

But as anticipated from his understanding of Western civilization, Fukuzawa loses no time in pointing out the differences between principle and reality in the economic world. 'The intercourse of states is fundamentally different from that of individuals, ... since people hold specific feelings towards their own country' (FYZ, 4/204). Correspondingly even though free trade is good as an abstract theory, it could not be applicable as a general rule.

Taking the examples of India and Turkey, he says in *Gakumon no Susume* (1874) that India was once a country well known for its literature, and Turkey was a great country of warriors. But now the Indian people are not so far from being British slaves, and their sole business at the present is to grow opium to supply to the Chinese. Only British merchants obtain great profit by the transaction. Turkey is also an independent country in name only, and the British and French govern her trade. By virtue of free trade, her natural products are declining day by day, and all manufacturing goods are entirely dependent on imports from Britain and France (FYZ, 3/107).

Fukuzawa undoubtedly grasps the reality of developed countries controlling underdeveloped countries by virtue of free trade. He recognized that a market mechanism that is expected to bring about universal opulence would not work as beautifully as theory indicates. He naturally applies this recognition to his own country. Japan must protect her manufacturing industries against advanced countries which would enforce free trade on Japan for their own sake: 'In trade between a manufacturing country and a growing country, the former makes use of unlimited human power and the latter limited produce of land … This is approximately what happens in our present state of trade with foreign countries. We shall lose out in the end' (FYZ, 4/193–4).

Thus Fukuzawa regards protective trade as a sensible and realistic economic policy for a weak country like Japan, which must avoid being placed on the losing side in foreign trade. The foundation of the strong and wealthy nation at the time must be based on protective trade, by which we could foster infant industries and catch up with developed countries. Free trade can hardly apply until Japan is able to stand on an equal footing with advanced foreign countries.

It was not until 1893 in his article 'Jitsugyo-ron' (On Business) that Fukuzawa proclaimed 'I avowedly advocate here free trade for the first time' (FYZ, 6/181). The development of the industrial revolution in Japan evidently enabled him to make this declaration. Now the Japanese economy had grown enough to supply manufacturing goods on her own which she was obliged to import before. There were even some manufactured goods which Japan was exporting. Cotton spinning above all was ranked as the champion of exports: 'As far as cotton spinning is concerned, India is not our rival any more and even British spinning, that worldly distinguished manufacturing, could not compete long with Japan' (FYZ, 6/142). Therefore 'it is the best way for Japan to become an Oriental trading nation by opening up various ports for unfettered imports and exports so that we can get cheap food and clothes domestically, and spread our wings wide internationally' (FYZ, 6/186–7). Whereby Fukuzawa changed his view from protective trade to free trade in correspondence to the change of situations.

From his early days as a writer, Fukuzawa persistently stressed the significance of foreign trade. He viewed Britain, his model to follow, as 'the most affluent country as well as the top trading country in the world', and emphasized the prosperity of Japan by means of foreign trade: 'we are not engaged in trade as a result of our riches. On the contrary, we can increase our wealth as a result of our engagement in trade' (FYZ, 9/351). In 'Jitsugyo-ron' he maintains this foreign trade-oriented view to say that 'the driving force of our business lies primarily in foreign trade and we cannot find any fields that are free from the influence of the progress of trade' (FYZ, 6/163).

But as seen above, one could say that Fukuzawa's stance towards the policy of foreign trade showed a change from protectionism to free trade around the 1890s according to the change of situation.

For Fukuzawa, 'value does not exist in things themselves, but in the way they work' (FYZ, 4/37). Nothing is in itself either good or bad, but it is only the way in which it is used that makes it so. This practical, utilitarian and

functional stance of thinking for the attainment of the preservation of national independence and development of economy penetrated both his attitude towards the reception of Western civilization and the policy of foreign
trade.

TAGUCHI AND HIS FUNDAMENTAL IDEAS

Ukichi Taguchi was born in Edo as a son of a low-ranked but direct feudatory
samurai of the Tokugawa shogunate. His family came from the lineage of a
noted Confucian scholar, Issai Sato. As if reflecting this heritage, at the age of
11 Ukichi won a silver prize in a test of reading Confucian classics held by
the Shogunate government and started serving as a lower Bakufu official.

After the collapse of the Tokugawa shogunate, Taguchi suffered many
hardships while continuing his study in Chinese classics, English, and medicine and pharmacy. But at the age of 17, obliged to earn a living, he entered
the translation board of the Treasury as a senior pupil. As the Treasury had a
large supply of current Western books at that time, Taguchi naturally shifted
his area of study from medicine and pharmacy to political economy and
history. After the abolition of the translation board in 1874, Taguchi trans-
ferred to the currency board and remained there until he quitted the Treasury
in 1878.

During his service at the Treasury from the age of 17 to 23, Taguchi mainly
studied the writings of H.D. Macleod, C.F. Bastiat and A.L. Perry which
more or less adhered to the *laissez-faire* economic doctrine. For Taguchi, who
had no opportunity to visit Europe and America as Fukuzawa did, the study
of political economy at the Treasury prescribed the foundations for his ideas
throughout his life.

Being often called 'Adam Smith in Japan', Taguchi was undoubtedly influenced by Adam Smith. But his economic thought fundamentally belongs to
the Manchester school and the third school of economics named by H.D.
Macleod as he declares: 'I never deny that people refer to me as the Manchester school characterized by *laissez-faire* or liberalism represented by Cobden
and Bright' (TUZ, 3/412); 'Political economy nearest to my view is that of
Macleod in Britain, C.F. Bastiat in France and A.L. Perry in America' (TUZ,
8/205). Along with these economic thinkers, Taguchi was also influenced by
H. Spencer as an advocate of *laissez-faire* doctrine and Buckle as a historian
of civilization.[8]

Being influenced and stimulated by the study of Western economics and
social ideas, Taguchi started writing his two most famous books whilst still
under service for the Treasury: *Nihon Kaika Shoshi* (A Short History of
Japan's Enlightenment, 1877–82) and *Jiyu Koeki Nihon Keizai-ron* (Free

Trade and the Japanese Economy, 1878). However it is notable that these early writings show, as we will see below, the influence of not only Western ideas but also Confucian learning that permeated Taguchi's mind through the education in his youth.

After his resignation from the Treasury in 1879 at the age of 24, Taguchi launched into his long-cherished publishing business and started issuing an economic journal, the *Tokyo Keizai Zasshi* (the Tokyo Economist, first monthly and then weekly, discontinued in 1923), with the aspiration to be a match for the London *Economist*.

Taguchi's aims in the *Tokyo Keizai Zasshi* were not only to report and comment on current economic topics, trends and problems, but also to propagate political economy as a science among people. Noting that there was no academic journal of political economy at that time, his purpose to disseminate the knowledge of political economy was highly worthy. In Taguchi's journal various economic schools ranging widely from British classical, protectionist, German historical, Austrian marginal to the socialist school were introduced and commented on in plain form by appropriate specialists apart from Taguchi's own *laissez-faire* standpoint. In this respect the *Tokyo Keizai Zasshi,* until around the turn of the century, played a pivotal role in the enlightenment of political economy in Japan.

Along with the issue of the *Tokyo Keizai Zasshi,* Taguchi presided over the Tokyo Keizaigaku Koshukai (The Tokyo Economic Lecture Society), and published a series of translations on the writings of Western social sciences amongst which was the first translation of Adam Smith's *The Wealth of Nations*.

In 1887 Taguchi organized the Keizaigaku Kyokai (The Economic Society), a non-governmental academic society with the purpose of spreading and promoting the progress of political economy in both theory and practice. The society contributed to the spread of economic knowledge by means of lectures, debates, policy propositions and publishing activities. He also served as a Member of Parliament from 1894 until his death in 1905.

There is no doubt that one of Taguchi's contributions to Meiji enlightenment lies in the introduction and dissemination of Western ideas through various organizations under his management. But what makes him stand out as a conspicuous figure in modern Japan is his uncompromising liberal economic thought and unyielding individualism. Behind his arguments for free trade and a *laissez-faire* policy lurks his conviction in the natural law or universal principle stemming from the influence of not only Western ideas but also Confucianism, Chu Hsi philosophy in particular.

TAGUCHI ON CIVILIZATION

In contrast to Fukuzawa, Taguchi does not highlight the difference between Western and Japanese civilization. On the contrary, Taguchi lays stress on the fundamental similarity between these two civilizations.

According to Taguchi, the elements that advance civilization are inherent within all countries, and there is a universal law of progress and development in the same way as the plant has its own law of growth. Just as plants are destined by their very nature to grow to a certain shape and size, so society is bound to progress along a certain line. 'There is no difference between the progress of society and that of organic things' (TUZ, 2/106).

In *Nihon Kaika Shoshi* which was written with reference to some of the classics of Japanese historians together with Western thinkers such as H.T. Buckle and H. Spencer and others, Taguchi says that 'the true nature of human beings lies in securing life and avoiding death' (TUZ, 2/11), and self-interest results from such nature.

Taguchi sees no difference in human nature between the West and Japan: 'Human nature is one and the same all over the world. Therefore the elements which have facilitated enlightenment of the Westerners must exist in the people of this country' (TUZ, 2/127).

The European enlightenment, Taguchi argues, is not the one led by the noble, but by the common people. Commerce and free trade have their origin in the demands of the common people. The impetus for various inventions that have brought about the present European civilization derives from those demands made by the majority of society. Thus Taguchi understands that the enlightenment is nothing but an advance from an aristocratic civilization to a democratic one led by the common people. He contends:

> Civilization and enlightenment, as shown in Western books, lead society to an average condition. The difference in the style of travel between the noble and common people has narrowed as a result of the invention of railway and steamship. The invention of weaving machinery has also reduced the difference in the clothes worn by the noble and the commoner ... In accordance with technical progress and the invention of various instruments, the noble and the commoner have become closer to each other in life style. (TUZ, 2/119)

It is true, says Taguchi, that the Western countries are running ahead of Japan at the present in the tendency towards an average of social condition which characterizes the progress of civilization. But the elements advancing civilization are inherent in Japan as well. In fact, he contends, 'we can find them in the labouring society of this country' (TUZ, 2/127). The clothes of labourers such as *momohiki* (long underwear or close-fitting trousers), *harakake* (workman's waistcoat), and *hanten* (workman's short coat) demonstrate it. They are very like Western trousers, vest, and overcoats respectively. The people of high society in the Tokugawa era abhorred eating meat and adhered to plain fish and vegetables, whereas meat was eaten in labouring society (TUZ, 2/128).

By enumerating these examples, Taguchi puts emphasis on the existence of the elements of social progress in Japan and concluded that 'learning the merits of the West is quite different from being subordinate to the Westerners' (TUZ, 2/521). Moreover he sees Western civilization as 'really nothing other than a result of the enlightenment that our lower society will necessarily reach in the end' (TUZ, 2/118). The progress of mankind, either in Europe or Japan, advances along a path which leads the social condition of various ranks towards an average. Thus Taguchi urges 'to remove every aristocratic trait, either tangible or intangible, from our civilization, and hereby increase wealth, develop knowledge and reform our race' (TUZ, 2/137). We Japanese should study Western learning such as physics, political economy and other sciences, not because the West has discovered them, but because they embody universal truth. The Japanese wish to set up a constitutional government, not because it has Western origins, but because it accords with human nature (TUZ, 2/522).

Taguchi asserts that Europe and Japan are equal in terms of their possession of the elements of civilization, and that the Japanese do not need to feel inferiority relative to Western civilization in this respect. We can see in this assertion Taguchi's proclamation of nationalism colouring Meiji enlightenment in general.

FREE TRADE, POLITICAL ECONOMY AND THE FUNDAMENTAL PRINCIPLE

Taguchi's argument that civilization has a tendency towards an average state arouses a resonant response in his argument on free trade.

The high or low cost of production caused by 'bounty or stinginess of natural endowment' induces countries to adopt an international division of labour in which they export those products with which they are naturally endowed and import those products in which they have a scarcity of natural endowment. Through this sort of trade, economic resources will be evenly distributed among countries all over the world. Taguchi says in *Jiyu Koeki Nihon Keizai-ron* that 'the exports and imports in foreign trade are caused by the movement in which various goods go out and come in seeking for an average level' (TUZ, 3/16). The rise and fall of prices is nothing but a reflection of the movement towards this average.

Taguchi compares the economic movement to the flow of the atmosphere in nature. Gases and fluids are repeatedly in states of 'endosmose' (penetration) and 'exosmose' (exudation). Their movements are caused by a mutual desire of gases and fluids to reach an average level, and their movements cease upon reaching a balanced state, that is equilibrium (TUZ, 3/16). Just as gases and fluids move to obtain an average ratio of mixture, so goods move to seek an average ratio of exchange. The nature of both movements is the same in essence in spite of their apparent differences.

Taguchi reiterates a similar argument in his article entitled 'Gaikoku Kawase Soba-ron' (On Foreign Exchange Rate, 1893). Free trade causes goods of the north to flow to the south in response to the demand, just as the winds flow northwards and southwards alternately as a natural phenomenon. Like natural phenomena, wine flows into Japan from Europe, for which in return tea and raw silk flow out to Europe in order to balance them (TUZ, 3/291).

Taguchi further explains free trade on the analogy of the circular flow of blood in the human body. Like the human body in which various organs interact with each other, there exist various countries mutually related to each other in the world economy. France, Italy and Spain are no more than grape-vine countries in terms of the economic world, and China and Japan are placed as tea producing countries. These countries are mutually dependent on each other just as the organs of the body are dependent on each other for healthy life. The free movement of products through exports and imports results in an average distribution of the products. Taguchi asserts that there is no adequate term to describe this mechanism other than 'an exquisite wonder of the Creator' (TUZ, 3/21). We could not reach the perfect situation if we artificially disturb this wonder. Therefore he sees that the path to wealth lies in setting economic phenomena as free as natural phenomena are. There should be no more political rivalry among countries than rivalry between various organs in the human body. Taguchi says that 'there would be no state so far as trade is concerned' (TUZ, 3/277).

On this understanding of the economic world, Taguchi goes so far as to say in the article 'Gaikoku Kawase Soba-ron' as follows: there are some who apprehend that the specialization of the Japanese industry to the production of tea and raw silk would necessarily bring about the destruction of sugar and cotton in Japan. But 'there will be no problem even if sugar and cotton industries are broken down'. Because when we think of what the real wealth of a country consists, we can say with confidence that a country is defined as rich when the total sum of products increases. 'If the total sum of production of tea and raw silk increases, we can say definitely the country is rich, even if the sugar and cotton of the country are destroyed' (TUZ, 3/291).

This straightforward free trade argument of Taguchi was exactly the same as his opinion in the controversy on free trade versus protectionism (1880–81) which had taken place between the *Tokyo Keizai Zasshi* and the *Tokai Keizai Shinpo* (The Tokai New Economic Review, edited by Tsuyoshi Inukai and published between 1880 and 1882).[9] In the same *laissez-faire* vein, he had controversies with the members of the Japanese social policy school and was against the factory legislation.

Taguchi's argument on free trade, which reflects his organic concept of society, undoubtedly shows the influence of Spencer's *Social Statics* (its Japanese translation was published by Taguchi's firm in 1881–83).

At the same time, however, we have to take notice of a considerable imprint of Confucian classics on his ideas. Although Taguchi criticized Confucian classics education which simply enforced students to recite its passages, the tone of his criticism was not so high pitched as that of Fukuzawa. Noteworthy on this point, Taguchi referred to Chinese classical philosophers to describe the doctrine of *laissez-faire* in the beginning of the first chapter of *Keizai Saku* (Economic Policy, 1882): 'the ancient Chinese sages made non-interference the foundation of the way of government. Their words may appear simple, but in fact they contain the true principle of wise economy' (TUZ, 3/83).

The concept of *li* (the natural reason, or principle) in Chi Hsu's Confucian learning that embraces nature, human beings and society with the one and the same supreme ultimate principle probably helped Taguchi to accept the Western doctrine of *laissez-faire* when he learnt it at the Treasury. Organic and functional social philosophy of Confucianism seemed to provide him with a sort of resonance board which enabled him to accept the social theory of Spencer and construct his harmonious view of the economic world. As a matter of fact, he says that 'the economic world naturally has its own *dai-li* (fundamental principle). We can never gain wealth and strength by means of artificial intervention' (TUZ, 3/143).

Then what is *dai-li* in the economic world? At first sight it seems to be the law of supply and demand. Taguchi says that 'there is the social law of supply and demand working in social life, just as the natural law of gravitation is working among heavenly bodies, and the natural law of circulation of blood is working among the human body' (TUZ, 2/622). However Taguchi then goes a step further and says that 'science, whatever it may be, in its nature must persist in carrying one fundamental element through to the end' (TUZ, 3/394). Therefore political economy would not be able to call itself a science, provided it sticks to the interactions of the two elements of supply and demand. It must inquire into the one and fundamental element that wields the economic phenomena. Taguchi finds such a fundamental element necessary to the following logic:

Assuming that you supply writing brushes and a peasant supplies some rice, what determines the exchange rate of those two items? The proportion of your demand for his rice and his demand for your writing brushes must determine it. Because when your demand for his rice is stronger than his demand for your writing brushes, you have to give him more writing brushes than the quantity of rice he gives you in value (TUZ, 3/322). The law of supply and demand means a competition between a buyer and a seller, but behind this competition is the human nature of self-interest which virtually means man's inborn desire for securing life and avoiding death. Demand in the market, therefore, is nothing but the expression of this inherent human nature, and 'the conflict of self-interest of sellers against that of buyers results in price' (TUZ, 3/396). So 'value is equivalent to a balance between my demand and your demand ... The ups and downs of the price of goods depend on the balance between the demand of a person who possessed a goods and that of another person who wants to buy it' (TUZ, 3/322).

After following this logic, Taguchi concludes that 'cost is purely a mental phenomenon and hereby political economy is a mental science' (TUZ, 3/410). Thus 'to define political economy as a science to deal with price is adequately to define it as a mental science' (TUZ, 3/402).

This kind of argument brings Taguchi close to the third school of economics named by Macleod. The characteristic of the third school is to regard political economy as the 'science related to exchanges' of wealth. In this respect they call economics the science related to value. And it is not the production cost which is the cause of value, but value that is the inducement to the production cost. Macleod says that 'demand is the sole form, or cause, of value', and that 'value is not a quantity of an object, but an affection of the mind'.[10] Taguchi agrees with this view and contends that political economy is the 'science of value, or science of exchanges' (TUZ, 3/395).

According to Taguchi, therefore, the task of political economy as a science lies in the elucidation of the law of economic phenomena that consists of competitions of self-interest expressed in the form of demand in the market. The essence of political economy does not lie in proposing policies. Political economy does not debate about what the government should or should not do. It is very far from policy, precept, or maxim. Therefore the truth of political economy changes in response neither to the differences of the times nor of the situations of countries. The profitable way is always adaptable to any country, and the unprofitable way is always harmful anywhere and anytime. The argument of political economy is invariable and unchangeable. It is absolutely true just as one plus two always equals three (TUZ, 3/247).

Taguchi thus condemns the ideas expressed by the German historical school, which maintains that sound economic policies should naturally vary according to the differences between countries, and the times and stages of economic development. The proponents of such views, claims Taguchi, do not understand the true principle of political economy.

In his methodology to make a rigid distinction between science and policy, how does Taguchi justify free trade and *laissez-faire* doctrine as a science?

Does not free trade belong to the realm of economic policies? Taguchi never bends the knee to this sort of criticism. He insists that the economic law penetrating the economic world expresses itself correctly through free trade. With Taguchi free trade is an expressive materialization of the natural law, or *dai-li*. Thus the truth of free trade is nothing less than the truth of political economy as a science. The various elements that constitute the economic world will be arranged in harmonious order, only if left to the domain of *laissez-faire* doctrine.

The economic prosperity of Britain based on free trade, argues Taguchi, is the result of making her policy conform to the fundamental principle. His dream was to have Tokyo grow to become 'London in the East' by following *dai-li*. Fukuzawa also certainly looks up to Britain as a model Japan should follow. But Fukuzawa with a hint of ambivalent feeling is very aware that the model does not necessarily exemplify free trade as theory teaches. Rather Fukuzawa respects Britain mainly because of her imperialistic power, whereas Taguchi considers Britain as the homeland of free trade throughout his life.

The geographical location of Japan faces the Chinese continent and the Korean Peninsula to the west, Siberia to the north, with the American continents across the Pacific Ocean. This bears a close resemblance to Britain's location which faces both the European and the American continents. By taking advantage of her geographical location, Taguchi contends, Japan will become Britain in the East, only if she pursues a free trade policy like Britain. In contrast to Fukuzawa, Taguchi senses little threat from the Western powers. There is no doubt that this originates from his conviction of the fundamental principle which he regards as permeating the economic phenomena. Taguchi as 'a free citizen of the economic world' lays it down that 'there is no distinction between high and low, or right and wrong in the economic phenomena' (TUZ, 3/11, 148).

Taguchi's pressing concern as a free trader rather concentrates on how to make Japan replace China in the Asian and Pacific trade. It was China that was taken seriously by Taguchi as the main rival of trade. He discusses in an article entitled 'Shina no Jitsuryoku' (Real Power of China, 1884) that Japan ought to make every possible effort to control the Oriental trade by overwhelming China (TUZ, 5/178).[11]

It was in 1885 that Fukuzawa brought out a famous article 'Datsua-ron' in which he insisted that Japan should say farewell to China and other Asian countries, and join the European circle. It is noteworthy that Taguchi's article on the mighty power of China came out almost at the same time that Fukuzawa was displaying straightforward contempt for the Chinese.

Taguchi supported the Sino–Japanese war on the basis that the deprivation of the independence of Korea by China could not go unheeded in view of

Japan's self-defence (TUZ, 5/348–9). Nevertheless, some years after the Sino–Japanese War, he refuted those who advocated the war as 'a righteous war', and described the war as 'a silly undertaking to spend enormous money for conquering a foreign country', besides sacrificing thousands of compatriots (TUZ, 5/407). Taguchi did not believe that Japan was predetermined to be responsible for keeping peace under arms in the East, since it was against the economic interests of Japan as well as his conviction in the universal validity of free trade (TUZ, 5/408).

CONCLUDING REMARKS

The enlightenment in Japan started with the introduction of Western ideas accompanied by nationalism to a substantial extent. As the predominant country in the West in the times of Japanese enlightenment was Great Britain, quite a few of the intellectuals of Japanese enlightenment possessed pro-British feelings, and this applies to both Fukuzawa and Taguchi. They persisted in upholding British liberalism even when German ideas that stressed the necessity of the state's interference in various fields of life increased their momentum after the 1890s. Through the wide readership of their writings, they seemed to breed pro-British feelings among the learned people regardless of their social rank or occupation.

Fukuzawa's reception of Western ideas that is characterized by his utilitarian, practical and functional approach evidently derives from the complicated task he assumes as an intellectual of Meiji enlightenment. Japanese intellectuals from then on have been destined to follow his approach towards Western ideas to varying degrees.

In his approach to political economy, Fukuzawa was also naturally practical. He considers political economy as a tool for administration.[12] It is self-evident for him that economic power is closely connected with national military power as shown in *Jiji Shogun* (1881): 'War is the art of extending the rights of independent governments, and foreign trade is a sign that one country radiates its glory to others' (FYZ, 4/191). He therefore sees that the role of political economy lies in increasing the financial power of the nation. Political economy is fundamentally regarded as an art of the state.

Taguchi is practical in character as shown in his wide range of interests and careers, that is, publisher, journalist, organizer of several societies, planner of emigration to the southern islands in the Pacific Ocean, entrepreneur of a private railway, and a Member of Parliament. But he seems to represent a 'man of principle' in comparison with Fukuzawa. He accentuates the similarity of civilization between Japan and the West, and hoists a banner of the universal adaptability of political economy underpinned by the human nature of self-interest to secure life and avoid death. He further insists on the adoption of free trade and *laissez-faire* as the true policy.

Through his arguments, Taguchi played the role of introducing the concept of economic balance or equilibrium which had a decisive significance in the formation of political economy in European enlightenment ages, though Taguchi's arguments were tinged with the third school of economics. In this mixed comprehension of economic thought, Taguchi, like other contemporary thinkers, seems to represent a peculiarity of enlightenment in Japan which attempts to incorporate the ideas of the eighteenth century, the century of enlightenment, into the ones of nineteenth century without being conscious of definite differences between them.

NOTES

1. Chuhei Sugiyama, *Meiji Keimoki no Keizai Shiso* (Economic Thought in the Meiji Enlightenment Ages, 1986), p. 151. But Sugiyama perceives Fukuzawa as a consistent advocate of mercantilism as far as his foreign trade is concerned. See op. cit. p. 144.
2. Masao Maruyama appropriately defines the characteristic of Fukuzawa's ideas as a 'situational thinking' (*Maruyama Masao Shu*, 1965, vol. 5, p. 211).
3. Though being a son of a low-ranked samurai of a minor retainer in the Nakatsu–Okudaira clan – a weak hereditary vassal to the Tokugawa shogunate, Fukuzawa seized opportunities to voyage to San Francisco in 1860, Europe in 1862, and Washington and other eastern cities of America in 1867. His Dutch and English studies helped to bring him these opportunities.
4. FYZ: abbreviation of *Fukuzawa Yukichi Zenshu* (Complete Works of Yukichi Fukuzawa). 8/65–6: abbreviation of vol. 8, pp. 65–6. Hereafter these abbreviation forms will be used.
5. Fukuzawa learnt Chinese classics in his childhood and became sufficiently versed so as to have the privilege of giving occasional lectures (FYZ, 7/12). Fukuzawa not only estimates Confucius and Mencuis as 'first ranked great scholars with rare ability' (FYZ, 4/61), but also insists on the study of Chinese classics along with Western learning in the Keio Gijuku school (FYZ, 19/380) which was established by him as 'a guide to European civilization' (FYZ, 9/529).
6. Having said so, Fukuzawa changed his mind again in an article written in 1884, and said that 'We cannot fail to follow the Western way in religion' (FYZ, 7/212). Nine months later he put forward 'Datsua-ron' (Going out of Asia).
7. TUZ: abbreviation of *Teiken Taguchi Ukichi Zenshu* (Complete Works of Ukichi Taguchi). 6/128–9: abbreviation of vol. 6, pp. 128–9. Hereafter these abbreviation forms will be used.
8. In an article 'Mourned over the death of Mr Herbert Spencer', Taguchi regards Spencer as 'a giant of modern thought', and as 'an outstanding figure among others'. He perceives the core of Spencer's *Social Statics* (1851) as 'the argument very similar to free trade that denounces intervention of government' (TUZ, 2/622). As to H.T. Buckle, Taguchi describes his *Introduction to the History of Civilization in England*, 2 vols (1857–61) as 'the most persuasive' on the history of civilization (TUZ, 2/137).
9. For more on the controversy, see Sugiyama, *Origins of Economic Thought in Modern Japan* (1994), pp. 85–97.
10. H.D. Macleod, *The History of Economics*, London, 1896, p. 110; *The Principles of Economical Philosophy*, 2 vols 1872–75, London, vol. 1, pp. 323 and 331.
11. As shown in *Shina Kaika-shi* (A History of Chinese Enlightenment, 1888), Taguchi embraced a considerable respect for Chinese culture. Nevertheless, after the Sino–Japanese

war, he gradually showed his contempt for the Chinese (TUZ, 4/572). Furthermore in 'Nihon Jinshu-ron' (An Essay on the Japanese Race, 1895) and *Ha-Kouka-ron* (Refutation to the Yellow Peril, 1904), Taguchi attempted to differentiate the Japanese from the Chinese in terms of language, feature and intelligence, and identified the Japanese with the Aryan race.

12. See *Minkan Keizairoku Nihen* (Popular Political Economy, vol. 2, 1880), FYZ, 4/343.

REFERENCES AND FURTHER READING

Anzai, Toshizo (1995), *Fukuzawa Yukichi to Seiyo Shiso* (Yukichi Fukuzawa and Western Thought), Nagoya: Nagoya Daigaku Shuppan-kai.

Bellah, Robert N. (1957), *Tokugawa Religion: The Value of Pre-Industrial Japan*, New York: Free Press.

Blacker, Carmen (1964), *The Japanese Enlightenment: A Study of the Writings of Fukuzawa Yukichi*, Cambridge: Cambridge University Press.

Fujiwara, Akio (1993), Francis Wayland no Shakai Keizai Shiso (The Study of Francis Wayland's Social Economic Thought), Tokyo: Nihon Keizai Hyoron-sha.

Fujiwara, Akio (1998), *Fukuzawa Yukichi no Nihon Keizai-ron* (Yukichi Fukuzawa on the Japanese Economy), Tokyo: Nihon Keizai Hyoron-sha.

Fukuzawa, Y. (1958–63), *Fukuzawa Yukichi Zenshu* (Complete Works of Yukichi Fukuzawa), 21 vols, Tokyo: Iwanami Shoten.

Fukuzawa, Y. (1969), *An Encouragement of Learning*, translated and introduced by David A. Dilworth and Umeyo Hirano, Tokyo: Sophia University.

Fukuzawa, Y. (1973), *Fukuzawa Yukichi's. An Outline of a Theory of Civilization*, Translated by David A. Dilworth and G. Cameron Hurst, Tokyo: Sophia University.

Fukuzawa, Y. (1981), *The Autobiography of Fukuzawa Yukichi with Preface to the Collected Works of Fukuzawa*, translated by Eiichi Kiyooka, Tokyo: Hokuseido Press.

Fukuzawa, Y. (1985), *Fukuzawa Yukichi on Education. Selected Works*, translated and edited by Eiichi Kiyooka, Tokyo: University of Tokyo Press.

Hirota, Masaki (1976), *Fukuzawa Yukichi Kenkyu* (A Study of Yukichi Fukuzawa), Tokyo: Tokyo Daigaku Shuppan-kai.

Iida, Kanae (1984), *Fukuzawa Yukichi* (Yukichi Fukuzawa), Tokyo: Chuou Koron-sha.

Jansen, M.B. (ed.) (1965), *Changing Japanese Attitudes toward Modernization*, Princeton: Princeton University Press.

Koizumi, Shinzo (1966), *Fukuzawa Yukichi* (Yukichi Fukuzawa), Tokyo: Iwanami Shoten.

Maruyama, Masao (1995–96), *Maruyama Masao-shu* (Collected Works of Masao Maruyama), vols 2, 3, 5, 13 and 14, Tokyo: Iwanami Shoten.

Matsumoto, Sannosuke (1996), *Meiji Shisoshi* (History of Thoughts in the Meiji Era), Tokyo: Shinyo-sha.

Matsunoo, Hiroshi (1996), *Taguchi Ukichi to Keizaigaku Kyokai* (A Study of Taguchi Ukichi's Economic Thought and the Political Economy Club), Tokyo: Nihon Keizai Hyoron-sha.

Morris-Suzuki, Tessa (1989), *A History of Japanese Economic Thought*, London: Routledge.

Najita, Tetsuo and Irwin Scheiner (eds) (1978), *Japanese thought in the Tokugawa Period 1600–1868,* Chicago and London: University of Chicago Press.

Oxford, Wayne. H. (1973), *The Speeches of Fukuzawa: A Translation and Critical Study,* Tokyo: Hokuseido Press.

Shively, D.H. (ed.) (1971), *Tradition and Modernisation in Japanese Culture,* Princeton: Princeton University Press.

Sugihara, Shiro (1971), *Kindai Nihon no Keizai Shiso* (Economic Thought in Modern Japan), Kyoto: Mineruva Shobo.

Sugihara, Shiro (1972), *Seio Keizaigaku to Kindai Nihon* (Western Political Economy and Modern Japan), Tokyo: Mirai-sha.

Sugihara, Shiro and Kazuyoshi Okada (eds) (1995), *Taguchi Ukichi to Tokyo Keizai Zasshi* (Ukichi Taguchi and the Tokyo Economist), Tokyo: Nihon Keizai Hyoron-sha.

Sugiyama, Chuhei (1986), *Meiji Keimoki no Keizai Shiso* (Economic Thought in the Meiji Enlightenment Ages), Tokyo: Hosei Daigaku Shuppan-kyoku.

Sugiyama, Chuhei and Hiroshi Mizuta (eds) (1988), *Enlightenment and Beyond: Political Economy Comes to Japan,* Tokyo: University of Tokyo Press.

Sugiyama, Chuhei (1994), *Origins of Economic Thought in Modern Japan,* London and New York: Routledge.

Taguchi, U. (1927–28), *Teiken Taguchi Ukichi Zenshu* (Complete Works of Ukichi Taguchi, 8 vols), Tokyo: Teiken Taguchi Ukichi Zenshu Kanko-kai, reprinted (1990), Tokyo: Yoshikawa Kobun-kan.

Takahashi, Seiichiro (1947), *Fukuzawa Yukichi* (Yukichi Fukuzawa), Tokyo: Jitsugyo no Nihon-sha, reprinted (1979), Tokyo: Nagasaki Shuppan.

Tanaka, Hiroshi (1993), *Kindai Nihon to Jiyushugi* (Modern Japan and Liberalism), Tokyo: Iwanami Shoten.

Tooyama, Shigeki (1970), *Fukuzawa Yukichi* (Yukichi Fukuzawa), Tokyo: Tokyo Daigaku Shuppan-kai.

Uchida, Yoshihiko (1989), *Uchida Yoshihiko Chosaku-shu* (Collected Works of Yoshihiko Uchida), vol. 5, Tokyo: Iwanami Shoten.

Uete, Michiari (1974), *Nihon Kindai Shiso no Keisei* (The Formation of Modern Thought in Japan), Tokyo: Iwanami Shoten.

3. The Japanese social policy school: its formation and breakup

Takashi Fujii

INTRODUCTION OF THE ECONOMICS OF THE GERMAN SOCIAL POLICY SCHOOL

In 1886 almost 20 years after the Meiji Restoration a young graduate of Tokyo University set off from Japan for the universities of Europe. In Germany he studied at Heidelberg, Halle, Berlin, and other universities for two years. There he learned the economics of the German social policy school especially from Professor Adolf Wagner (1835–1917), Gustav von Schmoller (1838–1917) and others. He next travelled to Britain where his interest was more focused on surveying conditions of poverty. Upon returning to Japan in 1890, he took up the post of professor at his alma mater. This marked the proper introduction of the economics of the German social policy school to Tokyo University, the only national university in Japan at the time.

The name of this youth was Noboru Kanai. He was born in Shizuoka Prefecture in 1865 and died in 1933 at the age of 68. In addition to teaching many students as a professor of the law department of Tokyo University, he led Japanese economics in the 1890s and 1900s and wrote a number of works including *Shakai Mondai* (Social Problems), *Shakai Keizaigaku* (Social Economics), and *Shakai Seisaku* (Social Policy). However in the course of Japanese economics history, rather than as an economist he is recognized as the central figure of the Japanese Association for the Study of Social Policy (henceforth referred to as the Association) and as the man who introduced and established the economics of the social policy school to Japan (Kawai, 1969).

The study of economics at Tokyo University did not start with Kanai, but it was a young American philosopher named Fenollosa (1853–1908) who was the first person to teach economics there. This man is explained in Japanese school textbooks as a famous art critic and the first person to introduce the beauty of Japanese images of Buddha overseas. However it was with the aim of teaching economics that this teacher arrived in Japan in 1878. According to the notes of students who attended his lectures, his teaching of economics was based on the thinking of J. S. Mill with some of the theories of H.C. Carey incorporated where necessary. The basic teaching of Fenollosa was founded on the classical school, although he used the theories of various schools of thought (Sugihara, 1980).

In the middle of the 1880s, professorship for the teaching of economics at Tokyo University passed from Fenollosa to Kenzo Wadagaki (1860–1919). Wadagaki had studied abroad in Britain and Germany, and he became a supporter of the economics of the German social policy school. It was because of this leaning towards the German social policy school that Wadagaki invited Kanai, who had thoroughly mastered the economics of the German social policy school, to teach at Tokyo University (Sekiguchi, 1986).

SOCIAL BACKGROUND OF THE JAPANESE SOCIAL POLICY SCHOOL

The study of economics in Japan in the 1880s and 1890s was led by the private universities such as Keio University and Waseda University. Prominent theorists of the British classical school of the time were Yukichi Fukuzawa (1835–1901) of Keio University and Tameyuki Amano (1859–1938) who dominated the teaching of economics at Waseda University. Moreover, the journalist Ukichi Taguchi (1855–1905) actively published economic arguments centred on the British classical school in the *Tokyo Keizai Zasshi* (Tokyo Economist). These thinkers played an important enlightening role in the development of capitalist industry and argued that the government should maintain a liberal economic system. (Refer to Chapter 2 for a description of the economic theories put forward by these thinkers.)

Despite this trend in economic thought, there were a number of reasons why the government of Japan decide to introduce German economics around 1890. Following the Meiji Restoration of 1868, a large divide arose among government leaders as to whether basic policies of modernization should be based on the British model or the German model. This matter was eventually settled in 1881, and since then Japan has maintained a legal system based on the German model. The single largest outcome of this policy was the Constitution of the Empire of Japan in 1889.

It was necessary for Japan to achieve a similar level of industrialization as countries in Europe and America. Japan had to compensate for its slow start. Britain possessed the highest industrial capacity at the time, but Germany was also showing an astonishing vigour in closing the gap. The fundamental reason why the German school of thought became the mainstream within the Japanese government was admiration for German progress. As a result, Japan also adopted the German model in its school system. Kanai's decision to choose the German social policy school as an overseas student was based on this Japanese basic policy of industrialization at the time.

These political considerations, however, were not the only reason for the successful introduction and establishment of German social policy school economics in Japan. Other reasons were the academic tradition of Japan and the fact that the advance of industrialization was leading to the generation of major economic problems (known as 'social problems') in Japan at that time.

In the Tokugawa era in Japan the shogunate strongly demanded that the ruling warrior class should study Confucianism. Although Japanese Confucianism was a moral learning that espoused the necessity of spiritual cultivation it also came to be regarded as a school of learning for governing the masses because it was also an ideology of the ruling classes. Because of the advance of the market economy the middle of this period saw a warrior class declining into poverty while the growing income disparity between the rich and the poor ignited riots. Under these conditions, Confucianism developed as a school of learning for discussing what sort of rule (economic policy) was necessary for the government (shogunate) to govern the masses (Nomura, 1950). This academic tradition was carried on by the learned sections of society following the Meiji Restoration. In particular because the economics of the social policy school strongly leaned towards the study of policy to achieve rule over the masses, it was an extremely understandable school of learning for thinkers heavily influenced by Confucianism.

Of course the Japanese academic tradition of teaching Confucianism alone is not sufficient to explain why the social policy school dominated the mainstream in Japan. In Japan, economic problems similar to those seen in Germany were occurring.

From around 1890 onwards, economic problems requiring the approach of the social policy school were starting to occur in Japan, albeit in a rudimentary form. Japan's victory over China in the Sino–Japanese War of 1894–95 proved that Japan had already achieved a certain degree of industrialization. Industrialization brought with it labour problems. The representative export industries in Japan at the time of the Sino–Japanese War were cotton and silk, and young women formed the bulk of the workforce in these textile industries. In order to give an internationally competitive edge to their products, the employers in these industries kept wages down and forced the female workers to work long hours late into the night. As a result the number of women dying from tuberculosis and other serious diseases increased so rapidly that bureaucrats and academics came to look on the problem with deep concern.

In addition at around the time of the Russo–Japanese War of 1904–5, heavy industry had come to lead the economy. The establishment of the state-owned Yawata Iron and Steel Works in the 1900s was a typical reflection of this, and this sparked the development of armaments factories, shipyards, machine factories and other iron-consuming sectors. It is no exaggeration to say that Japan's victory in the Russo–Japanese War was largely due to the country's industrial base and in particular the firm establishment of heavy industry. In heavy industry, too, fierce competition in international markets resulted in harsh working conditions being forced on the workers. Because the workforce in such heavy industries was composed of men in their prime, any dissatisfaction they felt in working conditions came to be expressed in the form of labour disputes. In 1900, the government enacted the Public Peace and Police Law in an attempt to suppress the labour movement. But this did not necessarily resolve labour problems.

In line with the occurrence of labour problems, the start of the twentieth century was also a time when widespread interest came to focus on socialist ideas. Socialism had been introduced to Japan before then, but only as an ideology discussed among learned thinkers. In the 1900s, as a result of the increase in the number of workers, socialism came to fuse with the workers who were its bearers. *Waga Shakaishugi* (My Socialism) by Sen Katayama (1859–1933) and *Shakaishugi Shinzui* (Essence of Socialism) by Shusui Kotoku (1871–1911) were published in 1903 and attracted many readers. It was in 1901 that Katayama, Kotoku and others formed Japan's first socialist political party, the Social Democratic Party, centring around Isoo Abe (1865–1949), but the government immediately prohibited this organisation (Matsunaga, 1976).

HISTORY OF THE ASSOCIATION FOR THE STUDY OF SOCIAL POLICY

It was with this historical background and through the efforts of Kanai that the economics of the German social policy school was introduced and became established in Japan. The supporting role played by the powerful aristocratic diet member, Kumazo Kuwata (1868–1932) should also not be forgotten. Kuwata, who had a realistic view of the political world was not just a member of the Association, but also played a prominent part in planning various social policies. But it would be wrong to search for the reasons behind the establishment of German economics in Japan solely in the activities of Kanai and Kuwata, and others. Even in the 1890s when the British classical school was popular, the journalist Sadamasu Oshima (1845–1914) criticized the *laissez-faire* theory of international trade and argued that protective trade was necessary in order to develop modern industry in Japan on the same level as Europe and America. In addition to translating Friedrich List's *National System of Political Economy* into Japanese, he proposed through a number of economic reviews that Japan should have the right to raise its own tariffs (at the time Japan did not possess tariff autonomy). Although Oshima's proposals were only supported by a minority, the fact that he showed that economics does not totally rely on *laissez-faire* but sometimes requires protective measures by government when necessary, played an important role in the establishment of the social policy school in Japan (Iida, 1984; Morris-Suzuki, 1989).

Research into the history of the social policy school starts from the pioneering work of Etsuji Sumiya (1895–1987) and runs through to the more recent works of Koichi Sekiya, Toshiro Oka, Takehito Sakamoto, Makoto Ikeda and Kanae Iida. In the English literature, Tessa Morris-Suzuki briefly touched on the subject in her *A History of Japanese Economic Thought*, and Kenneth B. Pyle argued on the relation between economics and bureaucrats in 'Advantages of Followership: German Economics and Japanese Bureaucrats, 1890–1925'. Each of these works show differences in detailed points, but all the researchers generally agree that the Japanese social policy school was introduced in the 1890s with the introduction of social policy thought from Germany, became established with the national conference of 1907, and collapsed in the 1920s with the rise of Marxian economics and the neoclassical school.

The great work of Sumiya is good for gaining a comprehensive understanding of the ideological features and personages of the social policy school; the essay by Iida is effective for understanding the most recent level of research; and the work of Morris-Suzuki is recommended for understanding the positioning of the movement within the economic history of Japan (Sumiya, 1958; Sekiya, 1958; Oka, 1970; Pyle, 1974; Sakamoto, 1972; Ikeda, 1977; Iida, 1984; Morris-Suzuki, 1989).

How did the classical school, the mainstream of economic thought in the 1880s, look on labour problems? The above-mentioned Ukichi Taguchi in his thesis 'Rodo Hogo Mondai' (The Problem of Labour Protection) (1901) opposed the idea that the government should regulate working hours, saying that a reduction in working hours would lead to a fall in wages. The view of Taguchi that policy to protect labourers was unnecessary despite the fact that labour problems existed in reality was an indication that *laissez-faire* had ceased to properly deal with the problems.

In contrast to this, Kanai and other social policy school advocates considered the direct research of measures for the prevention and resolution of labour problems to be the issue. They classified labour problems and various other economic problems as 'social problems' and in doing so expressed the view that the fundamental causes of labour problems lay not on the side of individual workers but on the side of society. In other words, the fact that labourers must work under poor conditions is not because of their own low skills and capacity but the result of deficiencies in the legislative system. Therefore if the fundamental cause lies in society, it is the responsibility of society to find a solution to the problems. To sum up, whereas the classical school proponents of *laissez-faire* believed that it was impossible to prevent and resolve labour problems, the common understanding of the social policy school was that if the government established laws and prepared social systems according to necessity based on a policy of social improvement, labour problems could be prevented and resolved even in a system with private ownership. Social systems that were proposed in the Plea of the Japanese Association for the Study of Social Policy (1901) included factory legislation, trade unions, friendly societies, accident insurance, cooperative societies, and others. Young and rising economists and pioneering bureaucrats, imitating the Verein für Socialpolitik in Germany, established the Association for the Study of Social Policy in order to discuss measures to prevent and resolve social problems. The Association discussed the advantages and disadvantages of social policy and put forward its own social policies, and in this sense it was an academic group which played an enlightening role. This was the only nationwide economics association in Japan at the time.

The Association was established in April 1896 (the year after the end of the Sino–Japanese War) and at first it had only a few members and was a study group for them. But its supporters increased in line with the growing seriousness of labour problems, and it eventually came to include almost all economic thinkers in academic and bureaucratic positions. [1] In addition to Kanai, Kumazo Kuwata, Iwasaburo Takano (1871–1949, Tokyo University), Tokuzo Fukuda (1874–1930, Tokyo University of Commerce), Hajime Kawakami (1879–1946, Kyoto University) and others were included as leading members.

The increase in members meant that the Association could no longer be run on a study group basis, but it became necessary to hold national conferences and to be more open. In 1907, 40 years after the Meiji Restoration, the first national conference of the Association was held at Tokyo University. On the first day of the conference factory legislation was treated as the common theme and members and guests gave their various opinions. On the second day individual papers were read regarding subjects such as 'means of protecting labourers', 'air in factories and labourers' health', 'agriculture and social problems', and others. On the third day observation tours to a printing factory and a cotton spinning mill, and others were planned. Following the example set by *Schriften des Vereins für Sozialpolitik* in Germany, a conference report was published under the title *Kojoho to Rodomondai* (Factory Legislation and Labour Problems). Journals of economics of the time also printed detailed reports describing the conference (Shakaiseisakugakkai, 1977).

The fact that factory legislation was selected as the common theme for the first conference indicates how it was important to the members. Britain and

other advanced industrialized nations had already established factory legislation, and the Association believed that debate should also begin in Japan on
whether or not to regulate working hours and conditions through legislation
in the same way. The government had been advocating the necessity for
factory legislation since around 1890. In 1903, *Shokko Jijyo* (Labourers'
Working Conditions), which was a multifaceted study of working hours,
employment relations, wages, living environment, and other related issues,
was published (Noshomusho, 1976). But due to the strong opposition of
capitalists to the regulation of working hours by law, no law was passed in
the National Diet. The selection of factory legislation as the common theme
for the national conference of 1907 by the Association implied support for
the government policy. The contents of the conference will be briefly described in the following paragraphs.

In his opening address, Kanai declared that factory legislation would be
the common theme of the conference and that the goal of the Association was
the achievement of 'social harmonization'. Kanai, Kinji Tajima (1867–1934,
Kyoto University) and Kuwata then gave reports in which they each argued
that factory legislation was necessary and consistent with the earning of
profits by firms. Kuwata proposed his own personal factory legislation pack-
age containing age restrictions, restriction of working hours, and the prohibi-
tion of all-night working, and so on. The entrepreneur Eiichi Shibusawa
(1840–1931), who attended the conference as a guest, stated that he had
considered the time too early for factory legislation but, after attending the
conference, he now believed the time to be right.

As may be inferred from the above, despite being an academic association
conference, there was no real debate or argument. It would be no exaggeration to say that the conference was a political meeting calling for the establishment of factory legislation. The remarks of Juichi Soeda (1864–1929),
however, drew objections from some of the rising economists.

Soeda, who was a former minister of finance and was then president of
the Japan Industrial Bank, stated his support for factory legislation but, in
rounding off his speech, proposed that management based on the feudalistic
master and servant relationship, in which employers were compassionate to
workers and workers respected their employers, was necessary in order to
achieve 'harmony between workers and capital'. In response to Soeda's
argument that reevaluating the master and servant relationship would enable factory legislation to function more effectively, Takano, Kiheiji Onozuka
(1870–1944, Tokyo University) and in particular Fukuda, who argued that
the standard of living of workers does not improve because of the very
existence of such a master and servant relationship and that the relationship
between workers and employers has to be made equal, objected strongly.
Takano then gave his cherished opinion, arguing for the need to form labour

unions in order to make the relationship between workers and employers equal.

This argument is brought up later in recollections. In his reminiscences, Takano describes how Kumazo Kuwata had cautioned himself and other young members, saying that their criticism was impolite to Soeda. This indicates that it was still unusual in Japan at that time to discuss freely, even in the case of a learned association conference. This trend to avoid mutual criticism and argument among participants indicates how the first conference, rather than being a debate among economists discussing various facets of factory legislation, was more similar to a political meeting simply calling for the establishment of factory legislation.

Be that as it may, factory legislation, with the support of the Association, eventually came to be passed by the National Diet in 1911. However it was not until five years later in 1916 that the legislation actually came into effect. Moreover the contents of the legislation were not necessarily far-ranging enough, being limited to restrictions on the employment of minors, restrictions on the working hours of minors and girls, employers' maintenance obligations in cases of work accidents, and so on. Although there was room for improvement, the initial objective of establishing restrictions on working conditions by law had been achieved.

The national conference of the Association was held once a year, 13 times in all. The following themes adopted from the second conference onwards indicate what the economists of the time regarded as important social problems: 'The Tariff Question and Social Policy' (1908), 'The Problem of Migration' (1909), 'Municipal Enterprises' (1910), 'Accident Insurance' (1911), 'Problems of the Cost of Living' (1912), 'Labour Disputes' (1913), 'The Problem of Tenant Farmer Protection' (1914), 'Tariff Problems Seen in Terms of Social Policy' (1915), 'The Problems of Government-run Enterprises' (1916), 'Small-scale Industry' (1917), 'Women Workers in Japan' (1918), 'Trade Unions' (1919), 'Problems of the Middle Class' (1920), 'The Wage System and Wage Distribution System' (1921), and 'Problems of Japanese Tenant Farmers' (1922) (Shakaiseisakugakkai, 1977). In addition to labour problems, discussion also focused on problems relating to agriculture and small-scale industry. The dramatic development of capitalism in Japan also resulted in the appearance of economically vulnerable groups such as labourers and small-scale businessmen (farmers, small-scale industries and others), and the character of the Association as a body for proposing policies to protect such weak groups in society can be seen in the themes selected for its conferences.

In time, however, the national conference of the Association lost its vigour and the number of participants declined. Social policy administration was organized with the establishment of the Social Division of the Ministry of the

Interior in 1920; a series of worker protection legislative acts (factory legislation, employment aid legislation in 1921, and so on) was implemented; and even policies for the protection of farmers and small-scale industries had come to be introduced. As a result, a body such as the Association, which only played an enlightening role in proposing policy, gradually lost its appeal. There are no records of the conference in 1923 and 1924, and it is not even clear whether or not it was held in these years. In the end, the Association lost all its momentum and went out of existence in 1924.

Towards the end, not only did the number of Association members decrease, but academic and ideological differences between the major members were beginning to appear. Some economists were of the firm belief that a socialist economic system in which private ownership was abolished and replaced with state and public ownership was the only way to resolve fundamental social problems. Representative of this belief was Hajime Kawakami who started off as a social policy theorist but eventually developed into an economist of socialist and in particular Marxist learning. Although the Association was at one time strongly opposed to socialism (see later), members supporting socialism increased in number and, when the noted socialist Hisashi Aso (1891–1940) applied for membership later on, he was eventually accepted in spite of some minor opposition.

The rise of socialism at the same time led to an increase in the number of anti-Marxist economists such as Tokuzo Fukuda.[2] Fukuda, who studied under Lujo Brentano in his younger days, espoused the 'Seizonken no Shakai Seisaku' (Social Policy for the Living Right of the People) in 1916 in which he criticized Kanai et al. , and in the 1920s he became an active supporter for the introduction of the neoclassical school. The vigorous research activities and contrasting academic development of Kawakami and Fukuda are described in detail in Chapter 4.

IDEOLOGY OF THE SOCIAL POLICY SCHOOL

As well as being a learned society for researchers specializing in social policy, the Association also adopted an academic stance that was known as the social policy school. The fact that the same members formed the Association and the school is a feature that was also seen in the social policy school in Germany.

The social policy school in both Germany and Japan was conscious of danger in the fact that the income disparity between the labourers' side and employers' side was growing and that class divisions were becoming more and more pronounced. [3] The 1899 Prospectus of the Association for the Study of Social Policy contains the following passage:

Recent efforts by Japan have resulted in great progress and significantly increased the national wealth. ... However, this has also resulted in wider disparities between rich and poor and, consequently, signs of a gradual decay in social harmony can now be seen. In particular, clashes between capitalists and labourers can already be seen. ... Unless countermeasures are taken now, this will be the cause of major problems in the future. The Association is organised here to study this problem.

The Association warned of future troubles unless measures were taken to counter 'clashes between capitalists and labourers'. This passage implies criticism of *laissez-faire*, which did not propose to consider any countermeasures, and socialism, which would be the inevitable outcome of the said clashes. The Prospectus carries on to say the following:

We oppose *laissez-faire*. The reason for this is that the extreme exercise of this self-interest and uncontrolled free competition would result in an excessive gulf between rich and poor. We also oppose socialism. The reason for this is that the destruction of the existing economic structure and the abolition of capitalists would be harmful to the progress of the national destiny. (Quoted in Morris-Suzuki, 1989).

The Prospectus thus states that destruction of the existing economic structure would be harmful to the progress of the 'national destiny', and it goes on to state the measures by which the problems of class struggle can be resolved:

Our beliefs are as follows: we support the existing economic system of private property and wish, within this system, to prevent class conflict and promote social harmony by means of both individual action and the authority of the state. (Quoted in Morris-Suzuki, 1989).

'Support of the existing economic system of private property' implies compliance with the Constitution of the Empire of Japan. The Association aimed to achieve social harmony by respecting individual action and applying the authority of state within the bounds of the existing state system. In short the Association, from the standpoint of improving society, aimed to achieve harmonization between capital and labour by means of social policy.

As the influence of the classical school, which ignored the existence of labour problems, grew weaker, the Association came to direct its criticism at socialism. When the government prohibited the Socialist Political Party that was formed in 1901, the Association issued the aforementioned Plea of the Association for the Study of Social Policy in which it scathingly criticized socialism, stressing the fundamental difference between itself and socialism centring around the latter's opposition to the system of private property. In this way the Association was slowly developing into an anti-socialist body.

Also the Association passed a resolution recommending that Sen Katayama should resign as a member in 1899.

Since the Japanese Association for the Study of Social Policy was modelled around the German one, there were many similarities in the thinking of both. But since the Japanese Association aimed at the resolution of social problems in Japan, it possessed some uniquely Japanese features. Hyoe Ouchi (1888–1980) raises the following three points as features that were unique to the Japanese Association: first, it turned the interest of a large proportion of the population towards labour legislation and other social problems; second, the influence of Wagner was strong; and third, it was solely concerned with proposing policy and paid little attention to the basic study of social problems (Ouchi, 1978).

Ideology that existed within the Association can broadly be divided into the following three strands.

First there was socialism, which was an exceptional existence within the Association. Socialists such as Isoo Abe belonged to the Association in its early days but they regarded social policy as just one step towards the ultimate realization of socialism. For the socialist members, there was no intrinsic difference between social policy and socialism.

The second ideology was also supported by a minority group and consisted of liberals professing private sector led social policy such as Iwasaburo Takano, Tokuzo Fukuda and Kunio Yanagita (1875–1962, bureaucrat) and others. This faction differed from the socialists in that it sought to resolve social problems under the existing Constitution (Takano and Yanagita were sympathetic to socialism in that the former supported the labour union movement and the latter supported the cooperative movement, but Fukuda was strongly opposed to socialism). However Takano came to desire the healthy growth of labour unions, and Fukuda and Yanagita became supporters of Taisho Democracy. Both Takano and Fukuda studied under Brentano in Germany.

The overwhelmingly large proportion of members belonged to the third ideological group. They espoused state-led social policy and, although they did not totally ignore the private sector, they placed their greatest expectations on state legislation as the means of achieving harmony between labour and capital. Noburu Kanai, who was the main proponent of factory legislation, was the representative member of this group. Since Kanai, who had been strongly influenced by Wagner, maintained a position of leadership within the Association for a long time, his thinking became the mainstream of the Association.

Having said that, the influence of Kanai alone is not sufficient to explain why the third ideology became the mainstream. The constitution of 1889 made the role of the state large and limited the rights of citizens, in reflection of the international relations and economic power of Japan at that time. The reason why supporters of state-led social policy formed the majority of Association members was probably related to the fact that, in the age of imperialism, a great deal was sought from the state in order for Japan's economy to catch up with the advanced industrial nations.

A FORGOTTEN LEGACY OF THE ASSOCIATION

As the industrialization of Japan's economy advanced and heavy industry, in particular, started to develop full-scale after the end of World War I, the labour movement gained in momentum and supporters of socialism increased. It has already been mentioned how, in the Association too, a rift developed between economists such as Hajime Kawakami who supported socialism and especially Marxism, and neoclassical school economists such as Fukuda who opposed this.

As was described earlier, Hyoe Ouchi, in his recollections of the history of Japanese economics, pointed out that the Japanese social policy school was characterized by an over-emphasis on policy recommendations and a disregard for basic research. That is to say that the social policy school economists did not place great importance on theoretical research or empirical research. As a result, all of the early research work on the social policy school carried out by Etsuji Sumiya and others concentrates on economists who vigorously debated policy proposals. The basic research referred to by Ouchi contains both theoretical research and empirical research, but it was the theoretical research that was dramatically deepened by Kawakami, Fukuda and others. The previously mentioned thesis by Iida analyses in detail the process whereby the Marxist economists and neoclassical school emerged as internal critics from within the social policy school (Iida, 1972–73, 1984).

In this section, an introduction is given to the formation of the Japanese historical school by Ginzo Uchida and the research into the standard of living conducted by Iwasaburo Takano and Kunio Yanagita, both of which are economic areas that received little attention in Japan at that time. The academic experiments of these men were unable to become the mainstream of Japanese economics and have been almost totally ignored in earlier research on the social policy school. However, I believe that the work of these men had the potential to open up new possibilities in the study of economics in Japan.

Uchida was born in 1872 and passed away in 1919 at the early age of 47. After studying at Tokyo University and Waseda University, he became a member of the Association. After teaching the first course on 'History of the Japanese Economy' at Tokyo University in 1899, in 1902 he travelled to Europe to study and returned home in 1907. After that he was appointed as a professor at Kyoto University and devoted himself to the research of

Japanese history. After his death in 1919, *Uchida Ginzo Ikoushu* (the Posthumous Manuscripts of Ginzo Uchida), containing all his writings in five volumes, was published in 1921. His doctorate thesis was written on the land system and currency system in the Edo era. His research method could be described as careful and steady positivism. He carefully collected old manuscripts, carried out strict inquiries based on his own theories of history, and drew out hypotheses after applying much careful thought.

Uchida was a pioneer in the research of economic history in Japan. A famous student of his was Eijiro Honjo (1888–1973, Kyoto University), and he and others were described as the Japanese historical school (Ichikawa, 1976), although they did not advance any arguments that directly resulted in the proposal of policy. Moreover, they put little effort into deepening economic theory, and did not possess the influence to compete with the research of economic history viewed from the standpoint of Marxism which was so popular at that time. The character of their school was modest. However the vast amount of historical literature on the Japanese economy, which was collected by Honjo, Seiichi Takimoto (1857–1932, Keio University) and Takao Tsuchiya (1896–1988, Tokyo University), became the essential literature for the research of Japanese economic history from that time on.

Another stream of positive research was the study of the standard of living of labourers and farmers. The activities of Kawakami and Fukuda greatly contributed to the advancement of the research of economic theory. However something big was also lost as a result. That was the viewpoint of the 'lifestyle' of citizens, that is, the viewpoint concerning the kind of lives being led by labourers and farmers. Here introduction is given to Iwasaburo Takano and Kunio Yanagita, who were representative of economists who advanced research in this area.

Takano was active within the Association from its establishment right through to its break-up. He had a strong interest in labour problems but, rather than proposing policy, he was more concerned with research to gauge the actual living conditions of labourers. He attempted to gauge actual living conditions by surveying the family budgets of labourers. The well-known *Tsukishima Chosa* (Investigation at Tsukishima) of 1918 was a good example of this (before that he also provided guidance in the *Saimin Chosa* (Investigation of Poor People) that was implemented by the Ministry of the Interior in 1911). Tsukishima in Tokyo was a residential district for low income classes, and Takano, concentrating not on poor people in general but labourers only, had labourers report their income and expenditure on survey forms and tried to numerically express the hardship faced by labourers in everyday life. Takano later resigned from Tokyo University in 1919 and managed the Ohara Institute for Social Research, and he made a great contribution to the research of labour problems in Japan (Oshima, 1968).

Yanagita, on the other hand, who studied social policy at Tokyo University, focused on the fact that the standard of living of farmers was lower than that of labourers, and he started out by concentrating on research of farmer problems. Since labourers were concentrated into certain areas within cities, it was possible for Takano personally to carry out investigation of family budgets. But because farmers were dispersed in rural areas throughout the country, Yanagita could not conduct the same kind of research. Thus Yanagita systematically attempted to research the history of farmers in Japan by using folk tales, legends, place names, and so on passed down through generations of farmers. He believed that the fundamental reason for the poverty of farmers lay in the small area of their farmland and, by investigating the history behind the appearance of such small-scale farming, he attempted to create a capitalistic form of farm management (Fujii, 1995).

However, the unprecedented research of Takano and Yanagita remained only a minor area within the study of economics in Japan, since they had no successors who attempted to understand the actual living conditions of labourers and farmers from the viewpoint of 'standard of living'. [4] Therefore, the work of these two individuals never became an established area of research in Japan.

CONCLUSION

Industrialization of the Japanese economy from the 1890s onwards brought with it labourer and farmer problems. The government of Japan, which was advancing modernization based on the German model, attempted to resolve social problems by introducing the economics of the German social policy school into Tokyo University, the sole national university in the country at the time.

Although the social policy school was weak in theoretical research and positive research, its strong point was that it focused attention on the practical problems of reforming the system for economically vulnerable groups. The school made a major contribution to the establishment of factory legislation, but with the increase in supporters of socialism brought about by further industrialization, opinions became divided among members of the Japanese Association for the Study of Social Policy in the 1920s, and the Association eventually broke up because of the internal divisions.

The members became bored with policy proposals not backed up by economic theory, and many economists such as Kawakami and Fukuda turned to theoretical economic fields such as Marxism and the neoclassical school. A few economists such as Uchida concentrated on research of Japanese history, whereas others like Takano and Yanagita moved on to research the actual lifestyles of labourers and farmers.

However, few economists built upon the work of Takano and Yanagita, and the mainstream of Japanese economic study in the 1920s paid little attention to analysing the actual living conditions of the poor. They moved more towards research of theoretical economics imported from Europe and America. After the demise of the social policy school, economists paid little attention to its strong points and emphasized its weak points.

NOTES

1. Since the 1900s the government pursued the policy of expanding higher education by establishing universities and commercial colleges. This caused the number of economists and eventually the number of the members of the Association to increase. New national universities were established in Kyoto, Sendai, Fukuoka, and Sapporo while new commercial colleges were established in Tokyo and Kobe.
2. Tokuzo Fukuda was critical of Marxism. It is therefore ironic that his books criticizing Marxism played a role in introducing Marxism to Japan. He even became an editorial supervisor for the first translation of *The Capital* by Motoyuki Takabatake.
3. Up until the 1920s the labour and socialist movements had not become powerful enough to menace political stability. It was not until the end of World War I that clashes between capitalists and labourers became fierce and the Association broke down.
4. Iwasaburo Takano no longer taught at any university after his resignation from Tokyo University in 1949. Kunio Yanagita continued his studies after he resigned as a bureaucrat. Thus one of the main reasons they did not have successors was the fact that they did not remain at university

REFERENCES

Fujii, Takashi (1995), *Yanagita Kunio: Keiseisaimin no Gaku* (Kunio Yanagita: his Social Policy), Nagoya: Nagoya Daigaku Shuppan-kai.

Ichikawa, Takamasa (1976), 'Nihon-shi Kenkyu to Keizaigaku' (Relation between the Study of Japanese History and the Study of Japanese Economy), in *Iwanami Koza Nihon Rekishi*, vol. 25, Tokyo: Iwanami Shoten.

Iida, Kanae (1972–73), 'Senzen Wagakuni Keizaikenkyu ni okeru Shakaiseisaku Gakkai no Yakuwari (1) (2) (3)' (The Roll of the Association for the Study of Social Policy in the pre-war Japanese Economic History) *Mita Journal of Economics* (Keio University), vols 72–73.

Iida, Kanae (1984), 'Nihon Shakaiseisaku Gakkai to Keizaigaku Kenkyu' (The Japanese Association for the Study of Social Policy and Economic Studies) in The Society for the History of Economic Thought (eds) *Nihon no Keizaigaku* (The History of Economic Studies in Japan), Tokyo: Toyo Keizai Shinpo-sha.

Ikeda, Makoto (1977), *Nihon Shakaiseisaku Shisoshi Ron* (Essays on the Japanese Social Policy School), Tokyo: Toyo Keizai Shinpo-sha.

Kawai, Eijiro (1969), *Meiji Shisoshi no Ichidanmen* (One Aspect in the History of Meiji Thought), Tokyo: Shakai Shiso-sha.

Matsunaga, Shozo (1976), 'Shakai mondai no Hassei' (The Origin of Social Problems in Japan), in *Iwanami Koza Nihon Rekishi*, vol. 16, Tokyo: Iwanami Shoten.

Morris-Suzuki, Tessa (1989), *A History of Japanese Economic Thought*, London and New York: Routledge.

Nomura, Kanetaro (1950), *Nihon Keizai Shisoshi* (A History of Japanese Economic Thought), Tokyo: Keio Tsushin.

Noshomusho (1976), *Shokkojijo* (Labourers' Working Conditions), Tokyo: Shin Kigensha.

Oka, Toshiro (1970), 'Kindai Nihon ni okeru Shakaiseisaku Shiso no Keisei to Hatten' (Formation and Development of the View of Social Policy in Modern Japan), in *Shiso* Tokyo: Iwanami Shoten, 12.

Oshima, Kiyoshi (1968), *Takano Iwasaburo Den* (The Life of Iwasaburo Takano), Tokyo: Iwanami Shoten.

Ouchi, Hyoe (1978), 'Nihon Shakaiseisaku Gakkai no Unmei to Gengai Nihon Keizaigaku no Shimei' (The Mission of Contemporary Economics and the Destiny of the Japanese Association for the Study of the Social Policy), in *Nihon Shakaiseisku Gakkai Shiryo* (Original Materials concerning the Japanese Association for the Study of Social Policy), Tokyo: Ochanomizu Shobo.

Pyle, Kenneth B. (1974), 'Advantages of Followship: German Economics and Japanese Bureaucrats, 1890–1925' in *Journal of Japanese Studies* **8** (1).

Sakamoto, Takehito (1972), 'Shakaiseisaku Gakkai no Seiritsu to Hatten' (Formation and Development of the Association for the Study of Social Policy), in Takahashi, Kohachiro (eds) *Nihon Kindaika no Kenkyu* (An Inquiry into the Modernization of Japan), Tokyo: Tokyo Daigaku Shuppan-kai.

Sekiya, Koichi (1958), 'Nihon Shakaiseisaku Gakkai Shoshi' (A Short History of the Japanese Association for the Study of Social Policy), in *Nihon Shakaiseisku Gakkai Shiryo* (Original Materials concerning the Japanese Association for the Study of Social Policy), Tokyo: Ochanomizu Shobo.

Sekiguchi, Hisashi (1986), *Tokyo Daigaku Hyakunenshi Bukyokushi 1* (History of Tokyo University), Tokyo: Tokyo Daigaku Shuppan-kai.

Shakaiseisakugakkai (1977), *Nihon Shakaiseisku Gakkai Shiryo* (Original Materials concerning the Japanese Association for the Study of Social Policy), Tokyo: Ochanomizu Shobo.

Sugihara, Shiro (1980), *Nihon Keizai Shisoshi Ronshu* (Essays on the History of Japanese Economic Thought), Tokyo: Mirai-sha.

Sumiya, Etsuji (1934), *Nihon Keizai Gakushi no Hitokoma* (One Age in the History of Japanese Economic Thought), Tokyo: Ohata Shoten.

Sumiya, Etsuji (1958), *Nihon Keizai Gakushi* (A History of Japanese Economic Thought), Kyoto: Mineruva Shobo.

Taguchi, Ukichi (1901), 'Rodo Hogo Mondai' (The Problem of Labour Protection), in *Teiken Taguchi Ukichi Zerishu* (The Complete Works of Ukichi Taguchi), vol. 2, Tokyo: Yoshikawa Kobunkan.

4. Two inquirers on the divide: Tokuzo Fukuda and Hajime Kawakami

Takutoshi Inoue and Kiichiro Yagi

INTRODUCTION

Tokuzo Fukuda (1874–1930) was born on 2 December in Tokyo. He was baptized a Protestant at the age of twelve and maintained a strong interest in religion throughout his life.[1] He was one of the most brilliant students who had ever enrolled in the Tokyo Higher Commercial School, which had been and still is called 'Hitotsubashi' after its location up to 1927. After one year's teaching experience at the Kobe Commercial School, he returned to Hitotsubashi to enter the graduate course. As soon as he finished this course, he received an appointment as a lecturer in economics at his alma mater. Following the government's policy for the training of young professors, he was sent to Germany from 1898 till 1901 and studied under K. Bücher in Leipzig and under L. Brentano in Munich. He received a doctorate from Munich University with his thesis, *Die gesellschaftliche und wirtschaftliche Entwicklung in Japan* (Fukuda, 1900) . This was published in Stuttgart in 1900 and read widely in the German-speaking world as an excellent introduction to the economic history of Japan. As he was impressed by the founding of commercial colleges (Handelshochschule) in Germany, he became one of the enthusiastic advocates for the reform of as well as the promotion of advanced commercial colleges in Japan to an equal academic rank with the Imperial Universities.[2] However, because of a dispute with the principal soon after his return to Hitotsubashi, he had to leave his alma mater from 1905 till 1919.

Hajime Kawakami (1879–1946)[3] was born on 20 October in Iwakuni, Yamaguchi Prefecture. He entered the College of Law at the Tokyo Imperial University and studied further at its graduate school. He taught economics and agricultural economics as a part-time lecturer at several colleges in Tokyo and published two books in 1905. One dealt with basic concepts of economics, *Keizaigaku jo no Konpon-Kannen* (Fundamental Concepts of Economics), another advocated the significant place of agriculture in the economy as a whole, *Nihon Sonno-Ron* (Japanese Arguments for Agriculture).

However, he had to wait for a while before he was called to the Kyoto Imperial University in 1908. During this period Kawakami devoted himself to journalism, beginning with the serial *Shakaishugi Hyoron* (A Critique of Socialism) in a popular newspaper (the *Yomiuri Shimbun*) under a pseudonym (1905b) and ending with the editorship of the *Nihon Keizai Shin-shi* (New Journal for Japanese Economy).

The reason that Fukuda, five years senior to Kawakami, became interested in Kawakami may be because Fukuda found a similar vein in Kawakami. First, both shared a deep interest in the ethical problems raised by Christianity. Though Kawakami was not baptized, he was greatly influenced by Christians such as Kanzo Uchimura (1861–1930) and Naoe Kinoshita (1869–1937) and deeply attracted by the altruistic teachings of the Bible. Kawakami even pushed himself to join an altruistic religious collective by the name of Mugaen, namely 'the Garden without Self' although, disappointed, Kawakami soon left it. Fukuda might have felt some sympathy towards Kawakami's frank disposition, as he himself experienced conversion several times. Second, in contrast to senior professors who were satisfied to imitate their foreign mentors, both intended to establish their own systems in economics and energetically explored various directions of economics. A common interest in economic policies as well as in economic history might be further added.

While both Fukuda and Kawakami began their research under the heavy influence of the German Historical School, they widened their perspectives by assimilating various new trends in economics. Probably under the guide of L. Brentano's sympathetic introduction to the German edition of Alfred Marshall's *Principles of Economics*, Fukuda was interested in the Cambridge school of economics and found his favourite at last in the welfare economics along the line of A. Marshall and A.C. Pigou. Kawakami, on the other hand, was attracted by E.R.A. Seligman's economic interpretation of history as well as by the marginalist economic theories of F.A. Fetter, J.B. Clark and I. Fisher. However, in his 40s Kawakami's interest in socialism and Marxism superseded the theoretical inquiry into marginalist economics he pursued in his 30s. After that most discussions between the two became a rather barren dispute between an anti-Marxist and a Marxist.

In the transition from the authoritarian Meiji state to the age of parliamentary politics of the Taisho era, both economists participated in democratic movements in their own way. In 1918, Fukuda, along with Sakuzo Yoshino (1878–1933), professor of politics at the Tokyo Imperial University, established the Reimei-kai which aimed 'to abolish evil and anti-democratic thought of despotism, conservatism and militarism' and 'to promote and consolidate the life of the nation in accord with new trends of thought after the World War which are guided by liberal, progressive and democratic principles' (Shinobu 1968, pp. 493–4). As an avowed leader of the Taisho Democracy, Fukuda endeavoured to establish a new economics which was to serve for the consolidation of the well-being of the nation. However, Kawakami was critical of the limitations that the leaders of the Taisho Democracy realistically set to the extension of democracy in Japan. After awakening the interest of the public to the social problems of industrialized nations by the best-seller, *Binbo Monogatari* (A Tale of Poverty) in 1917, Kawakami started to publish a private journal *Shakai Mondai Kenkyu* (Studies on Social Problems) in 1919 to 'propagate ideas of Marxism' (1947, V, p. 236). At this point, Kawakami's influence on Japanese intellectuals surpassed that of Fukuda's. As Toshihiko Sakai (1871–1933) put it, the tide had changed 'from the Fukuda era to the Kawakami era'.[4]

Both Fukuda and Kawakami did not hesitate to become involved in social movements. Fukuda supported the moderate trade unionism of the Yuaikai (Friendly Society), later the Sodomei. However Kawakami influenced the radical wing of Sodomei, which caused its organizational split later. Fukuda and Kawakami once crossed swords on the topic of social democracy. In Fukuda's view 'social democracy' contradicts the ideal of democracy due to its subjection to the interest of a peculiar class. To Kawakami, however, it was the inevitable course of historical change that progress is made under the special interest of some particular class. Criticized for his insufficient understanding of Marxism by a younger generation, Kawakami made every effort to transform himself into a consistent Marxist scholar. As a result, he was forced to resign from Kyoto Imperial University because of several subversive phrases in his publications and because he had the support of groups of communist students. It was at the age of 53 (1932), when he became a member of the illegal Japanese Communist Party, that he felt that his lifelong quest was finally completed.[5]

DEBATES BETWEEN FUKUDA AND KAWAKAMI

Fukuda and Kawakami engaged in more than ten disputes, which were not just over economic theories but also over social issues. From 1905 to 1907, the two economists exchanged their views on the taxation of rice imports and on the decline of independent farmers. They next debated many topics related to the methodology of economics. After 1917 the focus of discussions moved to the problems of Marxian economics and the cleavage between the two became gradually apparent.[6]

To confirm the basic difference of the two economists, we first explore the views they held in the first series of debates on the rice problem.[7] The main issue was whether the special rice import tax, which had been introduced to cover the expenses of the Russo–Japanese War, should be maintained or not.

At that time, Japan was in a favourable position concerning choice in the basic policy of trade and development, since the long wished for revision of the unequal customs treaty had been accomplished. Many free traders as well as protectionists joined the debate. On the other hand, this debate was related to another issue: the future prospect of Japanese agriculture based on small peasant farmers. Many were alarmed at the impoverishment of small farmers and the menacing spread of landowner–tenant disputes. Generally the protectionists associated themselves with the camp of agrarians like Tokiyoshi Yokoi (1860–1927), while free traders such as Tameyuki Amano (1861–1938) and Kotaro Noritake (1860–1909) combined their arguments with their vision of mercantile and industrial development. Policy advisers, such as Noboru Kanai (1865–1933) and Kumazo Kuwata (1868–1932), occupied a mixed position of the parallel development of commerce, industry and agriculture on the basis of protectionism.

Fukuda supported the abolition of the rice tax and opposed the protection of small peasant farming. He maintained that the proper distribution of agricultural products would be realized only through the market, and protectionist policies would only benefit landowners at the cost of the well-being of consumers. At the same time, he argued that traditional farming was the main cause of the declining tendency of Japanese agriculture and that introduction of competition on a commercial base into agriculture would contribute to the growth in the scale of cultivation run by independent farmers or by some joint production unit. Fukuda's arguments came from his conviction that Japan should be a nation of commerce and industry based on agriculture driven by the rational spirit of capitalism.

Kawakami began his argument for agriculture with his conviction that 'agriculture is the foundation, while commerce is the periphery' (1905b, p. 262). He supported maintenance of the rice tax and the protection of independent farmers. However he distinguished himself from the extreme position of protectionism, since he opposed the artificial high price on which traditional inefficient cultivation could be preserved. In principle, Kawakami trusted in the high quality of the work ethics of Japanese farmers and expected that they could improve cultivation in the most appropriate way to Japan. Compared with the agrarian argument of Tokiyoshi Yokoi, Kawakami stressed the independence of farmers (not the obedience of tenants to landowners) and further advocated a harmonized development of commerce and industry on the base of agriculture. According to Kawakami, the increase of independent farmers would provide the country with food and industrial materials as well as a broad domestic market for industrial products, thus helping the prosperity of commerce and industry.

Despite the difference in their attitude to the rice import tax, Fukuda and Kawakami shared an optimistic view of the possibilities of the future development of Japanese agriculture. Unlike most other economists then, who thought at the time that Japanese agriculture was destined for decline due to the scarcity of cultivatable land and the decline in the price of agricultural products in the world market, the two argued for the development of the national economy as a whole through the intersectoral relationship between the agricultural sector and other sectors. However, as regards the content of the ethical base of agricultural development, the two economists showed a marked contrast. According to Fukuda, the lack of a profit motive was the basic problem for the sound development of agriculture based on the self-interest of farmers. On the other hand, Kawakami believed that the industrious work ethic of Japanese farmers lay in their unselfish way of life by which they could be considered as representative of the national interest as a whole.

This difference also appeared in their ideas about how the nation should deal with its economy. Fukuda stood for liberalism in social policies. He believed that the self-motivated activities of individuals were the basic elements that made society move forward, and that government interference in private affairs should be kept to a minimum. However, rejecting the selfish profit-seeking motives of merchants, Kawakami quested for a non-capitalistic ethical basis for Japan as a nation.[8]

FUKUDA'S LIBERALISM IN SOCIAL POLICIES

After returning from Germany, Fukuda advocated factory legislation so as to secure labourers from disease and accidents and to improve their capability and independence. Fukuda's position in the field of social policy is best defined by the term 'liberalism in social policies'. He borrowed this term from L. Brentano's 'sozial-liberale Ideenrichtung' (social liberal direction) to indicate the reformist position in which initiatives of individuals and voluntary associations should be guaranteed. Unlike authoritarian senior economists in the camp of the Japanese Association for the Study of Social Policy, Fukuda argued that 'the state, society, and other organizations should refrain from intervention in people's social and economic affairs unless they have difficulty helping themselves' (Shakai Seisaku Gakkai 1909, p. 101).

Since writing his dissertation in Munich, the backwardness of Japanese society had been one of the continuing themes in Fukuda's thought. He noted that the individual, the nation, and society in the West supported each other in their movement forward and that the progress of the economy and politics rested on the base of a solid individualism. However 'in the economic society of contemporary Japan, the necessary conditions for the modern economic life in the age of global economy are not fully established'. Fukuda further argued: 'In the age when the concept of an individual as a fundamental unit of society and economy is an indispensable condition for a society to advance, we cannot be a mighty and wealthy nation by suppressing ideas of individualism at the same time' (1925–26, V, pp. 589–90). His faith in individualism was strengthened by his belief in historical development, 'as for people's advancement, the difference is just that they are a bit way ahead of us' (1925–26, V, p. 584).

In fact, Fukuda expected the emergence of economic actors who would follow the rational principle of 'gaining the maximum return from the minimum effort'. Such actors, he believed, had never previously existed in Japan. 'After the fundamental change in the economic organizations of societies due to the affiliation to a world economy', he explained, 'all economic conduct should be based on contracts by the free will, division of labour among equally free individuals, and exchange through free competition'. This is the modern economic man that Fukuda expected for the development of Japanese society.

In the first edition (1890) of his *Principles of Economics*, A. Marshall defined economics as 'a study of man's actions in the ordinary business of life; it inquires how he gets his income and how he uses it'. He later revised this to 'a study of mankind in the ordinary and social action which is most closely connected with the attainment and with the use of the material requisites of wellbeing' (4th edition). Noburu Kanai criticized the former definition, as 'it gives consideration only to the individual and neglects the nation and society as a whole organic entity'. Fukuda not only rejected this criticism, but also expressed his doubt about the revision made by Marshall. According to Fukuda, the revised definition obscured the clear message of the principle of individualism (1925–26, I, p. 20).

FUKUDA'S INTEREST IN CAMBRIDGE ECONOMICS AND MARXISM

Together with Brentano, Marshall was one of the major sources from whom Fukuda gathered his ideas. Fukuda used Marshall's *Principles of Economics* (1905) as the textbook for his course at the Keio Gijuku from 1905 to 1918. His lectures were published in 1909 as *Keizaigaku Kogi* (Lectures on Economics). He continued revising this book until his late years.

Fukuda maintained a keen interest in mathematical economics and advised his students to study it and translate classic literature in this direction. The Japanese translation of A.A. Cournot's *Recherches sur les principes mathématiques de la théorie des richesses* (1838), W.S. Jevons's, *The Theory of Political Economy* (1871), L. Walras's *Eléments d'économie politique pure* (1874), and H.H. Gossen's *Entwicklung der Gesetz des menschliches Verkehrs*

(1854) were produced thus by Fukuda's encouragement. As for Marshall's *Principles* Fukuda encouraged Kinnosuke Otsuka (1892–1977) to attempt a translation; Otsuka published a partly abridged translation in 1919 and then a complete translation in 1928.

Fukuda, on the other hand, began his study of Marxism around 1906. In Japan, the first stage of the study on Marxism was based mainly on American literature, as was the case with Toshihiko Sakai, Hitoshi Yamakawa (1880–1958) and Shusui Kotoku (1871–1911). Fukuda was one of the first Japanese scholars who studied Marx using the original German texts. In his article 'Marx-Kenkyu' (A Study of Marx) compiled in *Zoku Keizaigaku Kogi* (A Sequel to Lectures on Economics, Fukuda, 1911), Fukuda dealt with the distinction between 'constant capital' and 'variable capital', and presented his criticism of the inconsistencies between the labour value theory in the first volume of Marx's *Das Kapital* and that of production price in its third volume. He also denounced Marx's concept of 'surplus value', and made use of E. von Böhm-Bawerk's theory of capital and interest.

Though Fukuda remained critical of Marx and Marxism throughout his life, he also encouraged earnest theoretical research into this area. In those years when Kawakami was interpreting the Marxian concept of surplus value in terms of price theory, Fukuda's understanding of Marxian economics was surely outstanding. Fukuda supported Motoyuki Takabatake's (1886–1928) project of translating Marx's *Das Kapital* up to its completion (1925). On the other hand, Kawakami launched the publication of his own translation in serial form in 1927. However Kawakami's engagement in politics after his dismissal from Kyoto Imperial University hindered him from continuing this project. When he was in prison after his arrest in 1932 and declared his resignation from any political activity, Kawakami wished to resume this project as his last task as a scholar. This, of course, was not allowed even in his secluded life after his release in 1937 (Kawakami 1947, VI, pp. 121–4).

In accordance with his growing interest in modern marginalist economics, Fukuda, who had once regarded himself as 'the last economist of the Historical School in Japan',[9] gradually became sceptical about the future of the Historical School. In particular, he opposed the authoritarian advocates of the *etatist* conception of social policy such as A. Wagner. On the other hand, Fukuda attacked Marxism and expressed his sympathy for E. Bernstein's criticism of Marxian orthodoxy. Taking over the social-liberal tradition and creating his own system of welfare economics was the task adopted by Fukuda, who wished to provide an alternative to Marxism.

KAWAKAMI'S SWAY AFTER *BINBO MONOGATARI*

Kawakami's *Binbo Monogatari* was the book that taught modern Japanese of the new social problems in the industrialized nations. This originally appeared first as a series in the *Osaka Asahi Shimbun* (1916) when Japan was enjoying the economic boom caused by World War I. Kawakami warned Japanese against their euphoria from the very opening sentence, 'it is the poverty of the mass in present civilized nations that surprises us' (1917, IX, p. 9), and its truth was effectively shown also in Japan by the Rice Riots of 1918. In book form, the *Binbo Monogatari* was printed 30 times in a short period from 1917 to 1919, until Kawakami ordered an end to the printing. As Hyoe Ouchi (1888–1980) put it, 'every intellectual who is proud of the sense of social problems is willing to confess their indebtedness to this book' (Ouchi 1947, p. 182).

However the conclusion of this book is a very strange one for a famous Marxian economist in prewar Japan to reach. As a measure to solve the poverty problem, this book recommended a voluntary abolition of the consumption of luxuries by the rich prior to two other remedies for poverty, namely the correction of inequality in distribution and the transformation of production from private to public hands. In other words, the author regarded a moral revolution as being of paramount importance.[10] In reality, Kawakami was not at all a Marxist at this stage.

The theory used in *Binbo Monogatari* was far from Marxian theory. The reasoning that a voluntary abolition of the consumption of luxuries would result in an increase in the provision of necessities for the masses presupposed a full employment of capital despite the elimination of the demands of the rich, as well as a full conversion of the unconsumed income (saving) to capital accumulation. Kawakami conceived this reasoning from Hartley Withers's similar argument in *Poverty and Waste* (1914). However, this kind of optimistic view of the smooth adaptation of the market economy was just the sort that Marx would have opposed.[11]

Neither would Marxists agree with Kawakami's reasoning that luxury is the cause of poverty, because they believe that the income of the rich derives from the exploitation of the surplus value from the poor. In Marxian terms, the relation between the rich and the poor is a class relation between capitalists and wage labourers. This was the point that Tamizo Kushida (1885–1934), Kawakami's first disciple, used in criticizing his mentor. But Kushida himself was not well versed in Marxian economics at that time. Kushida argued that social problems were 'problems of distribution' not 'problems of production', from his understanding that the class struggle in wage determination could be regarded as a sort of 'bargaining' between two parties. Kawakami rejected Kushida's criticism promptly by repeating his idea that the problem of poverty was a 'problem of production' where production of necessaries was reduced by some reason (luxury consumption of the rich).[12]

However, after one year Kawakami confessed his disquiet as an economist in an essay entitled 'Miketsu-kan' (House of Detention) which appeared in the *Osaka Asahi* in the beginning of 1918. He compared the situation of contemporary economists who had no definite criterion to judge the priority between an increase in production and fair distribution with that of unconvicted prisoners in detention. Kawakami made an analogy between the incredible efforts of a prisoner who escaped from the skylight and Adam Smith's ten years devotion to the completion of his *Wealth of Nations* and called for the emergence of a second Adam Smith who could solve the theoretical indetermination by unbending endeavour (1918a, IX, p. 219).

Raising fairness in distribution as an independent criterion besides an increase in production was by itself a correction of the position developed in *Binbo Monogatari*. Pushed by his inner uneasiness, Kawakami started to examine the views of eminent economists about the priority between these two criteria. Kawakami first took up Jeremy Bentham and James Mill with the supposition that utilitarianism would be the philosophical base for orthodox economics. There he found that utilitarian thinkers never leave their individualistic position and prefer the safety of possessions to any kind of equalization of income. The utilitarian principle of maximum happiness, which rejects redistribution, was nothing but a principle of maximum production. Thus Kawakami established a series of equations: individualism (egoism) = holiness of private property = social policy as productive policy (1918b, IX, p. 233). In contrast, Kawakami argued, the true social policy should be a distributive policy which did not serve any series of productive policy equations but prevailed over them.

The term 'social policy as distributive policy' had been originally the position of an older generation of scholars including Kawakami's mentor Kuranosuke Matsuzaki (1865–1919). It seems as if Kawakami returned to his starting position as an ethical nationalist, but Kawakami's intention was that he would bridge social policy and socialism by the principle of 'distributive policy'.

However this also failed when Kawakami examined Marx's view on production and distribution (1919a, X, pp. 205–18). In the text of Marx's *Das Kapital*, Kawakami found that Marx did not separate distribution from production and rejected any ethical criterion of fairness or equality in distribution in his criticism of capitalism. His view of socialism as a liberation of new productive powers from the constraint of capitalist economies had the features of the productive policy. Kawakami realized finally that he had to abandon his position of integrating social policy and socialism on an ethical foundation, if he wanted to follow Marx.

EGOISM AND ALTRUISM IN KAWAKAMI

In the first number of the *Shakai Mondai Kenkyu*, Kawakami declared that 'I review every social policy from the final criterion of the ultimate solution of the social problem' (1919b, X, p. 227). He distanced himself from those who supported social policy without questioning the existing economic system as a whole. However this does not mean that he adopted the materialist view of revolutionary Marxism fully: he still retained 'the ultimate of the ultimate criteria' in the coincidence with 'the goal of human life', namely 'moral perfection as a man'. As Kawakami wrote, 'it is not allowed to ruin the soul for the sake of the flesh', which was his ultimate criterion for judging the means of the solution of the social problem (1919b, X, p. 228).

As the existence of this criterion suggests, the 'unsettled question' in economics was but a representation of a deeper moralistic question in Kawakami's mind. The dichotomy of 'productive policy' and 'distributive policy' was a translation of the question of the individual choice between 'egoism' and 'altruism' into the ethical dimension. Even after his denial of phrases such as an 'integration of the economy and the morality' in *Bimbo Monogatari* and 'social policy as a distributive policy', Kawakami appealed for the emergence of a 'second Adam Smith' who could establish an alternative economics which would replace traditional economics based on selfish 'economic man'.

Though he finally decided to follow Marx, Kawakami felt uneasy about whether he could find a final solution in Marx's materialism to the ethical problem which had troubled him since his youth. After filling the first numbers of the *Shakai Mondai Kenkyu* with studies of Marx and Marxism, Kawakami allowed himself to reveal his sentiment as his 'confession' in a different dimension to his social science. Recollecting the days when he had left his family to join a religious collective, he wrote that he had reached a religious awakening to the identity of egoism and altruism. 'An utmost consistent altruism is perfectly harmonized with egoism': this was the 'confession' Kawakami acquired from his religious experience. The young Kawakami thought that he could not live in this world if he followed the teachings of altruism totally. But 'if we consider ourselves standing on the belief of an absolute altruism', as our soul and flesh are thus donated to God, 'we have to pay utmost attention to keep this donation, that is the true egoism'.[13] This was the recognition with which Kawakami left the religious collective to return to academic research.

In the development of Western economic thought, Kawakami discovered a similarity to his own history of oscillation between egoism and altruism. In particular, the justification of self-interest by B. Mandeville and A. Smith in its early stages and the opposite development of T. Carlyle, J.S. Mill and J.

Ruskin attracted him. In *Shihonshugi-Keizaigaku no Shiteki-Hatten* (Historical Development of the Economics of Capitalism, 1923) he described 'the historical transformation of the thought for the approval of selfish activities – its emergence, development, death, and replacement by the opposite' (p. 143). This interpretation of the history of 'bourgeois economics' survived in the first half of his *Keizaigaku-Taiko* (Outlines of Political Economy), combined with a loyal interpretation of Marx's *Das Kapital* in its latter half. In this book, published in the very year when Kawakami was expelled from academic life, Kawakami called Marxian economics an alternative 'proletarian economics' and anticipated a parallel development to 'bourgeois economics' in that it began with a bold approval of the selfish interest of the working class. In Kawakami's view, Mandeville's claim that 'private vices' lead to 'public benefits' applied also in the case of the 'proletarian class' who bore the historical mission of the liberation of mankind as a whole through their struggle. Then Kawakami as an individual could fulfil his own interests by being an unselfish devotee to God. Thus by replacing the ethical question of individuals by the historical mission of a class, Kawakami adapted himself to the requisite of Marxism.

FUKUDA'S WELFARE ECONOMICS

In 1930 Fukuda wrote in the preface to *Kosei-Keizai Kenkyu* (Studies on Welfare Economics):

> I expect much from the mathematical direction of economics advanced by L. Walras, F.Y. Edgeworth, V. Pareto, and I. Fisher. However due to my weakness in mathematics, I cannot think that I am qualified to do any research in that field by myself, nor do I have the courage to do so. I can only hope to learn what others have made clear. Fortunately, I know some economists in Japan who are quite active in this field, and I am sure that we can see the harvest of their research before long. ... Therefore only one choice is left to me, and that is to focus on welfare economics whose trail was set by such scholars as J.A. Hobson, A.C. Pigou, and E. Cannan. (1930, pp. 5–6)

Fukuda distinguished between two kinds of economics, 'price economics' and 'welfare economics'. According to him, the former is the conventional economics that has its origin in A. Smith and now exists in various theories of modern economics, including Marxist economics. The latter, on the other hand, does not exist in a perfect form, though some elements are to be seen in conventional price economics and some efforts to systematize it have been made by German economists of the 'ethical school' as well as by Alfred Marshall. After Marshall, Pigou was the next to convert to welfare economics with his *Wealth and Welfare* (1912) and *Economics of Welfare* (1920), followed by Hobson and Cannan in Britain, R. Liefman in Germany, S.N. Patten in America, W. Mitscherlich in Austria and others.

Glancing at the direction taken by contemporary economists in the world, Fukuda interpreted the reason why welfare economics had yet to be completed as follows:

> As long as welfare economics remains economics, it has to measure welfare in economic terms, that is, by monetary units. In many cases in economic welfare, what is to be measured overlaps with the price. Therefore it is not at all easy to draw the line between welfare economics and price economics. (1925–26, V, pp. 276–7)

Fukuda maintained that welfare economics dealt with the 'degree of satisfaction' while price economics was concerned with the degree of 'desiredness'. Because most economists made no clear distinction between these two kinds of economics, they treated the two concepts with the same word, 'utility'. In his view, this vagueness hindered most economists from advancing in the direction of welfare economics.

Fukuda suggested that if 'utility' was to mean 'degree of satisfaction', then another word should be used to represent the 'degree of desirability'. He stuck to this conceptual distinction on three grounds: firstly, money could measure the degree of desirability only; secondly, the degree of desirability would hardly correspond to the degree of satisfaction; thirdly, the fundamental difference between price economics and welfare economics was the clearest where the distinction between the degree of desirability and that of satisfaction was made (1925–6, V, pp. 282–3). Fukuda highly evaluated the theory of marginal utility because it paved the way for welfare economics by making economists realize the subtle differences between the two concepts.

In *Kosei Keizai Kenkyu*, published just before his sudden death in 1930, Fukuda tried to give a philosophical base to welfare economics and explored the details of its structure. First he based the validity of welfare economics on Aristotle's concept of commutative justice.[14] Then he criticized Marx because Marx's economic theory remained in the domain of price economics due to his neglect of the theory of 'commutative justice'.

The next step Fukuda took at the outset of the second article, 'Joyo no Seisan, Kokan, Bunpai' (Production, Exchange and Distribution of Surplus), was a survey of the history of economics from his viewpoint of welfare economics. He believed that economics had originated from ancient Greek thought, including ideas set forth by Aristotle. He pointed out that the original Greek theory of utility was revised by Thomas Aquinas from the viewpoint of Christianity and transformed into the theory of cost. In his view, this was the foundation for the labour theory of value presented by Adam Smith and completed by Marx (1930, p. 142).

According to Fukuda, orthodox economics considered the following three principles: the principle of distribution according to invested services, the principle of cost, and the principle of exchange, as characteristics of capitalist societies. Since it gave priority to the market equilibrium attained by free competition, economic policy in capitalist societies aimed to perfect free competition and maintain the equilibrium of supply and demand (1930, pp. 149–50). Based on this argument of orthodox economics, Marx established his theory of exploitation by means of the production of surplus value. In Fukuda's view, Marx focused too much on production and neglected the significance of distribution. Fukuda considered a capitalist society as a 'society in which production, exchange and distribution of the surplus are performed'. Since a capitalist society is an 'acquisitive society of income' which is based on the distribution of surplus value, and the source of surplus value lay not only in production itself but also in the original distribution of various productive conditions preceding production, Fukuda concluded that the priority should be given to the theory of distribution.

Fukuda placed 'income' at the centre of his distribution theory.

> We live by income. Its distribution keeps our capitalist society going and advancing. Price, and money as well, therefore, are nothing but a means for the determination of income. Nothing is more significant for our economic existence and our physiological survival than income. (1930, pp. 166–7)

Because he tried to establish welfare economics based on the concept of income, it was logical for him to be critical of Marshall, who replaced 'income' with the 'material requisites of wellbeing' in the fourth edition of *Principles of Economics*.

As Fukuda argued, the distribution of income became crucial in a society experiencing a population increase, a rise in consumption, and advancement and change in the technology of production (1930, p. 164). He asserted that the distribution of income had to be carried out through optimizing conduct called 'earning activities'. This was because only through such rational conduct could the welfare of the next period be attained.

Fukuda mentioned the process by which an increase in distribution or consumption and saving (or investment) would promote an increase in income when he referred to Liefman and others:

> In such a distributive society as ours, consumption means direct purchasing of consumption goods with income. Saving means purchasing productive goods with income. Consumption promotes the production of consumption goods, while saving promotes the production of capital goods. (1930, pp. 172–3)

Commenting on this process Fukuda argued that too much saving and too much consumption would 'diminish the productivity of society'.

In order to avoid such a predicament, we should keep a certain proportion in terms of distribution between saving and consumption. Saving is necessary for society to maintain and to improve productivity, while consumption is necessary for a society to keep up with the increase in productivity. A genuine equilibrium is needed. (1930, p. 174)

To maintain this equilibrium, Fukuda argued further, a sort of 'welfare struggle' between 'productive people and unproductive people', between capitalists and labourers, and between 'those who have income and those who levy on the income, that is, the state and municipalities' should be fought (1930, pp. 174–5). Here he found the basis for his view of social policies.

After this analysis, he gave a 'tentative conclusion' about what he thought of the principle of distribution in capitalist society:

Of the two distributive principles of community, 'according to the ability of individuals' and 'according to the needs of individuals', only the latter deserves to be a principle of communism. In the stage of proletarian dictatorship, this is applied only on the base of the performed productive service. (1930, p. 178)

This principle is supposed to be applied in a higher form of communist society. In fact, however, it can be applied in capitalist societies after a modification such as 'according to the effective demand of individuals'. (1930, p. 179)

This is probably what Fukuda meant by 'earning activities' in distribution.

He next gave several examples of such struggles for distribution. One was the movement for industrial rationalization in the United States and Germany; another was the policy taken in Britain to fight against unemployment. He regarded those who were engaged in such movements or those who were executing such policies as those engaged in 'struggles for surplus value' by means of 'labour agreements', 'minimum or subsistent wages', labour insurance, and unemployment insurance. Class struggle, taxation by capitalist nations, public organization, public services, and various public companies and buildings were also the way of distributive struggles. He asserted also that these struggles should be regarded not merely as 'price struggles' but also as 'humanity struggles' as well as 'welfare struggles'. Fukuda added that 'wage struggles of workers could be economically significant' (see Ikeda 1982, p. 165). Fukuda interpreted the significance of class struggle as a beneficial means of 'improving public welfare and giving the direction of social advancement' (1930, p. 421), while he refused to such struggles as a means of realizing a socialist society. Thus Fukuda integrated class struggles into his system of social policy guided by welfare economics.

CONCLUSION: JAPANESE ECONOMISTS FACE THE SOCIAL PROBLEM

Fukuda and Kawakami belonged to the generation of Japanese economists who were aware of their mission to establish a unique system and tradition in Japanese economics. Starting under the common influence of the German Historical School, both strove to explore economic theories widely and finally followed separate paths, one as a critic of Marxism, the other as a Marxist. From the viewpoint of the intellectual history, their quests can be interpreted as an impressive representation of the ethical problems of individuals in an industrializing nation which reached the stage of the emergence of social problems as well as struggles among classes. Fukuda made an effort to refine his evaluation of the economic rationality of individuals so as to integrate class struggle into his welfare economics. In clear contrast, Kawakami was annoyed by the moral dimension of the 'egoism' of modern economic man and finally devoted himself to an altruistic service for the 'proletarian class'. Though they shared a common interest in the foundation of social policies in an age of grave social problems, neither could accomplish their task due to the severe political tensions of the day. A more fruitful debate between the two could have produced a common base to mitigate the cleavage of Marxian economists and non-Marxian economists in later years. Despite all their failures, their sincere inquiry into the social and ethical aspects of economic theory teaches us much that we cannot expect from most modern academic economists.

NOTES

1. For example, Fukuda at the age of 31 practised Zen.
2. Concerning the development of the Tokyo Higher Commercial School, see Sugiyama and Nishizawa (1988), and Nishizawa (1987).
3. For an overview of Kawakami's life, see Bernstein (1976). Kawakami's Selected Works (*Chosaku-shu*) was published first by Chikuma-Shobo in 12 volumes from 1964 to 1965 and after a decade a new full-scale Collected Works (*Zenshu*) by Iwanami (Kawakami 1982–86) was completed. Hereafter, sources of the citation from Kawakami are shown in parentheses signifying volumes and pages of this Collected Works.
4. This was the title of the review by Toshihiko Sakai on the well-read journal, *Kaizo* (1919). From his Marxist position, Sakai expected more from Kawakami's progress towards socialism than Fukuda's critical stance to socialism.
5. See his impressive description in the Autobiography (*Zenshu*, seq. V. pp. 452–4).
6. For instance, they discussed the original edition of Marx's *Wage Labour and Capital* in 1919, the logic of the proliferation of capital from 1920 to 1921, and Marx's *Das Kapital*, though other economists of the times were involved in the debates.
7. On this issue we owe much to Miyajima's study on Fukuda (Miyajima 1984, 1985). See also Sumiya (1992) with respect to Kawakami's arguments for agriculture.
8. This is rooted in Kawakami's conviction as a man of letters: 'Watch this pen! A pen never

exists by its own force. It never quests for its own gain. As a being who owes its whole existence to the force of others, it loves others with its full capacity' (1905c, *Zenshu* II, p. 449).

9. From Tatsunosuke Ueda's comment on Fukuda in Ueda et al. (1950), pp. 122, 129.
10. Sugihara (1995, 1996) offers another hidden aspect of this book. According to him Kawakami regarded the German wartime economy as a real step towards socialism, along with Lloyd-George's social reforms in Britain.
11. Ouchi (1965) and Kobayashi (1994) regard Kawakami's economics in this period as 'a very simple bourgeois economics' (Ouchi) and 'equilibrium theory' (Kobayashi). See Sugihara (1977) also in this respect.
12. Kushida ([1916] 1935), I, pp. 268–75. Kawakami's answer is in *Zenshu* IX, pp. 207–9.
13. Kawakami (1919b), *Zenshu*, X, p. 386. In later years Kawakami considered himself as a peculiar Marxist who approved the truth in the religious experience. Deguchi (1965) tries to examine this duality of Kawakami's thought.
14. Chapter 1 of Fukuda (1930), pp. 1–140, 'Aristotle no Ryutsu no Kosei' (On Aristotle's Commutative Justice).

REFERENCES

Bernstein, Gail L. (1976), *Japanese Marxist: A Portrait of Kawakami Hajime, 1879–1946*, Harvard University Press.

Deguchi, Yuzo (1965), 'Kawakami Hajime ni okeru Ni-shurui no Shinri' (Two Categories of the Truth in Hajime Kawakami), in H. Suekawa (ed.), *Kawakami Hajime Kenkyu* (Studies on Hajime Kawakami), Tokyo: Chikuma Shobo.

Fukuda, Tokuzo (1900), *Die gesellschaftliche und wirtschaftliche Entwicklung in Japan*, Stuttgart: Cotta.

Fukuda, Tokuzo (1907–09), *Keizaigaku-Kogi* (Lectures in Economics), Tokyo: Okura Shoten.

Fukuda, Tokuzo (1911), *Zoku Keizaigaku-Kogi* (A Sequel to Lectures in Economics), Tokyo: Okura Shoten.

Fukuda, Tokuzo (1925–26), *Keizaigaku-Zenshu* (Collected Works), vols I–VI, Dobunkan.

Fukuda, Tokuzo (1930), *Kosei-Keizaigaku Kenkyu* (Studies on Welfare Economics), Toko-shoin.

Ikeda, Makoto (1982), *Nihonteki-Kyochoshugi no Seiritsu* (The Emergence of Japanese Style Conciliationism), Kyoto: Keibun-sha.

Kawakani, Hajime (1905a), *Keizaigaku jo no Konpon-Kannen* (Fundamental Concepts of Economics), Tokyo: Sendagi Sosho, *Zenshu*, I.

Kawakami, Hajime (1905b), *Nihon Sonno-Ron* (Japanese Arguments for Agriculture), Yomiuri Shimbun Nishu-sha, *Zenshu*, II.

Kawakani, Hajime (1905c), A passage without title, originally in *Yomiuri Shimbun*, December 1905, *Zenshu*, II.

Kawakani, Hajime. (1906), *Shakaishugi Hyoron* (Reviews on Socialism), Yomiuri-Shimbun-sha, *Zenshu*, III.

Kawakani, Hajime (1916), 'Shashi to Hinkon' (Luxury and Poverty), *Keizai-Ronso* (Kyoto University), **2**(4), *Zenshu*, IX.

Kawakani, Hajime (1917), *Binbo Monogatari* (A Tale of Poverty), Kyoto: Kobundo, *Zenshu*, IX.

Kawakani, Hajime (1918a), 'Miketsu-kan' (The House of Detention), *Osaka-Asahi Shimbun*, 14–17 Jan., *Zenshu*, IX.

Kawakani, Hajime (1918b), 'Seisan-Seisaku ka Bunpai-Seisaku ka' (Productive Policy or Distributive Policy), *Keizai-Ronso*, **6**(5), *Zenshu*, IX.

Kawakani, Hajime (1919a), 'Seisan-Seisaku to shiteno Shakaishugi' (Socialism seen as Productive Policy), *Keizai-Ronso*, **8**(1), *Zenshu*, X.

Kawakami, Hajime (1919b), '*Shakai Mondai Kenkyu* Hakkan no Jo' (Preface to the first issue of the *Shakai Mondai Kenkyu*), *Shakai Mondai Kenkyu*, no. 1, *Zenshu*, X.

Kawakani, Hajime (1919c), 'Riko-shugi to Rita-shugi' (Egoism and Altruism), *Shakai Mondai Kenkyu*, no. 6, *Zenshu*, X.

Kawakani, Hajime (1923), *Shihonshugi-Keizaigaku no Shiteki-Hatten* (Historical Development of the Economics of Capitalism), Kyoto: Kobundo, *Zenshu*, XIII.

Kawakami, Hajime (1928), *Keizaigaku-Taiko* (Outlines of Political Economy), *Zenshu*, XIII.

Kawakami, Hajime (1947), *Jijoden* (Autobiography), Tokyo: Sekaihyoron-sha, *Zenshu*, seq. V–VI.

Kawakami Hajime (1982–86), *Zenshu* (Collected Works), 28 vols. (1982–84), 7 sequel vols. (1985), and an index volume (1986), Tokyo: Iwanami Shoten.

Kobayashi, Kanji (1994), *Kawakami Hajime – Marukusu Keizaigaku ni itaru madeno Kiseki* (Hajime Kawakami: Trails before Marxian Economics), Kyoto: Horitsu Bunka-sha.

Kushida, Tamizo (1916), 'Kawakami Kyoju no Shashi to Hinkon wo Yomite' (Reading Prof. Kawakami's 'Luxury and Poverty'), Kokka-Gakkai-Zasshi, **30**(5), also in *Kushida Tamizo Zenshu* (Collected Works), vol. 1, Tokyo: Kaizo-sha, 1935.

Miyajima, Hideaki (1984), 'Shoki Fukuda Tokuzo no Keizaiteki-Jiyuushugi' (Economic Liberalism of Fukuda Tokuzo in the Early Days of his Career), *Socio-Economic History*, **18**(1).

Miyajima, Hideaki (1985), 'Meiji-matsuki no Kawakami Hajime to Fukuda Tokuzo' (Hajime Kawakami and Tokuzo Fukuda in the Final years of the Meiji Era), *Tokyo Kawakami Kaiho*, no. 55.

Nishizawa, Tamotsu (1987), 'Seiki-Tenkanki ni okeru Koto-Shogyo-Kyoiku-Undo wo megutte' (On the Movement for the Higher Commercial Education around the turn of Centuries), *Keizaigaku-Zasshi* (Osaka City University), **88**(1).

Ouchi, Hyoe (1947), 'Kaidai' (Explanations), in Kawakami Hajime, *Binbo Monogatari* (Iwanami Bunko ed.), Tokyo: Iwanami Shoten.

Ouchi, Hyoe (1965), 'Keizaigakusha to shiteno Kawakami Hajime' (Hajime Kawakami seen as Economist), in Kiyoshi Suekawa (ed.) *Kawakami Hajime Kenkyu* (Studies on Hajime Kawakami), Tokyo: Chikuma Shobo.

Sakai, Toshihiko (1919a), 'Fukuda Jidai kara Kawakami Jidai he' (From the Fukuda Era to the Kawakami Era), *Kaizo*, December 1919.

Shakai Seisaku Gakkai (ed.) (1909), *Kojoho to Rodo-mondai* (Factory Legislations and Labour Problems), Tokyo: Dobunkan.

Shinobu,Seizaburo (1968), *Taisho Demokurashi-shi* (History of Taisho Democracy), Tokyo: Nihon Hyoron-sha.

Sugihara, Shiro (1977), 'Fukuda Tokuzo to Kawakami Hajime' (Tokuzo Fukuda and Hajime Kawakami), *Keizai Seminar*, December 1977.

Sugihara, Shiro (1989), 'Kawakami Hajime to Fukuda Tokuzo' (Hajime Kawakami and Tokuzo Fukuda), *Keizai Ronso* (Kyoto University), **124**(5/6).

Sugihara, Shiro (1995), 'Nihon-Keizaigakushi-jo no *Binbo Monogatari*' (*Binbo Monogatari* in the History of Economics in Japan), *Nihon Keizai Shiso-shi Kenkyukai Kaiho*, no. 5.

Sugihara, Shiro (1996), '*Binbo Monogatari* no Sogen' (Origin of *Binbo Monogatari*), in Sugihara, *Tabibito Kawakami Hajime* (Kawakami Hajime as Traveller), Tokyo: Iwanami Shoten.

Sugiyama, Chuhei and Nishizawa,Tamotsu (1988), '"Captain of Industry": Tokyo Commercial School at Hitotsubashi', in Chuhei Sugiyama and Hiroshi Mizuta (eds), *Enlightenment and Beyond: Political Economy Comes to Japan*, Tokyo: University of Tokyo Press.

Sumiya, Kazuhiko (1992), *Kawakami Hajime Kenkyu* (Studies on Hajime Kawakami), Tokyo: Mirai-sha.

Ueda, Tatsunosuke et al. (1950), 'Zadankai: Hitotsubashi Keizaigaku no 75–nen' (Discussions around 75 years of the Economics at Hitotsubashi), *The Hitotsubashi Review*, **24**(3), 122, 129.

Withers, Hartley (1914), *Poverty and Waste*, New York: E.P. Dutton.

5. The debate on Japanese capitalism: the *Koza* faction and its perception of society

Takaho Ando

PRELUDE TO THE CONTROVERSY OF JAPANESE CAPITALISM

Major conflicts, such as the Sino–Japanese War (1894), the Russo–Japanese War (1904), and World War I (1914–18), strongly spurred Japanese industrialization, establishing Japan's position as the preeminent capitalist country in Asia. Cities and markets grew and prospered, with the bourgeoisie and enlightened landowners forming the foundation of an active movement for political and social reform on the one hand, while on the other, the general public emerged as a distinct class. Political reform movements, such as the so-called Taisho democracy, were intermittently tried on a national scale, while the popular uprising known as the Rice Riots of 1918 also took place.

If this period is viewed globally, as Lenin argued in *Imperialism as the Highest Form of Capitalism* (1916), the advanced capitalist countries continued to dominate and divide the world. In China, competition intensified as the great powers of Europe gained entry. In this kind of global environment, Japan's drive to rapidly modernize and industrialize gave a distinct character to the makeup of capitalism there.

More than anything, Japan needed to be a nation strong enough to withstand the opposition to the imperialism it practiced in order to increase its production capacity and secure its markets. Even though the country had essentially reached the stage at which a cheaper government was called for, Japanese capitalism conversely found it necessary to emphasize a stronger state. This condition led the nation's bourgeois foundation to form cosy relationships with the old powers, and made for a sort of nationalist-led capitalism resulting in distorted relationships and a feudalistic structure.

With the modern dismantling of feudalism still at an incomplete stage, the social contradiction of 'capitalistic–imperialistic', as well as labour problems, had already begun to emerge. The combination of the bourgeoisie and enlightened landowners who accepted responsibility for the Taisho democracy possessed little power as a combined force, and quickly fell apart. While the bourgeois tendency towards rapid progress remained, conservative and reactionary trends continued as well. Thus, a new and powerful socialistic trend emerged, causing the sociopolitical movement to begin exhibiting a more complex character.

Ideological trends as well as the fate of intellectuals and academia followed a convoluted course. The free-wheeling scientific renaissance was, overall, frail and short-lived. As nationalism gained strength in Japan, the academic system, quickly set up with Germany's national system of study as its core, started out by banning free academia from the Tokyo Imperial University, and pressure was brought to bear on academia and ideology to accept paternalism. Especially after World War I, the reactionary structure remained, and the foundation of liberalism for the masses was curtailed. Thus with free academia left no leeway to fulfill its mission, it was feared there would be a socialist storm, with attendant class conflict and populist movements (Ishida, 1982).

What supplanted the acceleration of liberalism was Soviet Russia's Leninism, transplanted by way of Marxism, that is to say, Russian Marxism. It was not only the leaders of social and democratic movements who subscribed to Marxist thought: there were many liberals who converted to Marxism as well. Hajime Kawakami (1879–1946), an economist who wrote *Binbo Monogatari* (A Tale of Poverty, 1917), a work based on humanitarianism, and the liberalistic political scholar Ikuo Oyama (1880–1955) were receptive to Marxism, and with Kawakami and an economist Tamizo Kushida (1885–1934) as pioneers, Marxists leapt to the forefront of Japan's social sciences. At this stage, along with the intellectuals' banishment from universities and other such national research and educational institutions, it also meant that these bases of thinking and academia fell into the hands of the opposition movement. In fact, in contrast to the national academic system, paternalistic and tinged with fanaticism as it was, there was a period of popular research, as demonstrated by the opening of such nongovernmental institutions as the 'Puroretarian Kagaku Kenkyujo' (Centre for Proletarian Science) and the 'Sangyo Rodo Chosasho' (Industrial Labour Research Centre, established in 1924), whose aim was to develop scientific surveys and pursue other research. Numerous such foundations and groups had strong connections to the Japanese Communist Party, which was formed in 1922, but was reconstructed in 1926 after having been dismantled.[1]

In this fashion, the locus of thought and academics in the 1920s shifted to the masses and became monopolized by Marxism as the only powerful counterforce available, both theoretically as well as practically, to the social changes taking place.

While Marxism was linked to the Comintern, it boldly challenged the peculiar makeup of the leviathan that was Japanese capitalism, led by the emperor system. Above all, however, a dispute emerged as to the character of Japanese capitalism centred on the placement of the emperor system, rapidly dividing the group into two major camps. On one side was the group that adopted the ideology of the Japanese Communist Party. The guiding principle in the development of their theory was the 'Treatise on Japan', issued by the Comintern in 1927. In this work, a two-stage revolution, 'a forced, rapid bourgeois democratic revolution to be followed by a socialist revolution' was prescribed as the strategy for revolution in Japan, with the 'capitalist/landowner block', identified as the source of the bourgeois hegemony that formed the base of the national power, the target of overthrow. Keeping this as their guiding principle, Communist theoreticians, with Eitaro Noro (1900–1934) as key author and major contributors including Moritaro Yamada (1897–1980), Yoshitaro Hirano (1897–1980), Shiso Hattori (1901–56), and Goro Hani (1901–83) soon published the *Nihon Shihonshugi Hattatsushi Koza* (Lectures on the History of the Development of Japanese Capitalism; 7 vols) in 1932, aiming to point out the semi-feudalistic land system that gave the peculiar structure of Japanese capitalism a foothold. Afterwards, this group came to be commonly called '*Koza-ha*' (*Koza* faction).

Opposed to the *Koza-ha* was a group of socialists, including Hitoshi Yamakawa (1880–1958), Toshihiko Sakai (1870–1933), Kanson Arahata (1887–1981), and Tsunao Inomata (1889–1942), who did not belong to the Communist Party, and followed a different route, publishing the magazine *Rono* (Labour and Agriculture) in 1927. The group argued that the bourgeois elements of Japanese capitalism were already mature, and demanded that systematic changes in Japan be based on a socialist revolution. This group came to be commonly known as the '*Rono-ha*' (*Rono* faction), and in 1929 established the '*Ronoto*' (*Rono* Party) as a legitimate political body (Hoston, 1986).

These two currents confronted one another and debated every aspect of the revolution, including capitalism's historical stage, as well as type, structure, landownership, the Emperor system, the state, and the character of the revolution. The debate was at its peak when *Nihon Shihonshugi Hattatsushi Koza* was published, but even after *Koza,* many works by representatives of the *Koza-ha*, including Moritaro Yamada's *Nihon Shihonshugi Bunseki* (An Analysis of Japanese Capitalism) and Yoshitaro Hirano's *Nihon Shihonshugi Shakai no Kikou* (The Mechanisms of Japanese Capitalist Society) (both 1934) and other works were published in book form. From the other side, controversialists from the *Rono-ha*, including Itsuro Sakisaka (1897–1985), Takao Tsuchiya (1896–1988), and others continued the debate with their criticisms of the *Koza-ha*. In the end, however, the debate was halted with the arrest of members of the *Koza-ha* in July of 1936, and the *Rono-ha* in February of 1938.

This clash was known as the Debate on Japanese Capitalism (Sugihara, 1992). This debate may be divided into two periods, first the time of the theoretical questions found in the publishing of Noro's *Koza*, and the second phase of the debate that took place under suppression after the publishing of *Koza*. Here, to gain an understanding of the peculiar patterns of Japanese capitalism, one should reconstruct each of the important points at issue in the debate at the time.

EITARO NORO AND THE THEORIES OF KOZA

The central figure of the *Koza-ha* was Eitaro Noro. Against the background of the financial panic of 1924, and centred on a critique of Kamekichi Takahashi's (1891–1977) theory of the imperialism of Japanese capitalism (Takahashi, 1927; Hoston, 1984a), Noro fiercely debated the *Rono-ha*'s leading proponent, Tsunao Inomata. The number of supporters for each increased, and the battle lines of the debate on Japanese capitalism were clear from this point for both factions.

In 1930, Noro published his seminal work, *Nihon Shihonshugi Hattatsushi* (The History of the Development of Japanese Capitalism). This book, against the background of the debate with Inomata, was a collection of essays written since 1924 that showed Noro's exhaustive grasp of Japanese capitalism. In this original concept of Japanese capitalism, Noro connected with organizations such as the 'Centre for Proletarian Science' and the 'Industrial Labour Research Centre', which were engaged in the study of the masses, and made full use of their studies and empirical research, along with the 'Treatise of 1927'. The book itself centres on the debate, and by scrutinizing each of the debates, one can reconstruct an outline of the debate on Japanese capitalism up to about 1930.

Noro's *History of the Development of Japanese Capitalism* comprises five essays. Of these, the second essay is a critique of Takahashi's theory of imperialism, and the fourth essay is a critique of Inomata's works. In the first, third, and fifth essays, one can reconstruct Noro's own understanding of Japanese capitalism.

In the first essay (written in 1924–25), Noro divides Japan's social history into two periods, the pre-history of capitalism prior to the Meiji Restoration (1868), and the history of capitalism's development afterwards. As well as being a political revolution, the Meiji Restoration was a social revolution pushed along by the rulers, the 'capitalists and capitalistic landowners'. However, the first leaders in the political reform of the Meiji Restoration were 'reactionary court nobles and like-minded samurai unable to shed their feudalistic thinking.' Secondly, because of the accelerating Industrial Revolution, the government's conservative policies were of great moment. Due to intensified international capitalist competition and the resistance of the proletariat, a compromise was reached between the landowners and commercial capitalists. These factors, Noro claimed, reinforced the 'tyrannical, absolute nature' of the development of Japanese capitalism.

In the third essay (written in 1927), Noro posits the material basis of the 'tyrannical, absolute nature' of the development of Japanese capitalism even more concretely, pointing out its connection with feudalistic exploitation. Here Noro argues that even after the Meiji Restoration, the rents that landowners exacted from tenant farmers were feudalistic land rent payments, as were land taxes that the state collected from the farmers and the landowners. This fact, in combination with the 'semi-feudalistic' land rents, ensured a domestic basis for linking Japanese capitalism to the authority of the Emperor system.

The fifth essay (written in 1929), gives an analysis of the contemporary makeup of Japanese capitalism. Noro views Japanese capitalism within the context of the development of world capitalism. After World War I, except for a relatively stable period after 1923, world capitalism at the end of the 1920s plunged into a 'general period of crisis', when international and domestic confrontation reached its peak. Under these conditions, Japanese capitalism enjoyed no period of stability, and a 'constant condition of semi-panic continued'. This is because the development of Japanese capitalism began at the point where exceedingly radical contradictions were a common condition in the global capitalist system ('the weakest link in the chain of world capitalism'). The development of Japanese capitalism after the Meiji Era was the emergence of a primitive form of capital accumulation founded upon government exploitation of the farmers. Almost all of the farmers' surplus was collected as land tax by the government, and what little remained was taken by the landowners as land rent and by exploitative merchants. The farmers' money went to the establishment of a protective system to cover the costs of maintaining a tyrannical state and the system of public loans that provided capital to the privileged. In Japan, capitalism did not develop into the liberal and democratic systems found in Europe, and the trend towards monopoly of industrial and financial capital accelerated. Because of this, the farmers, although comprising half of the total population, in the end were reduced to petty businesses and poverty by 'the double exploitation of capitalism and semi-feudal land policies'. Thus, with a cramped domestic market, Japanese capitalists had no choice but to 'urge the nation to exploit colonies for markets, resources, and investment opportunities'. Then the deepening contradictions within Japanese capitalism at the peak of the progressing 'general crisis' in the world capitalist system worsened the problem. While the monopolistic domestic system in Japan was further reinforced, the country embarked on an imperialist war.

The above is the picture of Japanese capitalism painted in *The History of the Development of Japanese Capitalism*. Through the use of a structure paralleling that of the 'Treatise of 1927', the semi-feudalistic structure of Japanese capitalism was brilliantly highlighted. In this case, the important characteristics of so-called Japanese capitalism are firmly involved in the world capitalistic system. Noro inherited his methods from Lenin's *Theory of Imperialism* and attempted to tie this theory of the development of the inequality of capital worldwide to his understanding of the patterns of Japanese capitalism. The peculiar nature of semi-feudalistic and monopolistic Japanese capitalism not only featured various domestic conditions, but was controlled by the world system of capitalism. This view was shared by others of the *Koza-ha*, but it was never in the forefront in the debate he fought with the *Rono-ha*.

In fact, at the beginning of the debate between Noro and Inomata, this difference in approach to the problem of differences in the understanding of imperialism was already emerging. In contrast with Noro's grasp of Leninism, in Inomata's eyes it was the friction between advanced capitalism and native capitalism in addition to the formation of socialism and the Soviet Union that was causing the development of capitalism to stagnate, thus constituting the main contradiction in the international system of capitalism. Capitalism, if this main factor of strife between the classes were removed, was to bring about the greatest period of growth ever seen (Inomata, 1927). So various global conditions were, for the time being, abstractions, and Inomata tended to argue on the basis of the domestic characteristics of Japanese capitalism.

In the time that saw the publication of *The History of the Development of Japanese Capitalism* and the period immediately following, the debate between the *Koza-ha* and the *Rono-ha* revolving around the concept of imperialism since the conflict between Noro and Inomata was spectacular, but on the whole, perhaps because of the reason mentioned above, there was a propensity to debate the abstraction of the shrinking world economy, with the strong point being the idea that the patterns of Japanese capitalism were of a semi-feudalistic character. In contrast to Noro and the *Koza-ha*, who stressed landownership and feudalistic power as the important points, the *Rono-ha*, comprising a great number of intellectuals, basically questioned the maturity of Japanese capitalism. Essentially, the focus of the debate was shown to be an agricultural problem. The *Rono-ha* view sought to demonstrate the capitalist connection to agriculture, refuting in particular the position of Noro and the *Koza-ha* that recognized the connection of feudalism with high prices and farm land rents.

Summing up the *Rono-ha* view of this problem was Tamizo Kushida. In his essay of June 1931 regarding goods and farm rents, which Noro had classified as a category of feudalistic land rent, Kushida countered that first, goods and rent had already in essence been monetized with the development of the relationship between capital and farming villages; and second, even with the excessively high prices, this was not related to forces outside of economics, but due to economic coercion, therefore making it clear that this was a matter of capitalist control of land and rent (Kushida, 1931). Noro refuted Kushida's point, averring that this was not a matter of the commercialization and leasing of land, that instead it was a question of actual landownership, that the relationship between landowners and tenancy had no connection with capitalistic farmers, and that it furthermore showed non-economic coercion based on traditional customary contracts.

In this way, revolving around the land control system as the foundation of this main Japanese capitalism, the *Koza-ha* and the *Rono-ha* continued their heated debate. However, in 1931, the new 'Draft of the Japanese Communist Party Political Manifesto' was released by the Comintern. This tract prescribed a revolution for Japan, a 'proletarian revolution to extensively serve the bourgeois democratic mission', a position rather close to that taken by the *Rono-ha*.

This was disturbing and confusing to the *Koza-ha*. In this new situation, from about the spring of 1931, to reformulate *Koza-ha* theory Noro gathered scholars who were being hounded out of universities under suppression and began planning *Lectures on the History of the Development of Japanese Capitalism (Koza)* to show overall the structure and history of Japanese capitalism. This covered the domains of politics, society, history, ideology, science, technology, and so on, the aim of which was to gain literally a total grasp of the subject of Japanese capitalism and which mobilized approximately 30 intellectuals from various fields. In February, 1932, 'Kankou Shuisho' (Publishing Prospectus) was released, and the actual volumes of Koza were published from May 1932 to August 1933.

Suppression by authorities promoting military fascism was severe and despite plans to distribute seven volumes bans and partial censoring were ordered from the fourth volume on, dealing the *Koza-ha* a major blow. However, a run of between 8000 and 13 000 copies was secured for each volume, with readers comprising not only those of the left, but reaching a wide range of social strata, including those connected with government offices, making Koza a very great success.

Based on a sample of the contents published at the time, we here indicate the makeup of each volume of the *Koza*.

Part 1   History of the Meiji Restoration
        1.   An Introduction to the History of the Reforms of the Restoration
        2.   History of the Closing Days of the Tokugawa Shogunate
        3.   History of the Reforms of the Meiji Restoration

Part 2   History of the Development of Capitalism
   1.   Introduction to the History of the Development of Capitalism
   2.   History of the Development of Capitalist Economics
   3.   The Influence that Capitalism Exerted on Labourers and Peasants, and their Movements
   4.   Political History
   5.   Cultural History
Part 3   The Current State of Imperialist Japan
   1.   Japanese Imperialism at the Foundation of Post-War Capitalism's General Crisis
   2.   The Recent International State of Affairs
   3.   Recent Economic Conditions and Economic Panic
   4.   The Economics of Farming Villages and Panic in Agriculture
   5.   Recent Political Conditions
   6.   Recent Colonial Policy and the Nationalist Movement
   7.   Recent Class Conflicts
Part 4   Commentary on Material for the History of the Development of Japanese Capitalism
   1.   Literature on the History of the Development of World Capitalism
   2.   Commentary on Historical Material on Financial and Economic Policies
   3.   Commentary on Historical Material on Agriculture
   4.   Commentary on Socialist Literature
Index

It is quite obvious that the *Koza* is organized to conform to the structure of Noro's *History of the Development of Japanese Capitalism*. In other words: first, in connection with the general crisis in capitalism's world system, the aim is to analyse the structure of Japanese capitalism;[2] second, the ongoing use of the indispensable opportunity to analyse Japanese capitalism's peculiar characteristics as a hangover from the feudal system emerges strongly.

In reality, because of the oppression to which they were subjected, the *Koza* camp was forced to suffer a number of alterations and setbacks. First, the ideological leader, Noro, had planned an essay containing summarizations of Parts 1, 2, and 3, but was forced to live underground, and so was unable to write. Second, because of the ban, no accounts concerning class conflict, war, absolutism and the emperor system, and problems in the colonies were allowed, and many essays never saw the light of day. Third, researchers at the 'Centre for Proletarian Science' and the 'Industrial Labour Research Centre' were being suppressed, and as it was they who were in charge of publishing these works, production of Part 3 was understaffed.[3]

However, even with this result, the indisputable fact is that the *Koza* demonstrated the *Koza-ha*'s view of Japanese capitalism. As this was taking
place, the Comintern formalized the 'Treatise on the State of Japan and the
Duty of the Japanese Communist Party' in March of 1932. In this declaration,
the peculiar role in the emperor system played by the bloc of landowners was
emphasized, and again, as in the Manifesto/Treatise of 1927, the strategy of
forced change by means of a bourgeois democratic revolution leading to a
proletarian revolution was confirmed. The treatise was circulated in Japan in
July, while at the same time, the second volume of the *Koza* was being
published, but the similarity in the outlines of the treatise and the *Koza*
energized the *Koza-ha*.

For Noro, the *Koza* was not a work on Marxism in the narrow sense, but
rather the result of his strong desire to write a compilation of Japanese social
science. For example, when planning the compilation he had intended to
secure the participation of the civil scientist Nyozekan Hasegawa (1875–
1969) on one side, and that of Hyoe Ouchi and Takao Tsuchiya of the *Rono-
ha* on the other. Accordingly, in an environment where the institutionalization
of civil science was being suppressed, one can see the strong will of the
Koza-ha in pursuing the subject of civil ideology, and the desire to foster
academicism that valued the free discourse with the *Rono-ha*.

In this way, the *Koza* goes beyond a history of Marxist ideology, dramatically elevating the standards of Japanese social science to a whole new level.
The Koza exposed the new agenda in the debate on Japanese capitalism,
itemized the points of the debate, enlivened both the debate within the *Koza-
ha* as well as that with the *Rono-ha,* and had an impact on a broad range of
intellectuals, including civil libertarians. With the arrival of the *Koza*, the
debate on Japanese capitalism soared to a new plane.

The *Koza-ha* internal debate centring on manufacturing at the end of the Edo
Period was famous as the touchstone that drew the *Rono-ha* into the debate. In
a Koza essay, Shiso Hattori prescribed a level of post-Edo production capacity,
arguing that it should be at a manufacturing level (Hattori, 1932). He urged
caution regarding the considerable spread of manufacturing to such a wide
area, and, for a member of the *Koza-ha,* gave exceptionally high marks to
capitalistic control of the development of production. Soon afterwards, he also
argued that Japan should prepare its domestic markets to make the development of such manufacturing possible (Hattori, 1933). Katsujiro Yamada and
others in the *Koza-ha* countered that Hattori's view overemphasized the growth
of the bourgeois (K. Yamada, 1934), and this had repercussions on Takao
Tsuchiya's criticism of the argument that there was a growth in cottage
industry-type businesses prior to the Meiji Restoration (Tsuchiya, 1933).

The publication of the *Koza* stirred up even more the debate between the
Koza-ha and the *Rono-ha,* ranging over every field, from imperialist theory to

the ideology of the revolution in Japan. However, while admitting that there was groundbreaking work in new fields such as the debate over manufacturing, the tendency of the *Koza-ha* to frame their debates about the peculiar nature of Japanese capitalism in terms of the development of agriculture and land problems was no different than before the publication of *Koza*.

Of the various essays contained in the course, Moritaro Yamada's *Nihon Shihonshugi Bunseki* (An Analysis of Japanese Capitalist Society) and Yoshitaro Hirano's *Nihon Shihonshugi Shakai no Kikou* (Mechanisms of Japanese Capitalist Society) were published in 1934. Their organization is excellent, and Yamada's work especially shows his extensive understanding of all fields related to the economic structure of Japanese capitalism. Coupled with the fact that Noro's work never saw the light of day, Yamada's contribution was considered *Koza-ha*'s representative work, and was thus subjected to the concentrated fire of the *Rono-ha*. The criticism and support centred on Yamada's analysis thus formed the core of the debate on Japanese capitalism after the publication of *Koza* until the authorities terminated the debate in the summer of 1936.

THE DEBATE OVER *AN ANALYSIS OF JAPANESE CAPITALISM*

Moritaro Yamada, who was teaching economics at Tokyo Imperial University, was arrested in 1930 for being a professor with Communist sympathies. Although he then resigned from his position, he remained active as the central editorial contributor to Noro's *Koza*. Among the *Koza-ha*, it was he who had accumulated the most university research. While he was at Tokyo University, he had wanted to reconstruct Marxist ideology by his own analytical system for the sake of Japanese research, so he continued his ideological pursuit.

In his 'Kachiron no mujun to siyo' (Contradiction and Constraints of Value Theory, 1925) and 'Saiseisankatei bunseki joron' (Introduction to Analysis of the Reproduction Process, 1931), Yamada argued that values are the basic driving force of the overall economic structure, and that such had been duly established; moreover, in his analysis of the economic structure of one nation, as demonstrated in the third chapter of the second volume of Marx's *Das Kapital*, he believed the economic reproduction structure would be understood. Furthermore, since this reproduction structure shows the abstract form of overall capital in a society, it thus reflects the opposition to, and contradictions of, the overall capital. Accordingly, Yamada understood that it also appeared to show the total structure of the independent power that had to oppose and abolish capitalism throughout one nation.

Moreover, in Yamada's demonstration of the actual structure of capitalism for one nation, consideration had to be given to the historical environment. On the one hand, the capitalist structure taking shape in the developing stages was crucial; on the other, the landownership structure opposing capital was a decisive element as well. As found in *Das Kapital* (Chapter 7, Vol. I), the scenario has capital breaking up landownership, then taking over in a typical historical process. Here, with the fixed premise that capital will accumulate, Yamada held that the abstract reproduction structure is shown in Chapter 3 of Vol. II, and the actual structure in Chapter 3 of Vol. III (M. Yamada, 1980).

Does analysing Japanese capitalism this way work well in all cases? Broadly speaking, Yamada closely examines three conditions. First, Japan's path towards capitalism was set at the time when a significant number of nations then practising capitalism were moving to the stage of imperialism. Second, because the Meiji reforms were incomplete, feudalistic elements strongly interfered with capitalism's formation. Third, because the international environment of the first point operated in conjunction with the domestic historical circumstances of the second, those feudalistic elements of the time, especially landownership in farming villages, continued to be important in the foundation of capitalism in Japan.

Accordingly, the theories from Marx's *Das Kapital* could not be directly applied to Japanese capitalism. Some sort of mediating theory was necessary. One can see that for the problem posed by the world environment, Yamada employs Lenin's (and Noro's) theory of imperialism. For the issue of feudalism, Yamada turns his attention to Quesnay's *Tableau économique*. Quesnay understood the feudalistic connections to capital under the control of France's absolute monarchy, and explained this structure in *Tableau économique*. In it, he shows the structure of reproduction of capital under feudal landownership and its connection to the impending French Revolution. Grasping this, Yamada used Quesnay's *Tableau économique* as the foundation of his analysis of Japan's farming villages, and by supplementing this with Marxist reproduction theory, thought he had accomplished an analysis of the structure of Japanese capitalism (M. Yamada, 1980, Vol. I).

In the *Koza*, Yamada penned three essays on the formation of capitalism, development of industry, agricultural reform, and other important subjects. At their core was *An Analysis of Japanese Capitalism*, Yamada's independent contribution, published in 1934, that staked out his systematic theory of Japanese capitalism.

In the Foreword, first he compares England, France, Germany, and Russia, indicating that Japanese capitalism was formed in relation to conditions around the world. Then, from the reproduction theory standpoint, he warns that 'the basic structure of Japanese capitalism foretells its stance of opposition'. In this way, the structure of this book is extremely systematic, reflecting an awareness of the systematic approach.

This book is organized as follows: Chapter 1. Production Cycle – Reorganization: Manufacturing and the Various Types of Cottage Industry; Chapter 2. The Pivot of Transformation: The Military System – The Composition of Key Industries; Chapter 3. The Foundation: Semi-feudal System of Landownership – Petty Farming in the Peasant Servile Agricultural System.

Chapter 1 shows the form of capital used in building commodity-producing industries such as the cotton and spinning industries and how reorganization was carried out at the start of the Meiji Restoration. Chapter 2 shows the process of development in factory industries, that is, the production class dealing with the means of production, such as railroad, mining, machine tool and military-related industries. Chapter 3 shows that the industrial system was based on the system of landed property ownership and agriculture defined as the 'Semi-feudal System of Landownership – Petty Farming in the Peasant Servile Agricultural System'.

Here, Yamada strongly asserts that the feudal character of both land taxes and the landlord–tenant farmer system failed to be eliminated after property reforms in the Meiji era. It is clear that Yamada bases his view of the system of landownership in Japan on Quesnay's *Tableau économique*. He then goes on to discover, from a Quesnayesque viewpoint, the peculiarities of capitalism in Japan at the point at which capitalism had developed with support of the landownership system.

Yamada, however, emphasizes that it was not only the domestic conditions for development that created such a skewed construct of capitalism in Japan, but also a result of the global environment under capitalism, which was then gravitating toward imperialism. He particularly asserts that the structure of capitalism in Japan during the Sino–Japanese and Russo–Japanese wars was established under the overwhelming influence of these conflicts, and during this period events overlapped: the system controlling the military complex, that is, heavy industries needed to establish Japan as a great power, swung from feudalism to capitalism, the nationalization of the railroads was connected to the development of financial capital, and the rapid progress of imperialization proceeded.

Japanese capitalism could not outgrow its distorted structure based on the pre-modern system of labour, the semi-feudalistic system of farming (that is, a semi-feudalistic farm system of levying land taxes). As a backward, underdeveloped country, there was nothing for Japan to do on the foreign front but engage in an imperialist scramble for markets. In other words, the structure, based on the conditions of the purchasing power of American capital, comprised a domestic market with a silk industry from labour-based petty farming, and an imperialistic market for highly-focused, mechanized, large-scale industry and a supporting cotton industry, for which Japan embarked on an economic invasion of Korea, China and India. The peculiar structure of Japanese capitalism was restricted by the composition of these markets, and world markets composed of the socialist class structure from World War I and the Soviet Union were mandatory.

The above sketch of Japanese capitalism, upon analysis of such structure, also showed Yamada that there was a simultaneous concentration of powers against the establishment. In other words, there were ongoing analyses of both the feudalistic system of landownership in farming villages and the structure of industry, which conversely leaned towards military-related industries. Along with this, the workforce came together as capitalism (that is, general development of concentrated production and industrial rationalization) gathered steam, and 'the integration of regions, industrial sectors, and work processing meant an objective ordering and training of the labour rank and file, which led to the inevitability of the emergence of the proletariat' (Yamada, 1980, vol. 1). The development of a connection between a democratic revolution that started in the farming villages and a socialist revolution with labourers from leading industries at its core is the meta-message that Yamada inserts between the lines.

Noro provided a basic understanding of Japanese capitalism, and Yamada did not appear to stray far from his beaten path. However, Yamada gave a more articulate and specific analysis to aid understanding of the prescription for the development of industrial capital and the structure of the landownership system. He also broke down capital and labour into various categories and formulated them into concepts more precisely than Noro. Indeed, it was Yamada who, more than anything, clearly set forth a method of analysing Japanese capitalism, thanks to his large body of cumulative research which was so informed by the classics. Thus, what Yamada brought to the debate expanded the forum not only for the discussion of Japanese capitalism, but for the wider economic debate as well. For at first, the *Rono-ha's* criticisms of Yamada began with Tsunao Inomata and Soji Okada (1902–75) casting doubts on the view of feudalism's role in *An Analysis of Japanese Capitalism*, and then progressed to a systematic criticism of Istsuro Sakisaka and others.

Okada argued that the primitive accumulation of capital in Japan was derived from capital lent at high interest rates, national bonds, and numerous other features of the monetary system, showing it to be something that, even more than the development of capitalism, exploited wage labourers. Okada argued against overestimating the role of the peasant farmers by Yamada, emphasizing instead that of the bourgeois landowners. Also, citing the landowners' dependence on the current system of support of the financial bourgeoisie, Okada criticized Yamada's and the *Koza-ha's* idea of a two-stage revolution (Okada, 1934). In response to this, Junjiro Yajima and others from the *Koza-ha* defended Yamada's theory regarding the system of farmers and the landowners becoming bourgeois.

Moreover, the *Koza-ha*'s Hirano and Hattori were debating Hyoe Ouchi and Tsuchiya as well as others from the *Rono-ha* over the special character of Japanese farming villages and land rents and the issues surrounding manufacturing. Tsuchiya above all demonstrated the capitalist transformation in the connection between the spread of a commercial economy into farming villages and the system of landowners and tenant farmers before the Meiji period, and this grew into a strong criticism of the *Koza-ha* (Tsuchiya, 1937, 1977; Morris-Suzuki, 1989).

Itsuro Sakisaka was the *Rono-ha* member who confronted Yamada's overall system. First, focusing on the development of Japanese capitalism he claimed that, in the final analysis, Yamada had failed to grasp the concept of development. From Yamada's point of view, the type of capitalism established in the first decade of the 1900s, with its particularly slave-like agricultural and military characteristics, remained unchanged, having reached the stage of financial capitalism; similarly, the characteristics of feudalism for landowners, peasant farmers, and wage labourers were utterly unchanged. Rather than emphasizing the peculiarities of the system as Yamada had, Sakisaka wondered if it were not instead necessary to clearly show the process by which these characteristics would be negated by the general trends in the development of capitalism. Second, Sakisaka argued that Yamada's understanding of the classes fixed his view, never allowing him to abandon his idea of ushering in a two-stage revolution; for Yamada, the same classes would always be the vehicle for reforms in development. Third, Sakisaka asserted that Yamada's analysis of the transformation of landowners into bourgeoisie did not hold up. Fourth, and most important, Sakisaka said that by turning one's attention to the character of Japanese capitalism even temporarily, when the economic laws of Japanese capitalism were actually in place, one would inevitably come to recognize that development would result (Sakisaka, 1947).

In Sakisaka's critique of Yamada, he opposed Yamada's method of attempting to understand the relationship between the inequalities built into the system of global capitalism, and one can see the difference in their views emerge (much like the issue facing Noro and Inomata in their previously-mentioned argument about imperialism). Since Sakisaka emphasized only what would be accomplished through the general laws of capital, he had little awareness of the patterns of capitalism. However, despite their differences in opinion, the debate between Sakisaka and Yamada, centred on the connection between the stages and types of capitalism, raised basic economic issues and set trends in Japanese economics for years to come.

The debate over *An Analysis of Japanese Capitalism* on the whole now tended to focus more than ever on the issue of feudalistic structural interference in Japanese capitalism; both in theory and in fact, there was a progression at every level. The schematic of the *Koza-ha*, wedded to the concept of the feudalistic nature of Japanese capitalism, and the *Rono-ha*, stressing the general growth and development of capitalism, never changed, but the debate was fruitful in many ways, and continued to develop until the authorities began their brutal crackdown in 1936.

THE SIGNIFICANCE OF THE DEBATE ON JAPANESE CAPITALISM

As the emphasis of the debate on Japanese capitalism gradually shifted to economics, Japanese Marxists argued points across the entire academic spectrum: class in Japanese capitalism, society, the revolution, politics, history, and culture. Viewed in an historical context, one must not forget two conditions regarding ideology and theory. The first is that the rapid development of Japan, a backward country, left little opportunity for bourgeois ideology, theories, or movements to mature; this rapidly aggravated bourgeois contradictions, and meant there were a myriad issues for socialism to deal with. The second point is that Marxism, with its socialist core, was accepted along with Leninism in Japan, which kept it consistently under the strong influence of the Comintern's call for a global revolution.

The group that reacted most sensitively to these two conditions was the *Koza-ha*. As seen by Noro, *Koza-ha* had taken their lessons from Leninist theories of imperialism, and placed enormous weight on the argument that Japanese capitalism, with the inequalities inherent in its development, could not avoid taking on a nationalistic and militaristic makeup. Noro attempted to link this kind of structural distortion with the inadequate modernization of the Meiji restoration and the various lingering feudal relationships that were at the centre of farm village life, and to prove that semi-feudal landownership was the basis of the distortions in the developing structure of capitalism. As he analysed many various business and labour patterns, he believed that he had discovered the trinity of feudalism, industrial capital, and financial capitalism in every pattern he studied, and formulated his own original concept based upon this finding. Thus, the *Koza-ha* scenario of two-stage revolution became mainstream by promoting the issue of abolishing not only capitalistic connections, but simultaneously, those connected to landownership.

This *Koza* theory burned into the consciousness of the participants in the debate an awareness of the issues of the different types of capitalism that later appeared. The supposition was that pre-modern capitalism was formulated both on the level of global capitalism at the time as well as the contemporary domestic environment, with each aspect featuring peculiar nationalist characteristics. For Japanese economics in the days of the post-*Koza-ha* period, this was the starting point of an intense debate centred on class and patterns.

This way of thinking developed with two specific theoretical orientations. First, when capitalism is underdeveloped, as was the case in Japan, and control by foreign pressure is a major cause of its emergence, there is a tendency for nations to turn this dynamic to its own advantage. Along with the destruction of the *Koza-ha* and the increasing fascism of Japan's military, there were those within the *Koza-ha* who championed the viewpoint that forced industrialization by the state is a proper way to achieve modernization.[4] For example, in their search for new directions in social policy, Kazuo Okouchi (1905–84) and Yasoji Kazahaya (1899–1989) thought that a viewpoint based on the rationality of combined capital rather than on separate, individual capital, could result in policies protecting the interests of labour, even under military fascism. This is one line of thinking that diverged from the *Koza-ha* view, and it exerted a major influence on postwar social policy.

Capitalism, when underdeveloped, became a problem in the link between democracy and socialism. Criticized by *Rono-ha*, *Koza-ha* felt compelled to prove the semi-feudalistic nature of Japanese capitalism. Because of the severity of this issue, the point at which the study of democracy and *Koza-ha* met became clear, for example when conducting deep analysis of an issue in order to show the contemporary changes in non-economic forces, including coercive pressures stemming from such forces as customs and the limits imposed by communities. *Koza-ha*'s idea of simultaneously abolishing land-ownership and capital, which concerned the connection between socialism and democracy, was a pressing matter in terms both of their movement and its ideological dimension.[5]

Still, the relationship between democracy and socialism encountered some major difficulties not only in practice, but ideologically as well. Returning to Moritaro Yamada, his own theory on the abolishment of capital looked to Marx's theories on reproduction, and in regard to the matter of the abolishment of land ownership, to Quesnay's *Tableau économique*. But the underlying message of *Tableau économique*, that landownership is equivalent to throwing off the old style of agriculture, did not tie in well with the theory of capital for industry and the development of its markets. Therefore, it had no bearing on class conflict after the introduction of industrial capital. In this sense, even in the analysis of Japanese capitalism, one could not say that dismantling the system of landownership in farming villages was compatible with the labour force marshalling against leading industries. This drawback belied the *Rono-ha* theory of bourgeois transformation in farming villages.

The theorists who succeeded the *Koza-ha* after the war were most impressed by the theory that the dismantling of the feudalistic system went hand in hand with dismantling of communities along with the formation of industrial capital. A classic example of this was Hisao Otsuka (1907–95), with his peculiar combination of Max Weber's religious sociology and Lenin's market theory, formulating a concept comprising a pure form of contemporary industrial capitalism with individualized economic history as its core. Moreover, aware of the issues involved in Yamada's mixture of Quesnay and Marxist theories, many recognized the great number of theories connecting Marx to democracy, including those of France's Rousseau, England's Adam Smith, and Germany's List. These thinkers paid great attention to ideological history, and in the process of organizing Japan's postwar economics, had a hand in strongly linking economic theory with economic ideology. Furthermore, as catalysts in drawing attention to these thinkers' ideological concerns, the *Koza-ha*'s academics and view of democracy were closely involved in the process. Already Noro, the author of the *Koza,* was joined by the democratic political scientist Nyozekan Hasegawa. Those who took over from the *Koza-ha* after the war, for example, the economist Yoshihiko Uchida (1913–89), democratic political scientist Masao Maruyama (1914–96), as well as the forensic sociologist Takeyoshi Kawashima (1909–92), formed the *Koza-ha*'s academic battle front. In most of the illustrious achievements of postwar Japan's social sciences, one may find an awareness of the issues linking democracy and socialism.

The *Rono-ha* valued the general development of Japanese capitalism far more than the *Koza-ha*. They demonstrated the bourgeois transformation of the landowners and the capitalistic nature of land rents, maintaining that this did not leave the way open for unbridled feudalistic interference. *Rono-ha*'s theory was that, even in Japan, the realization of general laws governing the development of industrial capital would serve to heighten the class contradictions of the period of financial capital. Conversely, even while acknowledging the global market, they saw a slow shift to a certain level of imperialism. They had only a faint realization that theories regarding the development of capital inequities were important in formulating prescriptions concerning Japanese capitalism's domestic structure, considering imperialist markets to be but the outer layer of Japanese capitalism.

However *Rono-ha* also evolved as a result of their debate with *Koza-ha*. Their empirical analysis of the bourgeois aspect of Japanese capitalism, as in the case of Tsuchiya's work, demonstrated extremely high standards. Furthermore, their awareness of the differences in the patterns of Japanese and Western European capitalism grew, and because of their understanding of the stages of capitalism, it can be said that they did more than *Koza-ha* to give depth to the debate.

In this manner, the debate, as with the issue of the link between socialism and democracy, established the framework of postwar thinking while establishing basic methods for the various branches of social science and numerous other serious issues. More than a narrow debate with Marxism, the opening up of Marxism's internal debate was an epochal event that determined the basic structure of Japan's social sciences.

NOTES

1. As an indicator of the spread of Marxism, I would like to cite the publication of Motoyuki Takabatake's translation of *Das Kapital,* (1919–25) (Hoston, 1984b) and *The Collected Works of Marx and Engels* (1927–29; initial printing of 15 000 copies).
2. Goro Hani broke altogether new ground in his studies of the explosion of the imperialist contradictions in Asia as well as the problems of colonies and development of capitalism. A member of *Koza-ha,* he wrote *Toyo ni Okeru Shihon Shugi no Keisei* (The Development of Capitalism in the Orient) in 1932 for *Shigaku Zasshi* (Journal of History) (Hani, 1948) and introduced to *Koza-ha* theories not only of his view of Europe and Japan, but his insights into Japan in Asia as well. He thereafter continued to be a major influence on Asian theory. For *Rono-ha,* Tsunao Inomata held a similar perspective (Inomata, 1937).
3. In his commentary for a recent reprint of *Lectures on the History of the Development of Japan,* Kaichiro Oishi understood three points as evidence of the impact oppression had on *Koza* theory (Oishi, 1981).
4. It is believed that the problem with the ideological roots of postwar national monopolistic capitalism was not simply a matter of the high stage of capitalism's development; a fierce debate also arose over the role of the state in the backward countries in which there were inequities and so on in the development of capital, and there was also the experience of the prewar debate on Japanese capitalism.
5. With reference to this, I wish to point out that in developing its liberation strategy based on a two-stage revolution, a bourgeois democratic revolution leading to a proletarian revolution, as a way to enlighten the backward farmers and public, the *Koza-ha* emphasized the special significance of the Communist Party as being the avant-garde. When the so-called dictatorship of the avant-garde became a problem in Japan, the deep-seated causes could be ascribed to *Koza-ha* revolution theory, not just that repression had forced them underground. Around the time the Communist Party was reestablished in 1926, Kazuo Fukumoto (1894–1983) expounded the advanced nature of the avant-garde and the separation from the masses (Fukumotoism); this tack was always a part of Japanese Marxism.

REFERENCES AND FURTHER READING

Hani, Goro (1948), *Toyo ni okeru shihon shugi no keisei* (The Development of Capitalism in the Orient), Kyoto: Sanichi-shobo.

Hattori, Shiso (1932), 'Meiji ishin no kakumei oyobi hankakumei' (Revolution and Counterrevolution in the Meiji Restoration), in *Koza.*

Hattori, Shiso (1933), *Meiji ishin shi* (The History of the Meiji Restoration), Tokyo: Hakiyo-sha.

Hirano, Yoshitaro (1934), *Nihon shihon shugi shakai no kikou* (The Mechanisms of Japanese Capitalist Society), Tokyo: Iwanami Shoten.

Hoston, Germaine A. (1984a), 'Marxism and Japanese Expansionism, Takahashi

Kamekichi and the Theory of "Petty Imperialism"', Tokyo, 1989, *Journal of Japanese Studies* **10**(1), 1–30.
Hoston, Germaine A. (1984b), 'Marxism and National Socialism in Taisho Japan: The Thoughts of Takabatake Motoyuki', *Journal of Asian Studies,* **44**(1), 43–44.
Hoston, Germaine A. (1986), *Marxism and the Crisis of Development in Prewar Japan,* Princeton, NJ: Princeton University Press.
Inomata, Tsunao (1927), *Teikoku shugi kenkyu* (A Study of Imperialism), Tokyo: Kaizo-sha.
Inomata, Tsunao (1930), 'Botsuraku e no tenkoki ni tatsu nihon shihon shugi' (Japanese Capitalism on the Verge), *Kaizo* (Revision) March–July.
Inomata, Tsunao (1931), 'Marukusu shugi no zenshin no tame ni' (For the Advance of Marxism), *Kaizo* (Revision) March.
Inomata, Tsunao (1937), *Nouson mondai nyumon* (Introduction to Agrarian Issues), Tokyo: Chuo Koron-sha.
Ishida, Takeshi (1982), 'Staat und gesellschaft im modernen Japan im Zusammenhang mit der Entwicklung der Sozialwissenschaften', *Berliner Beitrage zur socialund wirtschaftlichen Japan-Forschung,* Nr. 20, Ostasiatisches Seminer, FU -Berlin.
Kushida, Tamizo (1931), 'Waga kuni kosakuryou no tokushitsu ni tsuite' (On the Particular Features of Farm Land Rents in Japan); in: *Ohara shakai mondai kenkyuujo zasshi* (Journal of the Ouhara Centre for Research of Issues in Modern Society) June.
Morris-Suzuki, Tessa (1989), *A History of Japanese Economic Thought,* London: Routledge .
Noro, Eitaro (1965), *Noro Eitaro zenshu* (Collected Works of Eitarou Noro), in 2 Volumes, Tokyo: Shinnihon Shuppan-sha.
Noro, Eitaro (ed.) (1982), *Nihon shihon shugi hattatsu shi koza* (Lectures on the History of the Development of Japanese Capitalism, 7 Vols, Reprint; Tokyo: Iwanami Shoten.
Oishi, Kaichiro (1981), 'Nihon shihon shugi hattatsu shi koza: kankou jijo' (Lectures on the History of the Development of Japanese Capitalism: Publication Status), in *Nihon shihon shugi hattatsu shi koza* (Lectures on the History of the Development of Japanese Capitalism), Reprint vol. 1.
Okada, Soji (1934), 'Nihon shihon shugi no kiso mondai' (Fundamental Issues of Japanese Capitalism), *Kaizo* (Revision) August.
Sakisaka, Itsuro (1947), *Nihon shihon shugi no shomondai* (Issues in Japanese Capitalism), Tokyo: Odo-sha.
Sugihara, Kaoru (1992), 'The Japanese Capitalism Debate', 1927–1937, Occasional Papers in Third World Economic History (4), 24–33.
Takahashi, Kamekichi (1927), 'Nihon shihon shugi no teikokuteki chii' (The Imperial Status of Japanese Capitalism), *Taiyo* (Sun) April.
Tsuchiya, Takao (1933), 'Tokugawa jidai no manufakuchua' (Manufacturing in the Tokugawa Period) *Kaizo* (Revision), September.
Tsuchiya, Takao (1937), *Nihon keizai shi ronshu* (Collected Essays on Japanese Economic History), Tokyo: Ikusei-sha.
Tsuchiya, Takao (1977), *An Economic History of Japan,* Philadelphia; Porcupine Press
Yamada, Katsujiro (1934), 'Manufakuchua ni tsuite' (On Manufacture), in *Rekishikagaku* (Historical Science), March.
Yamada, Moritaro (1980), *Yamada Moritarou chosakushu* (Collected Works of Moritaro Yamada) in 5 Volumes, Tokyo: Iwanami Shoten.

6.   General equilibrium theory and beyond: Yasuma Takata and Kei Shibata

Takashi Negishi*

1.   GENERAL EQUILIBRIUM THEORY AND JAPAN

The postwar contributions from Japan to the development of economic theory were most remarkable in general equilibrium theory. Japanese contributions number 18 among 171 entries in the bibliography of Arrow and Hahn (1971 pp. 428–37) which is a representative advanced textbook of general equilibrium theory. This ratio is very high, since the international share of Japan in researches in economics in general seems to be around 2 per cent, as is seen, for example, from the fact that of the total 1000 entries in *Who's Who in Economics* only 20 are from Japan (Blaug and Sturges, 1983).

There would not be such postwar contributions to general equilibrium theory, of course, without the basis laid by prewar studies of economics in Japan. In the 1930s, many Japanese economists seriously studied general equilibrium theory (Ikeo, 1996), but we concentrate on Yasuma Takata and Kei Shibata for the reasons outlined below.

No one can deny the fact that Michio Morishima was a leader of postwar contributions to general equilibrium theory from Japan. He was a student of Takata at Kyoto University, and then a leading member of the Institute of Social and Economic Research at Osaka University, founded and headed by Takata himself. Shibata was a colleague of Takata at Kyoto and was taught general equilibrium theory by the latter. There seems to be no direct relation between Shibata and Morishima, though there may be possible indirect influences through Nobuo Okishio with respect to studies of Marxian economics. Perhaps coincidentally, however, Shibata and Morishima are interested in the same problems, the non-stationary-state interpretation and over-determination of general equilibrium, though their proposed solutions are quite different.

Although they made some original contributions to general equilibrium theory, neither Takata and Shibata were satisfied with its current version and tried hard to go beyond it, emphasizing the importance of the consideration of more long-term problems.

Takata insisted that the neoclassical general equilibrium theory is only the first approximation to the real economy and that the second approximation based on the consideration of non-economic, social powers is necessary, particularly to explain the existence of unemployment. This is not surprising since he was also a leading sociologist in Japan who emphasized the importance of population problems to explain the long-term historical development of societies.

Shibata tried to solve long-term problems of Marxian economics by using a simplified general equilibrium theory. He was disappointed with the short-term nature of the recent neoclassical and Keynesian general equilibrium theories, since such theories are not useful to solve more important long-term problems like those of irreplaceable resources and environments.

The plan of this chapter is as follows. Section 2 sketches the life and works of Yasuma Takata, while Section 3 is devoted to giving a bird's-eye view of his five volume work *Keizaigaku Shinko* (New Lectures on Economics), from the point of general equilibrium theory. His most original contribution is the power theory of economics, which we discuss in Section 4. Section 5 is devoted to Kei Shibata's life and works. In Section 6 we sketch his monumental work *Riron Keizaigaku* (Theoretical Economics), which contains most of his contributions in the prewar period. Finally, we discuss Shibata's postwar studies of general equilibrium theory in Section 7.

2. YASUMA TAKATA

Yasuma Takata was born in 1883 at Sage in Japan. In the same year, Marx died and Keynes and Schumpeter were born. Graduating from Kumamoto high school in 1907, he entered Kyoto Imperial University and studied sociology. He also studied economics and, as a matter of fact, his study of Marxian economics was much earlier than that of Hajime Kawakami (see Chapter 4 of this book). In 1914, Takata was appointed lecturer at Kyoto Imperial University and taught economics there.

After he published *Shakaigakugenri* (Principles of Sociology) in 1919, he taught economics and sociology at Hiroshima Higher Normal School and Tokyo Higher Commercial School (the predecessor of the present Hitotsubashi University). He began to criticize Marxian economics severely and disputed with Kawakami and other Marxian economists in Japan.

Takata was appointed Professor of Economics in 1925 at Kyushu Imperial University and then in 1930 at Kyoto Imperial University. His five volume *Keizaigaku Shinko* was published between 1929 and 1932. He held the office of the dean of the economic faculty in 1938–1939. In 1944 he retired from Kyoto Imperial University on account of the age limit that applied there. Then Takata was appointed Professor at Osaka University in 1951, held the office of the dean of the economic faculty in 1953–1955, and founded the Institute for Social and Economic Research in 1954. After he retired from Osaka University he taught at Osaka Prefectural University and Ryukoku University.

In 1965 the Japanese government named Takata a person of cultural merits for his contributions to the development of sociology in Japan.

He published more than 100 books and about 500 articles, among which *Keizaigaku Shinko* was a great success as an advanced textbook in Japan, perhaps comparable to Marshall's *Principles* in English-speaking countries. He was nicknamed 'Japanese Marshall' by Bronfenbrenner (1956). Takata died in 1971 at the age of 88.[1]

3. *KEIZAIGAKU SHINKO*

Volume 1 contains a general survey and also the theory of production, the latter being rather descriptive and not very theoretical.

Volume 2 is concerned with the theory of price. In its Preface, Takata declares that he stands for the general equilibrium theory. While the text of this volume explains the Walrasian and Casselian versions of the general equilibrium theory, the appendix deals with the Paretian version with ordinal utilities and variable input coefficients. Unfortunately, Takata confuses simultaneous determination and causal relations and insists that factor prices are indeterminate unless they are exogenously given by social powers (pp. 250, 266, 344). This confused view will be, however, recanted in Volume 4. (NB, page numbers without dates refer to *Keizaigaku Shinko*.)

Takata clearly points out the possibilities of a rising (static) demand curve in the case of conspicuous consumption (p. 68). The premise that price enhances utility (utility is a function of price as well as consumption) is very old and can be traced back to Smith and Rae, though it was Veblen who made conspicuous consumption famous.[2] However, the conspicuous consumption premise is one thing, and it is quite another to recognize the possibility of a rising demand curve. In the case of the bandwagon effect (Leibenstein, 1950) or consumption externality, the recognition of a rising demand curve can be traced back to Cunynghame (1892) and Edgeworth (1905). In the case of conspicuous consumption or vanity, however, it seems that the possibility of a rising demand curve was first demonstrated by Leibenstein in 1950. If so, Takata's insight in 1930 is very remarkable.[3]

Takata clearly recognizes Marshall's careful distinction of a particular expenses curve and a supply curve. He calls the former the static supply curve, and the latter the dynamic one (pp. 87–91). This is also a remarkable fact, since economists in the English-speaking world soon forgot this distinction and accused Marshall of forgetting to take into consideration the producers' surplus (Ellis and Fellner, 1943). Marshall defined producers' surplus, of course, not by the supply curve, but by the particular expenses curve (Negishi, 1993). Takata rightly explains that producers' surplus is defined only with respect to the particular expenses curve (p. 281).

J.S. Mill argued that the value of a commodity brought from a foreign country, unlike those of domestic commodities, does not depend on its cost of production in the place whence it comes (Mill, 1909, p. 582). Using the so-called Cunyghame–Barone figure (Gandolfo, 1986, p. 42), Takata rightly criticizes Mill's view that the relative price is not equalized to relative cost in the exporting country, assuming incomplete specialization (pp. 296, 300). There is no difference between the case of domestic value and international value, in the sense that they are determined by demand and supply and they are not independent from the cost of production, as far as the supply is related to cost. In other words, assuming complete specialization, Mill overemphasized the role of reciprocal demands in the determination of international value.

Volume 3 deals with the theory of money. Referring mainly to German literature, Takata discusses such philosophical, definitional and institutional problems as what is money, as well as more theoretical ones like Gresham's law, the quantity theory of money and purchasing power parity theory. From the point of view of the general equilibrium theory, he argues that the price of a commodity is determined by demand and supply and that the relation between the cost of production and the price is not causal but merely functional. Similarly, he explains that demand and supply of foreign exchange determines the rate of exchange and that the relation between the purchasing power and the rate of exchange is not causal but functional.

In the Preface to Volume 4 which deals with the theory of distribution, Takata recants the position previously taken in Volume 2 and admits that the general equilibrium including equilibria in factor markets is determinate even if factor prices are not exogenously given by the social power. If such an equilibrium is not unique, however, the initial factor prices exogenously given in the adjustment process do matter for the final determination of the unique equilibrium (p. 81, see also Volume 5, p. 88).

Takata argues that demand and supply of labour determines wages and criticizes Tugan-Baranovsky (1913, pp. 31–9) who denied it and insisted that wages are exclusively determined by social powers. It is pointed out, however, that the existence of unemployment cannot be explained if the supply price of labour is not affected by the social power (pp. 109, 166). The effect of social power is also recognized for the case of land rent. It is interesting that Takata, unlike Marx, considers the absolute rent not only in agriculture but also in manufacture (pp. 201, 260).

Following Schumpeter, Takata considers that the profit of capital, from which interests are paid, is a quasi-rent in a dynamic economy (p. 352). As for the stationary state, he rejected the then prevailing interpretation and insisted that the amount of capital should be an endogenous variable (p. 325).[4] This is very interesting in view of the over-determinancy of Walrasian general equilibrium and the so-called Wicksell's missing equation problem raised in the later controversies on capital and interest.[5] When the supply of capital is limited, Takata admits that the rate of interest can be positive in such a stationary state as was considered by Walras, Cassel and Clark, which he calls the normal stationary state, while the rate of interest is zero in the stationary state considered by Schumpeter, which he calls the pure stationary state (pp. 317, 321, 333, 336). Of course, Takata points out the effects of social powers on the rate of interest (pp. 375, 438).

Finally, Volume 5 is devoted to the theory of changes. After he summarized his view of the stationary state (pp. 66, 69, 74), Takata develops his theory of trade cycles. The origin of trade cycles is the growth (quantitative change) and development (qualitative change) of the economy (pp. 179, 182). Particularly, the population increase is important. An increase in the population in a stationary state causes delayed and accelerated overadjustments with inertia in producers' goods industries (pp. 244, 273, 491). Takata's theory of trade cycle is a real theory and monetary factors are regarded as secondary ones. The persistence of trade cycles, repeated over- and underproductions with inertia, is explained by the overadjustments relative to the stable wages which are due to the existence of the social power (p. 438).

The book concludes with the author's emphasis that the ultimate autonomous variable in society is the population. The reason is, of course, it is the origin of social power (p. 501).

4.   POWER THEORY OF ECONOMICS

In the Preface of Volume 2 of *Keizaigaku Shinko*, Takata states that the originality of his book lies not in general equilibrium theory itself, but in the power theory of price. Takata's position changed three times, however, with respect to the power theory of economics. First, as in Volume 2 of his *Keizaigaku Shinko*, published in 1930, he insisted that general equilibrium theory cannot determine factor prices and they must be exogenously given by social powers. After he was criticized by such scholars as I. Nakayama, K. Shibata and T. Kimura, Takata changed his position in Volume 4 of the same book published in 1931. He admitted that general equilibrium theory as such can determine factor prices but argued that this first approximation to the reality should be supplemented by the second approximation of the consideration of social powers.

In 1934, Takata changed his position again and insisted that there can be no equilibrium with a positive rate of interest unless the effect of social powers are taken into consideration (Takata, 1934, 1935, p. 52). This position was based on his studies of the theory of interest of Böhm-Bawerk and Wicksell. Being confused by Lindberg's erroneous criticism on Böhm-Bawerk, Takata considered that the equilibrium solution of Böhm-Bawerk and Wicksell is not tenable and the effect of social powers must be introduced (1935, pp. 293–360).[6]

Therefore, Takata modifies the famous Wicksell mathematical model of Böhm-Bawerk's theory of interest, by introducing the effect of social power on tne supply of labour (1935, pp. 320–21). The modified model is as follows (notations are changed).

Let us suppose that the input of labour is uniform over the period of production t. Since the final output of consumer's goods at the end of t must be distributed between labourers and capitalists,

$$p = w\,[\,1 + (rt/2)] \tag{6.1}$$

where p, w and r signify respectively the value of output per labourer, the wage rate and the rate of interest. Takata considers that

$$p = f(t, K) \tag{6.2}$$

where K denotes the total amount of capital. The condition of the full employment is

$$L = g(w, p) \tag{6.3}$$

where L is given total labour population and g signifies the supply of labour determined by the social power of labourers. In other words, a certain level of w is insisted on by labourers to supply the given amount of labour. Since r must be maximized by capitalists, given w,

$$dp/dt = wr/2. \tag{6.4}$$

Finally, K is endogenously defined by

$$K = wtL/2. \tag{6.5}$$

Assuming L is exogenously given, Takata considers that five equations can determine five endogenous variables, p, w, r, t and K. Takata then emphasizes that the social power here is not the factor to modify the equilibrium value of variables determined without the effect of social power, but the factor without which the determination of the equilibrium value of variables is impossible (1935, p. 321). It is interesting to note that the amount of capital K is an endogenous variable which indicates the necessary amount to satisfy labourers' demands for wages insisted on by their social power (1935, p. 323). The model might be interpreted in this way as a normative one.[7]

Perhaps Takata's final position can be seen in Takata (1941).[8] He regained the position that the power theory of economics aims for a second approximation to the first approximation obtained by traditional general equilibrium theory (1941, pp. 23–6, 108; 1955, pp. 86–9, 177). In other words, the traditional general equilibrium theory, which he calls utilitarian economics, is logically consistent and can determine factor prices including the positive rate of interest and wages. In view of realism, particularly to explain the existence of unemployment, however, it is necessary to introduce power theory, since utilitarian economics cannot explain unemployment.

For Takata's coming back to this final position, it seems that Kimura's (1934) critical suggestion was influential (Takata, 1941, p. 110). Referring to Pareto (1927, p. 45), Kimura argued that non-economic factors influence the utility of entrepreneurs and labourers, and that the distribution of income is determined by these influenced utilities. It is interesting that Kimura referred to Pareto, since Pareto, like Takata, also studied sociology as well as economics and regarded pure economics (Takata's utilitarian economics) as the first approximation which should be supplemented by successive approximation, that is, considerations of not purely economic factors (Pareto 1927, pp. 12–13, 21).

In Chapter 6 (pp. 216–48) of Takata (1941),[9] he tries to follow Kimura's suggestion in his explanation of unemployment. The utility should include the utility of the satisfaction of the demand based on social power (p. 225). The labour is not supplied until the disutility of the loss of dignity caused by the wage level less than a proper rate disappears. When the proper wage rate is reached, the decision of how much labour to supply begins. Only then, the utility of consumption made possible by wage income is taken into consideration to decide how much labour to be supplied (p. 228). The question is not utility versus power. Within the utility in a wide sense, we should consider both the utility in a narrow sense and the utility obtained by the satisfaction of the demand based on the social power. In other words, we have to consider both utility in consumption and utility in possession or utility of dignity (pp. 229–230).

Perhaps we may formulate Takata's view of the supply of labour in the following way, since it may be easy for Takata, who knew the premise that utility is a function of the price in the case of conspicuous consumption (see Section 3 above), to consider that it is a function of the level of wages in the case of a labourer's dignity.

Suppose the utility of a labourer U is composed of utility of consumption V, disutility of labour supply D, and utility of dignity W as

$$U = V\,(wL/p)\ W\,(w - w^*) + D(L)$$

where w, p, L and w^* signify respectively the rate of wage, the price index of consumer's goods, supply of labour, and the proper wage rate. V is increasing with respect to the consumption wL/p and D is decreasing with respect to the labour supply L as such. As for W, let us assume that

$W = 0$, if $w < w^*$, and
$W = 1$, otherwise.

It is clear that $L = 0$ if $w < w^*$ and otherwise L is determined by the so-called second postulate of classical economics that the marginal utility of consumption with respect to labour supply L is equal to the marginal disutility of labour supply L as such.

Takata explains unemployment by the fact that labourers do not accept employment ($L = 0$) if the rate of wage offered is less than the proper one determined by their social power ($w < w^*$). According to Keynes (1936, p. 6), this is a kind of voluntary unemployment which is due to the refusal of a unit of labour, as a result of social practices or mere human obstinacy, to accept a reward corresponding to the value of the product attributable to its marginal productivity.[10]

As for Keynesian involuntary unemployment, Takata admits its existence but remains critical of Keynes in that the latter did not try to explain why workers will oppose a cut in money wages but not a cut in real wages (Keynes, 1936, p. 9). Takata insists that traditional utilitarian economics cannot explain it and does not believe any economic theory, which does not accept power theory, can do it. He explains why there is no competition from the unemployed to reduce the wage rate, by pointing out that workers' demands relating to dignity and prestige are at work (1941, pp. 42–3, 86; 1995, pp. 100, 131–2).

5. KEI SHIBATA

Kei Shibata was born in 1902 at Fukuoka in Japan. Graduating from Yamaguchi Higher Commercial School in 1921, he entered Kyoto Imperial University where he was taught Marxian economics by Hajime Kawakami (see Chapter 4 of this book). He was appointed lecturer at Kyoto Imperial University in 1929 and promoted to associate professor in 1931. Shibata learned general equilibrium theory from his senior colleague Yasuma Takata. After the publication of *Riron Keizaigaku* (Theoretical Economics) in 1935–36, he spent a year at Harvard in 1936, the year when Keynes's *General Theory* was published.

Shibata was appointed professor at Kyoto Imperial University in 1939. During the war, he was involved unsuccessfully in politics, and also unsuccessfully in his attempt to develop a totalitarian theory of economics. Shibata resigned from Kyoto Imperial University in 1946.

He came back to academic life in 1952 and was appointed professor at Yamaguchi University, where he held the office of the dean of economic faculty in 1953–54. In 1960, he resigned from Yamaguchi University and was appointed professor at Aoyama Gakuin University, where he held the office of the dean of economic faculty in 1969. Though his professorship was terminated in 1971 on account of the age limit, he continued his lectures at Aoyama Gakuin as a part-time lecturer until 1976.

Shibata died in 1986 at the age of 83. During his lifetime he published 22 books and 122 articles. The topics discussed ranged from the analytical and empirical problems of economics to criticism of the current theory of economics from the point of view of resources and environment problems, and to an idealistic philosophy of humanity and history.[11]

6. RIRON KEIZAIGAKU

Shibata's prewar contributions are published mostly in *Keizaironso*, the house journal of Kyoto Imperial University, and then included in his first book entitled *Riron Keizaigaku* (Theoretical Economics) published in 1935–36. Some important ones were later published in English in *Kyoto University Economic Review*.

Riron Keizaigaku consists of Preface, General Survey, Theory of Production, Theory of Circulation, and Conclusion.

In the Preface, Shibata states that properly simplified Walrasian general equilibrium theory is very useful for studies of economic problems. In the General Survey, he starts with the discussion of non-monetary exchanges of commodities and proceeds to that of monetary exchanges. Money is defined as the general medium of indirect exchanges (p. 55). The value of money, Shibata emphasizes, depends on its purchasing power in the past (p. 67). (NB, page numbers without dates refer to *Riron Keizaigaku*.)

Theory of Production is divided into Introduction, Theory of Income Distribution and Theory of Dynamic Relations in Production. The Introduction contains several important observations. In the explanation of the determination of the prices of the factors of production (pp. 155–8), Shibata points out the possibility of the overdeterminancy in the so-called Cassel's system, referring to his earlier paper (Shibata, 1930), which was published before the famous paper of Stackelberg (1933).

As for the problem of capital and profit in a stationary state, for which Takata showed an interesting view (see Section 3 in the above), Shibata also expressed an insightful view (pp. 163, 180). Shibata considers that the value of capital is an endogenous variable and argues that the rate of interest can be positive if the supply of capital (a function of the rate of interest) remains properly bounded.

General equilibrium system is simplified as promised in the Preface by some assumptions for the behaviour of households (pp. 185, 202; see also Shibata, 1933a and Lange, 1934–35). Shibata's system is not Walrasian, but rather classical and Marxian, since given real wages are assumed to be advanced as variable capital (pp. 195, 202) and money is assumed to be metallic one which can be produced in the industry (pp. 170, 186).

Shibata compares his analysis with that of Marx and insists that they are identical except that he considers the system of price of production only, which is more useful than the system of value, if one is merely interested in the behaviour of an economy quantitatively rather than in the conflict between social classes (p. 202). He argues that there is no difference between quantitative results of value analysis and those of price analysis, since prices of production are rightly derived from values by the Marxian solution of the so-called transformation problem, if it is carried out properly. Shibata demonstrates this by his numerical examples (pp. 204–15) and criticizes Takata (1931, pp. 107–8) who argued to the contrary (pp. 217–24).[12]

Theory of Income Distribution deals largely with very detailed studies of comparative statics (p. 225), of Marxian distribution problems and with occasional digressions on classical and neoclassical problems.

Perhaps the most important and most famous is the assertion that any technical change which reduces the cost of production necessarily increases the rate of profit (pp. 228, 241). The rate of profit is determined in Shibata's general equilibrium system by price–cost equations with constant input coefficients. Referring to Shibata (1933b) (see also Shibata, 1934), he gives a numerical example which is a counterexample to the famous Marxian assertion that the rate of profit tends to fall as the organic composition of capital is increased by technological improvements. Later, this assertion is strengthened in Shibata (1939) by an algebraic demonstration for a very simplified case and by Okishio (1961) who gives a proof for the general case.[13]

Shibata criticizes not only Marx but also Böhm-Bawerk (1914) who denied the role of economic power on markets. The question is the effect of an exogenous increase of the wage rate on the total wage income. Böhm-Bawerk's negative conclusion can be seen from his famous numerical tables for the determination of the rate of profit, wage rate and the period of production. Shibata conjectures that the validity of this conclusion depends crucially on the Austrian's special assumption on the production and capital structure, and produced a numerical counterexample, using a more standard neoclassical assumption (pp. 249, 274, 287; also Shibata 1935). Unfortunately, both Böhm-Bawerk and Shibata use an untenable supposition that the value of heterogeneous capital can be given exogenously. If this problem of the so-called Wicksell missing equation is solved by the proper use of the supply function of capital, the total wage income can generally be shown to be increased by an exogenous increase of the wage rate (Negishi, 1995).

Although Shibata failed to use the supply function of capital properly in his criticism of Böhm-Bawerk, he has a clear idea of how to use such a function (p. 163), as already mentioned above. He repeats this idea in his criticism (p. 291) of Takata's model of endogenous determination of the value of capital and the rate of interest with the wage influenced by the social power (see Section 4 above).

Ricardo admitted in the third edition (1821) of his *Principles* that the process of mechanization may prove injurious to the working classes, by constructing two numerical examples, the relevance of which we can confirm from the point of view of general equilibrium theory (Negishi, 1990). Ricardo has, however, been misunderstood by many later eminent economists including Wicksell, Kaldor, Stigler and Morishima, most of whom confused their own problems with the original problem of Ricardo (Negishi, 1998). It is very remarkable, therefore, that Shibata shows his correct interpretation of the problem based on a careful and detailed survey of related literature (pp. 301, 309, 317).

Theory of Dynamic Relations in Production deals with problems of adjustment processes from which comparative statics in Theory of Income Distribution are abstracted (p. 381). In other words, it deals with growth and trade cycles. Shibata's general equilibrium system here is very much like Marx's reproduction scheme, though not in terms of value, but in terms of prices.

First, trade cycles are discussed briefly with respect to changes beyond expectation in capital accumulation (p. 383). Then, detailed considerations are given for comparative dynamics of balanced growth with constant rates (pp. 393, 403) and non-balanced growth with changing rates (p. 438). Finally, effects of changes in input coefficients are considered. Shibata supports Tugan-Baranovsky's view that there can be no overproduction caused by the changes in organic composition of capital, provided that there are no monetary effects, and defends it against many Marxian critics (p. 492).

Theory of Circulation is composed of Introduction, Theory of Commodity Circulation and Theory of Monetary Circulation.

In Theory of Commodity Circulation, Shibata introduces commercial activities into general equilibrium theory (p. 565) and reworks his analysis in Theory of Production. What is particularly interesting is that he develops a regional general equilibrium model which assumes the inter-regional immobility of capital and/or labour (pp. 581, 613–27). Then the model is simplified to consider Ricardo's famous numerical example of comparative costs (pp. 628–33). Shibata rightly emphasizes the international difference in the rate of profit hidden behind Ricardo's numerical example and solves the equilibrium terms of trade and rates of profits by introducing supply functions of capital.[14]

The role of money is finally recognized fully in Theory of Monetary Circulation. Shibata reworks his analysis in Theory of Production, that is, Theory of Income Distribution and Theory of Dynamic Relations in Production. The latter is, of course, most important, since it covers trade cycles. Shibata's theory of trade cycles is a monetary theory of trade cycles (p. 838), which is explained in terms of the bank rate of interest, the natural rate of interest, and price expectation (p. 746). Under the gold standard system, Shibata concludes that the general price level is ultimately determined by the cost of production of gold (p. 749) and long-run cycles are explained by the conditions of gold production (pp. 782, 930).[15]

In the Conclusion, Shibata regrets that the book still falls short of his ultimate aim, that is, the study of the law which governs the historical changes in the social structure of production (p. 971).

7. POSTWAR STUDIES

While Shibata's prewar research was the application of the simplified general equilibrium theory to Marxian problems, one of his problems in the postwar period was the critical examination of the basic structure of Walrasian general equilibrium theory.[16] Let us consider a drastically simplified model, since it is not easy to see the point in the original version of the Walrasian general equilibrium model of capitalization and credit (Negishi, 1989, pp. 269–27; Nitta, 1991).

Assume that two goods (consumers' and capital goods) are produced from the input of labour service and the service of capital goods under constant returns to scale. Labour is assumed to be the sole primary actor of production and there is no inventory investment, nor is there money.

Let X_1 and X_2 be the level of output of the consumers' and new capital goods, respectively. The aggregate income of labourers and capitalists is

$$Y = w(a_1X_1 + a_2X_2) + q(b_1X_1 + b_2X_2) \qquad (6.6)$$

where w denotes the rate of wage, q denotes the price of the service of capital goods, a_1 and a_2 are the labour input coefficients in the production of the consumers' and capital goods and b_1 and b_2 are capital input coefficients in the production of consumers' and capital goods, respectively. Input coefficients are functions of w and q.

At the equilibrium, there is no profit for entrepreneurs, so that

$$p_1 = wa_1 + qb_1 \qquad (6.7)$$

$$p_2 = wa_2 + qb_2 \qquad (6.8)$$

where p_1 and p_2 are respectively the price of the consumers' and capital goods. Since markets for two goods have to be cleared,

$$D(p_1, p_2, w, q, Y) = X_1 \qquad (6.9)$$

$$H = X_2 \qquad (6.10)$$

where D denotes the demand for consumers' goods and H stands for the demand for new capital goods. Factor markets have also to be cleared so that

$$a_1X_1 + a_2X_2 = L \qquad (6.11)$$

$$b_1X_1 + b_2X_2 = K \qquad (6.12)$$

where L and K are respectively the given existing labour force and the given existing stock of capital goods. Since there is no money, suppose capitalists own capital goods and lend them to entrepreneurs or sell the service of capital goods to them. If gross saving is defined as the excess of income over consumption, then, capitalists save in kind or purchase new capital goods with saving so that

$$p_2H = S(p_1, p_2, w, q, Y) \qquad (6.13)$$

where S denotes the aggregate gross saving.

If equations (6.6) to (6.13) are interpreted as the description of a temporary equilibrium, there are eight equations to determine seven unknowns, Y, w, q, X_1, X_2, p_2, H, since we can choose the consumers' goods as *numéraire* so that $p_1 = 1$. The eight equations are not independent, however, and one of the equations can be derived from the other equations and Walras's law

$$Y = p_1 D + S. \tag{6.14}$$

In the determination of consumption and saving capitalists assume that goods and service of factors have the same prices in the future as they have at the present moment, and the difference between the resultant gross saving and the value of the depreciation of capital goods, that is, the net saving, can be either positive or negative. If it is positive, we have the case of a progressive economy which Walras wished to consider. The capital stock K is larger in the next period than in the current period, so that temporary equilibrium prices in the former are in general different from those in the latter, even though capitalists in the current period expected unchanged prices through periods.

The assumption of a saving in kind is unnecessary if we follow Walras to introduce a commodity E, consisting of a perpetual net income of a unit of *numéraire*, the price of which is the inverse of the rate of the perpetual net income or the rate of interest i. If this commodity is sold by entrepreneurs or firms wishing to buy new capital goods, and is purchased by capitalists wishing to save, the clearance of the market of this commodity through changes in i implies that aggregate gross saving = aggregate excess of income over consumption = aggregate demand for (E) × price of (E) = Aggregate demand for new capital goods × price of capital goods. Therefore,

$$p_2 H = S(p_1, w, i, Y) \tag{6.13'}$$

instead of (6.13) since capitalists are now concerned, not with p_2 and q but with i in the determination of consumption and saving. Similarly, (6.9) may be replaced by

$$D(p_1, w, i, Y) = X_1. \tag{6.9'}$$

At equilibrium, the rate of net income for capital goods has to be equalized to the rate of net income for the commodity E,

$$(q/p_2) - d = i \tag{6.15}$$

where d denotes the technically given rate of depreciation of capital goods. Since the introduction of a new unknown i is matched by the introduction of an additional equation (6.15), we still have equality between the number of unknowns and of equations (see Morishima, 1960).

Entrepreneurs and capitalists fail to predict future prices correctly in a progressive economy, since changes in prices are induced by changes in K in a series of successive temporary equilibria. The expectation of unchanged prices can be correct only in the case of a stationary state in which K remains unchanged through periods. The condition for a stationary state is that the aggregate gross saving is equal to the value of depreciation of capital goods,

$$H = dK \qquad (6.16)$$

in view of (6.13) or (6.13'). Since the number of equations is increased by the addition of (6.16), then the system is overdetermined, unless one more unknown is introduced. As far as we know, Yasui (1936) was the first to point out this overdeterminancy of the Walrasian system of capitalization and credit (Negishi, 1996). Yasui concluded that the existing stock of capital goods K should be no longer an arbitrarily given quantity, and has to be solved jointly with other unknowns from equations of general equilibrium. Then, we have nine unknowns, K, i, Y, w, q, X_1, X_2, p_2 and H, to be solved from any nine equations (6.6) to (6.8), (6.9), (6.10) to (6.12), (6.13), (6.15) and (6.16), since $p_1 = 1$ and one of the equations is not independent in view of (6.14).

Shibata also reached a similar conclusion concerning the over-determinancy of the Walrasian system of capitalization and credit. He accepted, however, neither the solution to make K unknown (Shibata, 1973, p. 214), nor the consideration of a stationary economy. Instead of (6.16), therefore, we have to introduce an investment function or a demand function for newly produced capital goods I such that

$$H = I\,(i, Y, w, q, X_1, X_2, p_2). \qquad (6.16')$$

If K is considered to be exogenously given, then, the system is still overdetermined. Shibata correctly realized, however, that (6.15) is actually a Walrasian investment function which presupposes that current prices are expected, correctly or incorrectly, to remain unchanged through future periods (Shibata, 1973, p. 209). With a more general investment function (6.16') introduced, then, (6.15) should be deleted from the system, so that it can now be demonstrated not to be overdetermined.

In view of Morishima (1977, pp. 100–122), it is a remarkable fact that Shibata (1973) considered (6.15) an implicit investment function which should be replaced by the investment function I in (16.6'). Introducing an investment function similarly in his Walrasian system, Morishima also found the system overdetermined, since both (6.15) and (6.16') are kept in the system. His solution is not to delete (6.15), but to replace the equality in (6.11) with the inequality, so that it is possible to have unemployment of labour (see Filippi, 1980, Negishi, 1980).

Shibata considered the problem of overdeterminancy also in the Keynesian system.[17] According to Nitta (1991), Shibata's Keynesian system may be summarized as follows.

The aggregate production function is

$$X = F(N, K) \tag{6.17}$$

where X, N, and K denote respectively aggregate output, employment and the given capital stock. Let us denote by F_n the marginal productivity of labour, that is, $F_n = \partial F / \partial N$. Then, the so-called first postulate of the classical economics is

$$F_n = w/p \tag{6.18}$$

where w and p signify respectively the given rate of money wage and the general price level. Demand and supply of money are equalized by

$$L(px, r) = M, \tag{6.19}$$

where L, r and M denote respectively the demand for money, the rate of interest and the given supply of money. Investment I and saving should be equal,

$$I(r) = s\, pX \tag{6.20}$$

where s is the given propensity to save.

Now four unknowns x, N, p, and r can be determined by four equations (6.17) to (6.20). Shibata first wished to include

$$F_k = r \tag{6.21}$$

where $F_k = \partial F / \partial K$, which he gave up to avoid the overdeterminancy. For Shibata, this is to realize that the Keynesian system is, after all, a short-run system.

On this conclusion, at least partly, Shibata's criticism of Keynesian economics is founded. The inability of Keynes, Shibata considers, to deal adequately with the phenomena of recent aggravation of stagflation can be traced to the absence of the concept of original goods, such as irreplaceable resources like oil and non-quantifiable resources like clean water and air (Shibata, 1977, p. 32; Nitta, 1991; Tsuru, 1984, 1985, pp. 245–7).

NOTES

*   This chapter has benefited from useful information and helpful suggestions provided by Aiko Ikeo, Hideomi Tanaka, Kiichiro Yagi, and Katsuya Yamamoto.

1.   For the details of Takata's life and academic activities, see Usui et al., 1976; Bronfenbrenner (1976); Hayasaka (1976); and Morishima's Foreword in Takata (1995).
2.   See Smith (1776), p. 190, and Rae (1905), p. 247. For Vebren, see Bagwell and Bernheim (1996).
3.   Morishima (1947) assumed that consumer's utility is a function of not only the consumption but also prices and derived the general expression for the effect of price changes on demand, though the possibility of a rising demand curve was not emphasized. See also Takata, 1995, p. 182.
4.   Walras assumed that the quantity of capital goods is given, while Böhm-Bawerk and Wicksell assumed that the value of total capital is given. See Yasui (1936), Negishi (1996) and Negishi (1995).
5.   See Negishi (1995) for Wicksell's missing equation problem and Section 7 of this chapter and Negishi (1996) for the over-determinancy problem in Walrasian stationary state equilibrium.
6.   Takata admitted later, however, that he misunderstood Böhm-Bawerk's theory and agreed that it can determine the equilibrium rate of interest without the interference of social power. See Takata (1937), p. 3.
7.   If it is to be a positive model, see Shibata's criticism in Section 6. For Takata's reaction to it in 1946, see Takata (1995, p. 154), where the supply function of capital is introduced, and L is considered to be an endogenous variable different from the given labour population, so that there can be unemployment.
8.   A part of Takata (1941), that is, pp. 1–108, is translated into English and included in Takata (1995, pp. 73–134, 164–177).
9.   It is based on his paper read at the 1936 meeting of the Japanese Association of Economics.
10.   For a different interpretation, see an Editor's Note, Takata (1995, pp. 183–6).
11.   For the details of Shibata's life and academic activities, see Sugihara (1987) and Tsuru (1984, pp. 222–48).
12.   See Okishio (1974) for his evaluation of Shibata's contribution.
13.   See Groll and Orzech (1989) for a recent evaluation of the so-called Shibata–Okishio Theorem.
14.   For the modern interpretation of Ricardo's comparative cost theory, see Gandolfo (1986, 1, pp. 7–32).
15.   For the evaluation of Shibata's empirical researches on long-run cycles (pp. 892–953, see also Shibata 1932), see Shinohara (1991), which concludes that Shibata is the first Kuznetsian and Friedmanian in Japan.
16.   Shibata, 1967, pp. 189–96, 1969, 1973, pp. 208–14. we owe much to Nitta (1991) in this section.
17.   Shibata, 1956, 1967, pp. 182–6, 251–61, 1969.

REFERENCES

Arrow, K.J. and F.H. Hahn (1971), *General Competitive Analysis*, San Francisco: Holden-Day.

Bagwell, L.S. and B.D. Bernheim (1996), 'Veblen Effects in a Theory of Conspicuous Consumption', *American Economic Review*, **86**, 349–73.

Blaug, M. and P. Sturges (eds) (1983), *Who's Who in Economics*, Brighton: Wheatsheaf Books.

Böhm-Bawerk, E. von (1914), 'Macht order ökonomisches Gesetz?' *Zeitschrift für Volkswirtschaft, Sozialpolitik und Verwaltung*, **23**, 205–71.
Bronfenbrenner, M. (1956), 'The State of Japanese Economics', *American Economic Review*, **XLVI**(2), 389–98.
Bronfenbrenner, M. (1976), 'Professor Takata Yasuma, A Foreigner's Recollections', in Usui et al., 1976, 471–84.
Cunynghame, H.H. (1892), 'Some Improvements in Simple Geometrical Methods of Treating Exchange Value, Monopoly, and Rent', *Economic Journal*, **2**, 35–52.
Edgeworth, F.Y. (1905), 'Review of *A Geometrical Political Economy* by Henry Cunyngham', *Economic Journal*, **15**, 62–71.
Ellis, H.S. and W. Fellner (1943), 'External Economics and Diseconomies', *American Economic Review*, **33**, 493–511.
Filippi, F. (1980), 'Morishima's Interpretation of Keynes: Some Comments and Criticism', *Zeitschrift für Nationalökonomie*, **40**, 355–67.
Gandolfo, G. (1986), *International Economics*, Berlin: Springer-Verlag.
Groll, S. and Z.B. Orzech (1989), 'From Marx to the Okishio Theorem', *History of Political Economy*, **21**, 253–72.
Hayasaka, Tadashi (1976), 'Nihon Keizaigakushi niokeru Takata Yasuma Hakushi' (Dr. Yasuma Takata in the History of Economics in Japan), in Usui, et al., 1976, 112–55.
Ikeo, Aiko (1996), 'The Advent of Marginalism in Japan', *Research in the History of Economic Thought and Methodology*, **14**, 219–47.
Keynes, J.M. (1936), *The General Theory of Employment Interest and Money*, London: Macmillan.
Kimura, Takeyasu (1934), 'Rogin niokeru Shakaitekinarumono' (Social Factors in the Determination of Wages), *Keizaigakuronshu* (Tokyo Imperial University), **4**, 93–146.
Lange, O. (1934–35), 'Marxian Economics and Modern Economic Theory', *Review of Economic Studies*, **2**, 189–201.
Leibenstein, H. (1950), 'Bandwagon, Snob and Veblen Effects in the Theory of Consumers' Demand', *Quarterly Journal of Economics*, **62**, 183–207.
Mill, J.S. (1909), *Principles of Political Economy*, London: Longmans and Green.
Morishima, Michio (1947), 'Shohishakatsudo to Kigyoshakatsudo' (Consumers' Behaviour and Firms' Behaviour), 1, *Keizaironso* (Kyoto University), 61, 83–115.
Morishima, Michio (1960), 'Existence of Solution to the Walrasian System of Capital Formation and Credit', *Zeitschrift für Nationalekönomie*, **20**, 238–43.
Morishima, Michio (1977), *Walras's Economics*, Cambridge, Cambridge University Press.
Negishi, Takashi (1980), 'Review of Morishima (1977),' *Economic Review*, **31**, 89–91 (in Japanese).
Negishi, Takashi (1989), *History of Economic Theory*, Amsterdam: North-Holland.
Negishi, Takashi (1990), 'Ricardo and Morishima on Machinery', *Journal of the History of Economic Thought*, **12**, 144–61.
Negishi, Takashi (1993), 'Marshallian Demonstration of the Tax-Subsidy Scheme under Variable Returns to Scale', Kyoto Institute of Economic Research.
Negishi, Takashi (1995), 'Böhm-Bawerk and Shibata on Power or Market', *Journal of Economics* (Zeitschrift für Nationalekönomie), **61**, 281–99.
Negishi, Takashi (1996), 'Takuma Yasui and General Equilibrium Theory in Japan', *Japanese Economic Review*, **46**, 227–34.

Negishi, Takashi (1998), 'Machinery', in H.D. Kurz and N. Salvadori (eds), *The Elgar Companion to Classical Economics*, Aldershot: Edward Elgar.

Nitta, Masanoni (1991), 'Toshikansu to Kajoketteiron' (Investment Function and Theory of Over-Determination), in Sugihara et al., 1991, 263–306.

Okishio, Nobuo (1961), 'Technical Changes and the Rate of Profit', *Kobe University Economic Review*, **7**, 85–99.

Okishio, Nobuo (1974), 'Seisankakaku-Heikinrijunritsu' (Price of Production – Average Rate of Profit), in Tsuru and Sugihara (eds), 23–46.

Pareto, V. (1927), *Manuel d'économie politique*, Paris: Marcel Giard.

Rae, J. (1905), *Sociological Theory of Capital* (C.W. Mixter's reprint of *The New Principles of Political Economy*, 1834), New York: Macmillan.

Shibata, Kei (1930), 'Kasserushi no Kakakukeisei no Kikou no Ginmi' (An Examination of the Mechanism of Price Formation as Explained by Mr. Cassel), *Keizaironso* (Kyoto Imperial University), **30**, 916–36.

Shibata, Kei (1932), 'An Examination of Professor Cassel's Quantity Theory of Money', *Kyoto University Economic Review*, **7**, 52–84.

Shibata, Kei (1933a), 'Marx's Analysis of Capitalism and the General Equilibrium Theory of the Lausanne School', *Kyoto University Economic Review*, **8**, 107–36.

Shibata, Kei (1933b), 'Shihonchikuseki to Shihon no Yukitekikosei no Henka' (Accumulation accompanied by the change of the organic structure of capital), *Keizaironso* (Kyoto Imperial University), **37**, 520–40.

Shibata, Kei (1934), 'On the Law of Decline in the Rate of Profit', *Kyoto University Economic Review*, **9**, 61–75.

Shibata, Kei (1935), 'On Böhm-Bawerk's Theory of Interest Rate', *Kyoto University Economic Review*, **10**, 107–27.

Shibata, Kei (1935–36), *Riron Keizaigaku* (Theoretical Economics), Tokyo, Kobundo.

Shibata, Kei (1939), 'On the General Profit Rate', *Kyoto University Economic Review*, **14**, 40–66.

Shibata, Kei (1956), 'Fatal Error Newly Uncovered in Keynesian Theory', *Kyoto University Economic Review*, **26**(1), 13–42.

Shibata, Kei (1967), *Kaitei Keizaigakugenri* (Revised Principles of Economics), Kyoto: Minerva Shobo.

Shibata, Kei (1969), 'A Theory of General Disequilibrium (1)', *Aoyama Keizaironshu* (Aoyama Journal of Economics), **21** 1–26.

Shibata, Kei (1973), *Chikyuhakai to Keizaigaku* (Destroying of the Globe and Economics), Kyoto: Minerva Shobo.

Shibata, Kei (1977), *Beyond Keynesian Economics*, Kyoto: Minerva Shobo.

Shinohara, Miyohei (1991), 'Shibata Keizaigaku to Chokihado' (Shibata Economics and Longrun Cycles), in Sugihara et al., 1991, 23–61.

Smith, A. (1776), *An Inquiry into the Nature and Causes of the Wealth of Nations*, London: Oxford University Press.

Stackelberg, H. v. (1933), 'Zwei Kritische Bemerkungen zur Preistheorie Gustav Cassels', *Zeitschrift für Nationalökonomie*, **4**, 457–63.

Sugihara, Shiro (1987), 'Shibata, Kei', in J. Eatewell, M. Milgate and P. Newman (eds), *New Palgrave*, **4**, London: Macmillan.

Sugihara, S. et al. (eds) (1991), *Shibata Keizaigaku to Gendai* (Shibata Economics and Today), Tokyo: Nihon Keizai Hyoron-sha.

Takata, Yasuma (1929–32), *Keizaigaku Shinko* (New Lectures on Economics), Tokyo: Iwanami Shoten.

Takata, Yasuma (1931), *Rodo Kachisetsu no Ginmi* (An Examination of the Labour Theory of Value), Tokyo: Nihonhyoron-sha.

Takata, Yasuma (1934), 'Seiryoku nakushite Rishi nasitoiu Riron' (A Theory that there is no Interest on Capital without Social Power), *Keizaigakukenkyu* (Kyushu Imperial University), **4**, 1–66.

Takata, Yasuma (1935), *Rishiron Kenkyu* (Studies in the Theory of Interest), Tokyo: Iwanami Shoten.

Takata, Yasuma (1937), *Rishiron* (Theory of Interest), Tokyo: Iwanami Shoten.

Takata, Yasuma (1941), *Seiryokusetsu Ronshu* (Essays in the Power Theory of Economics), Tokyo: Nihonhyoron-sha.

Takata, Yasuma (1995), *Power Theory of Economics*, London: Macmillan.

Tsuru, Shigeto (1984), 'A Survey of Economic Research in Japan, 1960–83', *Economic Review*, **35**(4), October, 289–306.

Tsuru, Shigeto (1985), *Gendai Keizaigaku no Gunzo* (A Group of Modern Economics), Tokyo: Iwanami Shoten.

Tsuru, S. and S. Sugihara (eds) (1974), *Keizaigaku no Gendaitekikadai* (Modern Problems of Economics), Kyoto: Minerva Shobo.

Tugan-Baranovsky, M.I. (1913), *Soziale Theorie der Vorteilung*, Berlin: Springer.

Usui, J. et al. (eds) (1976), *Takata Yasuma Hakushi no Shogai to Gakusetsu* (Life and Works of Dr. Yasuma Takata), Tokyo: Sobun-sha.

Yasui, Takuma (1936), 'Jikanyoso to Shihonrishi' (The Element of Time and the Interest on Capital), *Keizaigakuronshu* (Tokyo Imperial University), **6**, 1332–82.

7. Modernization and the studies of Adam Smith in Japan during and after World War II: Kazuo Okouchi, Zenya Takashima and Yoshihiko Uchida

Satoshi Niimura

ADAM SMITH IN JAPAN

Adam Smith is one of the most popular European thinkers in Japan. From the early Meiji era until now Smith has been read and studied by many Japanese scholars and ordinary people alike.[1] Why has Smith been so attractive to Japanese readers? The Japanese enthusiasm for Smith has changed over time, but his most important influence was related to the modernization of Japan. By reading Smith many Japanese easily understood what a modern man or society was and what prevented modernization in Japan.

Many high-level and influential studies of Smith appeared in Japan during and after World War II. In this paper we will consider three Smithian scholars of that period: Zenya Takashima (1904–90), Kazuo Okouchi (1905–84), and Yoshihiko Uchida (1913–89).

These scholars had some common characteristics. First, they studied Smith not only from an academic standpoint but also for a critical understanding of the reality of Japan in those days. We will show later how they understood and criticized Japan through their studies of Smith. Second, all of them were influenced by the so-called *Koza-ha* Marxism. Smith and Marx were the most popular thinkers in Japan, and both were often regarded as complementary rather than contradictory. We will consider later how deeply those Smithian scholars were influenced by *Koza-ha*'s recognition of Japanese capitalism. Third, they made much of 'civil society'. The phrase had a special meaning in Japan which was very different from that in Europe. In Japan 'civil society' often meant an ideal modern society or a normal capitalism. Fourth, they paid much attention to 'productive forces'. All of them interpreted Smith's political economy as a theory of productive forces. We will consider later in this study why they paid so much attention to the concept. Fifth, Okouchi and

Uchida made much of the 'domestic market'. They thought that it was much more important than the foreign market for the development of Japanese capitalism.

In the following we will consider these three persons, paying attention to the above points.

ADAM SMITH AND CIVIL SOCIETY: ZENYA TAKASHIMA

After July 1937, the war between Japan and China intensified and Japan shifted rapidly to a wartime regime (Nakamura, 1995, pp. 3–10). Three Control Laws were put in place in September 1937 and the Planning Agency, which became the centre of controlling and planning national economy, was established in October. The National General Mobilization Act was passed in April 1938. Direct economic control began with imports, exports and finance, then was extended to production and finally to personal consumption. Criticism of the direct control of the wartime economy was the main concern of Japanese intellectuals at this time .

Zenya Takashima entered the Tokyo University of Commerce in 1921. He read Menger, Wieser, Böhm-Bawerk, and Schumpeter in the seminars of Tokuzo Fukuda. The next year Takashima moved to the seminars of Kinnosuke Otsuka, and under his influence gradually became interested in Marx. Takashima studied Smith, Weber, and Sombalt, too. Forty years later, he confessed the state of his mind in those days as follows:

> I got interested in Smith gradually. As the situation of those days was so oppressive, studying Smith meant a kind of criticism or resistance against the times. Influence of *Koza-ha* Marxism was so strong in those days that I naturally came to think that studying Smith was a way of criticizing the relic of feudal system in Japan. ...
>
> Professor Otsuka said in his lecture or at another time. 'There is no civil society in Japan.' His words were immediately connected with Smith in my mind. ...
>
> As Japan became totalitarianistic, the number of scholars who praised List were increasing. ... Then I made up my mind to confront the current situation by criticizing List. ... It was a kind of passive confrontation. As I was not allowed to refer to Marx, I decided to compare Smith with List as a way to confront List. (Takashima, 1985, pp. 214–15)

After writing some monographs on List, Takashima published an inspiring and farsighted book, *Keizaishakaigaku no Konponmondai: Keizaishakaigakusha toshiteno Smith to List* (The Fundamental Problems of Economic Sociology: Smith and List as Economic Sociologists) in March 1940. This book consisted of four parts: (1) problems of economic sociology, (2) Adam Smith and problems of civil society, (3) Friedrich List and problems of national productive forces, (4) a conclusion. Some articles on List were added at the end of the book.

In the preface of the book Takashima said that his purpose was to establish economic sociology as 'the third science' by criticizing both pure (Walrasian) economics and national political economy (1941, p. 2). He thought that pure economics was rational, analytical, and objective, but it lost comprehensiveness, practicality, and historicity in theory. Takashima highly evaluated the theoretical significance of Schumpeter and Keynes, but he criticized their lack of historicity (1941, pp. 93–4). On the other hand, the political economy of Gottle was intuitive, comprehensive, and independent, but neither fully theoretical nor analytical. Accordingly Takashima intended to synthesize the theoretical method of pure economics with the historical method of political economy in his economic sociology.

Then Takashima explained what economic sociology was and who were the pioneers of economic sociology. He maintained that economic sociology was different from either the sociology of economy formed by Durkheim's school in France or Marxian political economy. Both economic sociology and Marxian political economy criticized pure economics by turning economics into sociology. However Marxian political economy intended to abolish the given conditions of pure economics, whereas on the contrary, economic sociology would just theorize and understand it (1941, pp. 30–31). The economic sociology Takashima was going to establish was similar to the sociological economics of Sombart or Gottle, but Takashima thought they also should be revised.

According to Takashima, Britain was 'the home of economic sociology' (1941, p. 46). From Hobbes to Adam Smith, economic sociology had been developed progressively as a science of civil society, and it was established in Britain where modern civil society was developed most typically. On the other hand, development of civil society in Germany gave birth to the theories of Hegel, List and the Historical School as 'the theory of German civil society'. And Takashima pointed out that Sombart, Weber, and Gottle were revealing the best and latest stage of economic sociology in Germany.

In order to establish economic sociology Takashima considered the theory of civil society of Adam Smith who was a pioneer of economic sociology. Takashima tried to understand Smith's theory more clearly by considering a criticism of List on Smith.

In the second part of the book, he examined Smith's three major works: *The Theory of Moral Sentiments, Lectures on Jurisprudence,* and *An Inquiry into the Wealth of Nations*, and he considered Smith's system of moral philosophy as a theory of civil society.

Takashima thought there were two 'fundamental problems of economic sociology' or ' problems of civil society' (1941, p. 125). One of them was 'the relationship between a civil society and a state' and the second was 'the analysis of social relations in a civil society as a mechanism of productive forces'. Takashima regarded a civil society as follows:

> Though the phrase 'civil society' often been used since Hobbes in Britain, its meaning is not always definite. ... However it was clear that a civil society meant economic relations above all, and especially the relations in a modern society which was liberated culturally, politically and economically, from medieval re- straints and formed in the seventeenth or eighteenth century. (1941, p. 126)

It is not easy for Western scholars in the field of the history of political or economic thought to understand the meaning of 'civil society' in Japanese literature. A civil society means a political society in the history of British political thought. However it often means an economic society in Japanese literature. Both Hobbes and Locke regarded 'civil society' as a synonym of 'political society'. In their theory of social contract, it was thought that the people in a natural state had established a civil government by a social contract or consent. And a political society or a civil society meant a society in which civil government was established. But Takashima did not regard a civil society as a political society but an economic one which was separated from and opposed to a state. His concept of civil society seemed to be deeply influenced by that of Hegel who regarded a civil society as opposed to a state.

On the other hand Takashima considered a modern civil society as a historical society which was established against feudalism. He said, 'the shaping of a modern civil society was a result of economic, political and cultural liberation from medieval or feudal restraints'. Therefore it was clear that the idea of civil society contained not only economic but also political and cultural aspects (1941, p. 129).

Takashima's concept of civil society was both structural and historical in the sense that a civil society was conceived as an economic society distin- guished from a state or government on one hand, and it was conceived as a modern society which was opposed to feudalism on the other hand. He did not think that these two meanings of a civil society were contradictory. Because a modern society was established through the revolution against absolute monarchy and feudalism, therefore the criticism of absolute monar- chy accompanied that of feudalism. According to *Koza-ha* Marxism, prewar Japanese capitalism was based on a semi-feudalistic society and controlled by the absolute Emperor. Therefore the criticism of Japanese capitalism included that of feudalism and that of absolute political power. The concept of civil society was regarded as an ideal against both feudalism and absolute political power.

Takashima pointed out that civil society was historical in the sense that it was formed as a result of liberation from feudalism, and a civil society or a commercial society was the fourth stage of society following the ages of hunters, shepherds and farmers. And in his view a civil society was socio-logical in the sense that it contained politics and culture as well as economy, but it was especially economic because economy was an essential part of society.

Then Takashima considered how ethics, laws, and economy were mutually related in Smith's concept of civil society, and what was the logic of unifying these three spheres. He thought that there were three spheres: moral, legal and economic, in Smith's system of moral philosophy. Takashima paid spe-cial attention to the importance of *Lectures on Jurisprudence* which he thought was an intermediate study relating *The Theory of Moral Sentiments* to *An Inquiry into the Wealth of Nations*.

Thus considering the relationship of three major works of Smith, Takashima concluded that there were moral, jurisprudential and economic spheres in Smith's philosophy and they were linked mainly by the principle of justice.

ETHICS AND ECONOMY: KAZUO OKOUCHI

When Kazuo Okouchi began his study of social policy, many people doubted the effectiveness of the traditional theory of social policy which insisted that an ethical state should protect the weak members of society. The panic and chronic recession after World War I strengthened such doubts. Facing the panic and financial distress people thought that rebuilding the national economy should be given priority over social policy.

Okouchi insisted that the social policy should not be based on an ethical request but on economic motives. From the viewpoint of economic rational-ity underlying capitalism, he regarded social policy as 'a policy of maintain-ing labour forces' (Okouchi, 1933, p. 212). Regular reproduction of labour forces with a certain quality and quantity was essential to maintain a capital-istic national economy and to develop it constantly. For that purpose the social policy of a state must restrain each capitalist from wasting labour forces. However such social policy did not exist in Japan.

Okouchi changed his thinking gradually (see Tozuka, 1971, pp. 183ff). At first he thought, under the theoretical influence of *Koza-ha* Marxism, that a normal type of social policy could be realized only after the revolutionary change of Japanese capitalism from a peculiar type to a normal version. But as a wartime regime established itself, all labour movements and socialist movements were suppressed, and Japanese capitalism had no possibility of revolution by the people. Therefore Okouchi thought that normal or rational capitalism could be realized in Japan only through regulation or reform by the state instead of revolution by the people.

Okouchi had thought at first that the expansion of productive forces in the arms industry was incompatible with the welfare of the working class and the stability of the national economy. However, under the wartime regime it was becoming more and more difficult to criticize the expanding policy of productive forces in the arms industry. Consequently Okouchi insisted that a rational social policy of maintaining labour forces was necessary even for the arms industry to expand productive forces. He asserted that the policy of maintaining labour forces was necessary for the smooth development of a wartime economy no less than for that of an ordinary economy. By this Okouchi intended to criticize the harsh treatment of working people and the life of austerity under the wartime regime in Japan.

Okouchi started his study of Smith from the practical concerns stated above. He inquired into what type of capitalism was most suitable for expansion of productive forces, and what sort of morals and policy were most suitable for development of such a type of capitalism. In order to answer these questions, he studied Smith and then published his book *Smith to List*. His study of Smith was not just a reading of a classic text, but also an inquiry into the solution of the actual social problems in the contemporary Japanese economy. Okouchi said in the preface of his book that any historical study should not be done for its own sake, but to contribute to the solution of contemporary problems (Okouchi, 1943, pp. 7–8).

This book consisted of two parts. In the first part Okouchi considered the relationship between ethics and economy and especially the significance of self-love for economy in Smithian theory. In the second part he considered List's theory of productive forces. We will show below the characteristics of his interpretation of Smith and how it was related to contemporary problems in Japan.

The most essential problem for Okouchi was: what were economic ethics? In other words, what was the relationship between ethics and economy? According to Okouchi, the German Historical School looked outside economy for ethics which were thought to be contradictory to economy (1943, pp. 5–6). On the contrary, Smith discovered ethics on the inside of economy and he found that ethics were promoting economy. Okouchi thought that ethics on the inside of economy were based on self-love as a virtue.

After examining the controversy of the so-called Adam Smith problem, Okouchi criticized the Historical School in that they had regarded self-love as immoral. Smith thought that self-love could be virtuous, though it was not always so. When self-love was sympathized with by 'an impartial spectator', it was approved of as propriety and it would be a virtue of prudence. Okouchi regarded sympathy as a kind of procedure capable of justifying a selfish principle in a civil society. Self-love can be approved of as a virtue of justice when it is within the range of 'laws of justice' or 'general rules of justice' .

Okouchi thought that self-love was virtuous because the welfare of society was achieved better by an 'invisible hand' of God when each person was self-interested enough under general rules or before an impartial spectator.

Okouchi agreed that Smith's 'homo aeconomicus' (economic man) as a bearer of the civil virtue of prudence was neither an abstract nor a non-historic being but the people of 'the middling and inferior stations of life', namely modern entrepreneurs and labourers who featured in modern British civil society (1943, p. 16). Therefore it was not in every age, but only in modern civil society that self-love corresponded to social welfare created by an invisible hand. And this self-love was not that of monopolistic merchants and manufacturers supported by mercantilism, but that of the modern independent entrepreneurs and workers in those days. In other words Smith did not approve of self-love in general. He criticized restriction and monopoly by justifying the self-love related to free competition and by criticizing the self-love related to monopoly .

Okouchi paid special attention to the Smithian theory of high wages (1943, pp. 222ff.). Smith criticized the mercantile policy of low wages and supported high wages. Mercantilists sought for the source of the wealth of nations in a foreign market, and they regarded wages as a cost of production in exporting industries, and insisted on the reduction of wages to increase the competitiveness of goods in a foreign market. In contrast Smith sought for the source of wealth of nations in a domestic market, and he regarded wages as a part of demand for consumption. In addition to it Smith criticized the mercantilists' theory of wages which insisted that high wages will result in laziness. Smith insisted that high wages maintained labour forces and improved the efficiency of labour.

Okouchi criticized the mercantile policy of low wages for the purpose of reducing a domestic market and creating pressure to export goods to a foreign market. This view followed *Koza-ha*'s criticism of Japanese capitalism. Okouchi thought that high wages kept labour forces in a good condition and raised the efficiency of production. This view was derived from his theory of social policy, and it criticized the policy of restraining consumption under the wartime regime on the grounds that it was incompatible with expanding productive forces.

POSTWAR JAPANESE CAPITALISM AND ADAM SMITH: YOSHIHIKO UCHIDA

Yoshihiko Uchida was the most influential Smithian scholar in postwar Japan. He entered the Faculty of Economics at the University of Tokyo in 1934, and studied Marx and Keynes. He wrote a graduation thesis on Keynes's *The*

General Theory of Employment, Interest and Money in 1937. Perhaps Uchida was one of the first students in the world to write a thesis on *The General Theory*. His recognition of the importance of the market for capitalism might partly have come from his early study of Keynes. Then Uchida studied industrial policy in graduate school. After leaving the university in 1940, he engaged in the investigation of natural resources in Southeast Asia as a member of the East Asia Research Institute. He was in a prison for four months in 1944 for violating the notorious Peace Preservation Law. He worked at Senshu University after 1946.

His concern covered large fields such as the history of economic and social thought in Britain and in Japan, Marxist thought, and the methodology of social sciences and arts. His most famous books were *Keizaigaku no Seitan* (The Birth of Political Economy) on Smith and *Shihonron no Sekai* (The World of *Das Kapital*) on Marx. We will trace Uchida's footsteps towards his study of Smith.

In his early published paper, 'Kokunaishijo-ron' (The Theory of Domestic Market) in 1947, Uchida asked how the postwar Japanese economy should be rebuilt and he answered by applying Smithian theory. According to Uchida, the Japanese government insisted on 'the economic development by foreign trade instead of by agriculture' (Uchida, 1947, p. 86). This insistence was based on the grounds that economic development in Japan must be achieved by the manufacturing industry instead of agriculture, and foreign trade was necessary to develop the manufacturing industry which exported goods to a foreign market. Against such a theory, Uchida insisted that Japan, of course, should take a strategy of economic development through manufacturing industry, but that the manufacturing industry should be established first for a domestic rather than for a foreign market. For that purpose there must be rich farmers to demand industrial products in a domestic market. Accordingly radical reform of farmland was necessary .

Uchida based such a plan for rebuilding the Japanese economy on Smithian theory. While depending on Okouchi's interpretation of Smith, Uchida related the distinction between a domestic and a foreign market to that of two kinds of self-love in Smithian theory. First the commercial society where productive forces were developing was realized as a domestic market when the self-love of the people in the middle and lower classes of society was fully liberated with regard to virtues of justice and prudence. On the other hand the self-love of merchants and privileged manufacturers engaging in foreign trade was likely to disregard justice instead of observing it. This second type of self-love did not contribute to the formation of normal commercial society and the rapid growth of productive forces.

As stated above, Uchida insisted that in order to rebuild the Japanese economy the manufacturing industry for a domestic market had to be developed, and for that purpose the purchasing power of farmers should be expanded by radical farmland reform. Following the views of Okouchi and Takashima, Uchida thought that capitalism controlled by the rules of justice could develop productive forces most rapidly, and that therefore it was the best type of capitalism.

Uchida made much of the productive forces. He was deeply influenced by the theories of Kazuo Okouchi and Yasoji Kazahaya in this area. In 1948 Uchida wrote a paper on the theory of productive forces which had been argued by Okouchi and Kazahaya during wartime. Uchida concluded that their theory of productive forces reflected the growing contradictions of economic structure in wartime Japan after the Manchuria Incident.

In 1949 Uchida published a paper on British mercantilism and Adam Smith, in which he displayed his detailed interpretation of Smith for the first time. Uchida analysed British mercantilism against a historical background of Smithian political economy in this paper. He clearly distinguished between absolutism and mercantilism. A lot of people had thought that Smith criticized feudalism and absolute monarchy. However, what Smith had criticized directly was neither feudalism nor absolute monarchy, but parliamentary mercantilism supported by modern landowners and merchants after the Glorious Revolution which overthrew feudalism and absolute monarchy in Britain. The parliamentary mercantilism after the Revolution originally went along with the interest of industrial capitals, while absolute monarchy was opposed to it. The central issue for Uchida was why parliamentary mercantilism was criticized by industrial capitals and accordingly by Smith. In this mercantilism, the interest of monopolistic trading capitals coincided at first with that of industrial capitals, because the industrial capitals needed colonies for overseas markets, and profit from the transit trade was returned to Britain and invested as productive capitals. But as time went on, industrial capitals reinforced their productive forces on one side, and the transit trade was getting more and more independent on the other side, until the interest of industrial capitals became opposed to that of trading capitals. Above all the increase of tax to maintain colonies became a big burden for industrial capitals. As a result of this, mercantilism was criticized by Smith who supported the interest of industrial capitals.

The distinction between absolutism and mercantilism was not only a subject in his interpretation of Smith, but also an important issue in postwar Japan to which Uchida intended to apply Smithian theory. *Koza-ha* Marxists thought that though Japan displayed highly advanced capitalism in the economic sense it was governed by a semi-feudal absolute monarchy in the political sense. Therefore they thought that a bourgeois democratic revolution to overthrow the absolute monarchy was necessary for Japan. However feudalism and absolutism in Japan were dismantled by defeat and the postwar democratization of Japan. Japanese Marxists were arguing about what was the true nature of postwar Japanese capitalism and its political power, and what type of revolution should be pursued.

As stated above, Uchida showed that the direct object of Smith's criticism was neither feudalism nor absolute monarchy but the parliamentary mercantilism that appeared after the Glorious Revolution and adopted the policy of protecting exporting industries and trading capitals. This interpretation of Smith seemed to suggest what should be aimed at in postwar Japan.

Uchida thought that though absolute political power had collapsed in postwar Japan, so long as a semi-feudal landowning system was not completely swept away, farmers and labourers were still very poor, therefore the domestic market was so small that manufacturing industry could develop only towards a foreign market. This economic structure had not changed since wartime. Therefore Uchida thought that democratic revolution was necessary to dismantle the feudal landowning system completely.

In the 1950s Uchida extended his interest to the moral philosophy of Smith which contained ethics and jurisprudence as well as political economy. And in 1953 he published his well-known book, *Keizaigaku no Seitan* (The Birth of Political Economy), which is said to be the most influential in the history of Smithian studies in Japan.

In this book Uchida intended to fill the gap between 'two streams' of studies of Smith in Japan. One of them was the study of the Smithian theory of value on the basis of Marxist theory, and the other was a study of Smith done by such scholars as Takashima and Okouchi as a part of a historical study of the growth of civil society in Britain. As stated above Takashima had intended to synthesize a historical method with a theoretical one in his study of economic sociology. Uchida followed this view of Takashima's, and he considered political economy as a science capable of analysing society historically and theoretically.

Uchida distinguished between the historical and theoretical effectiveness of political economy. In other words he made a distinction between how political economy was historically effective for the bourgeoisie to build a civil society, and how it was theoretically effective as a science of analysing the social system and history. In the first half of his book, he praised Smith highly as the founder of civil society who intended to overcome feudalism and mercantilism. And in the latter half, from a Marxian viewpoint, Uchida critically showed that Smithian political economy was an ideology which authorized capitalism.

Uchida was deeply conscious of the relationship between Smithian theory and contemporary Japan. He said in his book:

Perhaps some readers of this book may feel as if Smith is still alive in our time. Indeed I think contemporary Japan is full of the problems Smith made efforts to solve, and it is very important to point out that fact. ... However even though I pay attention to the positive aspects of Smith, it is not too much to say that I never think Smithian theory as it is can come true in contemporary Japan. On the contrary I dare say at first that I think we must fight against Smithian elements which will probably appear in Japan. (1953, p. 16)

Uchida regarded political economy, especially that of Smith and Marx, as 'a basic science for understanding social system and history', which was for Uchida an equivalent of Takashima's 'economic sociology'. According to Uchida, the political economy of Smith had two origins, that is, natural jurisprudence since Thomas Hobbes on one hand, and mercantilists' pamphlets on the other. Smith criticized and then synthesized both of these elements to establish his new science of political economy.

In the first half of his book Uchida considered what was the historical problem for Smith, and how Smith solved it through criticizing an old science and establishing a new one. He insisted that the historical subject for Smith was the criticism of 'two monopolies', both feudal and mercantile. Formerly, like other Smithian scholars such as Takashima, Uchida thought that Smith fought against feudalism. Then he gradually came to think that Smith criticized mercantilism directly instead of feudalism. Moreover Uchida asserted here that Smith criticized both feudalism and mercantilism in two senses.

First, Smith criticized both British mercantilism and French feudalism. They perpetrated 'old imperialistic wars' to obtain overseas colonies and consequently they made European civilized societies face a serious crisis. Uchida contrasted the thought of Smith with that of Jean Jacques Rousseau (1712–78) and concluded that they displayed two different types of thought which criticized the old imperialism in the eighteenth century. Second, Smith criticized British feudalism as well as British mercantilism because the former caused the latter. Smith thought that feudalism and absolute monarchy checked the growth of free independent farmers and consequently made a domestic market very narrow. That was why British mercantilism eagerly sought foreign markets.

In response to Smith's criticism Uchida believed that British mercantilism had two purposes or roles. One of the two was to secure private property acquired by labour and to support free independent producers who owned the fruits of their labour, and the other was to secure necessary conditions such as domestic and foreign markets for the development of capitalism. Such mercantilism was based on natural jurisprudence, which justified and authorized the mercantilism and also had two roles. One was to justify the acquisition of private property by labour, and the other was to authorize the mercantile policy on the basis of 'public utility'.

Smith intended to distinguish clearly between two aspects of mercantilism and natural jurisprudence, then he supported one and rejected the other. He proved that it was necessary to protect private property, but that a mercantile policy for public utility was useless. For that purpose Smith established a new political economy on the basis of his thought of 'homo aeonomicus and an invisible hand'.

Smith considered, in *The Theory of Moral Sentiments,* on what grounds a state could force justice on the people, and criticized the Humean view which regarded public utility as the grounds of justice. Smith showed that if a state was prevented from violating the life and property of individuals, the welfare of society will be realized as an unintended result. According to Smith, when the security of life and property was protected, homo aeconomicus, who wanted a rise in social position rather than natural wealth, acquired rich production and consumption of natural wealth as an unintended end result. This was what the Smithian 'invisible hand' truly meant. Smith established a new political economy through thus criticizing old natural jurisprudence.

CONCLUSION

At the beginning of this paper we asked why Smith was so popular in Japan. Now it is easier to answer this question. Many Japanese people, especially left-wing intellectuals during and after World War II, criticized the so-called 'pre-modern' elements in Japanese society such as feudalism, the feudalistic landowning system, absolute monarchy, monopoly, mercantilistic policy, low wages, war economy and so on, and indeed they were what Smith criticized in the eighteenth century.

Moreover Japanese people wanted to establish what they called a 'civil society' in Japan, which implied various elements such as liberty, justice, human rights, democracy, high wages, highly productive labour forces, a wide domestic market and peaceful international relations. These were what Smith had also tried to establish in the eighteenth century.

It has also been shown why Smith and Marx were often thought to be complementary rather than contradictory in Japan. It is not so surprising that mainstream Japanese Marxists did not aim at establishing socialism in Japan immediately. Instead they aimed to achieve democratic revolution which would not realize socialism, but normal or democratic capitalism in Japan. They thought that only after democratic capitalism was established, socialist revolution should be aimed at. Therefore there was no serious contradiction between the study of Smith and that of Marx for Japanese Smithian scholars who were influenced by Marxism.

NOTE

1. For a more detailed history of studies of Adam Smith in Japan, see Sugiyama, Omori and Takemoto (1993), Sugihara (1998), and Ikeo and Wakatabe (1998).

REFERENCES AND FURTHER READING

Adamu Sumisu no Kai (1979), *Honpo Adam Smith Bunken* (The Bibliography of Adam Smith in Japan), Tokyo: Tokyo Daigaku Shuppan-kai.

Ikeo, Aiko and Masazumi Wakatabe (1997), 'Adam Smith in Japan, reconsidered from a non-Marxian perspective', in Cheng-chung Lai (ed.), *Adam Smith across Nations,* Oxford: Oxford University Press.

Nakamura, Takafusa (1995), *The Postwar Japanese Economy: Its Development and Structure, 1937–1994,* second edn, Tokyo: University of Tokyo Press.

Obayashi, Nobuharu (1971), 'Keizaitetsugaku, Hohoron' (Economic Philosophy and Methodology), in Yukio Cho and Kazuhiko Sumiya (eds), *Kindainihon Keizaishisoshi* (The Economic Thoughts in Modern Japan), vol. 2, Tokyo: Yuhikaku.

Okouchi, Kazuo (1933) 'Rodosha Hogo Rippo no Riron nitsuite' (Of the Theory of Laws Protecting Labourers), reprinted in Kazuo Okouchi (1969), *Okouchi Kazuo Chosakushu* (The Works of Kazuo Okouchi), vol. 5, Tokyo: Seirin Shoin Sinsha.

Okouchi, Kazuo (1943), *Smith to List,* reprinted in Okouchi, Kazuo (1969), *Okouchi Kazuo Chosakushu* (The Works of Kazuo Okouchi), vol. 3, Tokyo: Seirin Shoin Sinsha.

Smith, Adam (1759), *The Theory of Moral Sentiments,* reprinted in D.D. Raphael and A.L. Macifie (eds) (1976), *Glasgow Edition of the Works and Correspondence of Adam Smith,* vol. I, Oxford: Oxford University Press.

Smith, Adam (1776), *An Inquiry into the Nature and Causes of the Wealth of Nations,* reprinted in R.H. Campbell, A.S. Skinner and W.B. Todd (eds) (1976), *Glasgow Edition of the Works and Correspondence of Adam Smith,* vol. 2, Oxford: Oxford University Press.

Smith, Adam (1978), *Lectures on Jurisprudence,* in R.L. Meek, D.D. Raphael, and P.G. Stein (eds), *Glasgow Edition of the Works and Correspondence of Adam Smith,* vol. 5, Oxford: Oxford University Press.

Sugihara, Shiro (1998), 'Adam Smith in Japan', in Cheng-chung Lai (ed.), *Adam Smith across Nations,* Oxford: Oxford University Press. Translated from Shiro Sugihara, (1972), 'Nihon niokeru Adam Smith', in Kazuo Okouchi, (ed.), *Kokufuron Kenkyu* (The Studies of *Wealth of Nations*), III, Tokyo: Chikuma Shobo.

Sugiyama, Chuhei, Ikuo Omori and Hitoshi Takemoto (1993), 'Adam Smith in Japan', in Hiroshi Mizuta and Chuhei Sugiyama (eds), *Adam Smith: International Perspectives,* New York: St. Martin's Press.

Sugiyama, Mitsunobu (1983), '*Keizaigaku no Seitan* no Seiritsu' (Formation of *The Birth of Political Economy*) in his *Sengo keimo to Shakaikagaku no Shiso* (The Postwar Enlightenment and the Thoughts of Social Sciences), Tokyo: Shinyo-sha.

Sugiyama, Mitsunobu (1995), 'Shiminshakairon to Senjidoin' (The Theory of 'Civil Society' and Wartime Mobilization), in Yamanouchi, Yasushi, Victor Koshimann, and Ryuichi Narita (eds), *Soryokusen to Gendaika* (The Total War and Modernization), Tokyo: Kashiwa Shobo.

Takashima, Zenya (1941), *Keizaishakaigaku no Konponmondai: Keizaishakaigakusha toshiteno Smith to List* (The Fundamental Problems in Economic Sociology: Smith and List as Economic Sociologists), Tokyo: Nihon Hyoron-sha.

Takashima, Zenya (1985), *Ningen, Fudo to Shakaikagaku* (Man, Climate and Social Sciences), Yokohama: Akiyama Shobo.

Tozuka, Hideo (1971), 'Shakai Seisaku-ron no Hensen' (The Change of the Theory of Social Policy), in Yukio Cho and Kazuhiko Sumiya (eds), *Kindainihon Keizaishisoshi* (The Economic Thoughts in Modern Japan), vol. 2, Tokyo: Yuhikaku.

Uchida, Yoshihiko (1947), 'Kokunai Shijoron: Kogyo Saiken no Hoko' (The Theory of Domestic Market: the Way of Rebuilding Manufacturing Industry), *Choryu*, 2 (4), Tokyo: Choryu-sha, reprinted in Uchida, Yoshihiko (1989).

Uchida, Yoshihiko (1948), 'Senji Keizaigaku no Mujunteki Tenkai to Keizai Riron' (The Contradictory Development of Wartime Political Economy and the Theory of Political Economy), *Choryu,* 3 (1), Tokyo: Choryu-sha, reprinted in Uchida, Yoshihiko (1989).

Uchida, Yoshihiko (1949), 'Igirisu Jushoshugi no Kaitai to Koten Gakuha no Seiritsu' (The Dissolution of British Mercantilism and the Shaping of Political Economy), in Yoshitaro Hirano et al. (eds) (1949), *Choryu Koza: Keizaigaku Zenshu* (The Works of Political Economy), vol. l, Tokyo: Choryu-sha, reprinted in Uchida, Yoshihiko (1989).

Uchida, Yoshihiko (1953), *Keizaigaku no Seitan* (The Birth of Political Economy), Tokyo: Mirai-sha, reprinted in Uchida, Yoshihiko (1988), *Uchida Yoshihiko Chosaku-shu* (The Collected Works of Yoshihiko Uchida), Tokyo: Iwanami Shoten, vol. l.

Uchida, Yoshihiko (1966), *Shihonron no Sekai* (The World of *Das Kapital*), Tokyo: Iwanami Shoten, reprinted in Uchida, Yoshihiko (1988), *Uchida Yoshihiko Chosaku-shu* (The Collected Works of Yoshihiko Uchida), Tokyo: Iwanami Shoten, vol. 4.

Uchida, Yoshihiko (1989), *Uchida Yoshihiko Chosakushu* (The Collected Works of Yoshihiko Uchida), Tokyo: Iwanami Shoten, vol. 10.

8. Economic development and economic thought after World War II: non-Marxian economists on development, trade and industry

Aiko Ikeo

1. INTRODUCTION

This chapter discusses the arguments advanced by non-Marxian economists relating to economic development and economic growth in Japan from 1945 to around 1970. Japanese non-Marxian economists intensively discussed the relationship between trade and development and the characteristics of the Japanese economy using observations of economic and political institutions around the world. Their arguments depended heavily on an historical context which was evolving in a complex fashion over time. They were concerned about economic stability and economic growth. They usually lacked a coherent theory or thought in their ongoing arguments.

I will pick up the topics which Japanese economists discussed most seriously and are relatively better known to a non-Japanese audience. I will give detailed discussion and the background, and point out several misunderstandings by non-Japanese scholars. Such a misunderstanding may seem a strange caricature to Japanese readers and at worst puts them off. The arguments made by the Japanese economists depended crucially on their contemporary context, and we must bear this context in mind at all times.[1]

Section 2 gives a general outlook on Japanese economic thought after 1945 and the shift in the balance of power from Marxian to non-Marxian economists in academia. Sections 3–5 discuss the famous flying-geese-pattern theory of economic development, the misnamed debate between pro-trade and pro-development strategies, and the criteria for which industries are promoted for development. They will show why some non-Marxian economists supported the government policy of the promotion of heavy and chemical industries. Section 6 examines a series of government economic plans including the Income Doubling Plan (1960), and argues that the Economic Council's deliberations in making the plans served to mould compromises among conflicting interests until the end of the growth era, although their planning lacked a scientific basis. Section 7 gives a brief summary of Japanese economic thought in the post-growth era.

2. THE MAJORITY AND MINORITIES

It is well known that the majority of economists in Japan were Marxist or Marxian economists from 1945 until the late 1960s. They were worried about big business wielding too much power over the market and believed in the central government's superior planning ability in the allocation of scarce resources and the correction of a more equitable distribution of wealth and income compared with market mechanism. The remaining economists of the day were not neoclassical, market-oriented economists, but rather development economists who payed careful attention to the 'real world' in recommending economic policies. They believed in an important role of the central government and local municipal governments in economic development, although they trusted entrepreneurship in the private sector. They were well aware that Japan's industrialization and economic survival relied heavily on international trade, especially imports, because Japan has scarce natural resources and a dense population (like the Netherlands). Therefore Japan must export goods in order to secure the import of natural resources such as iron ore, precious metals, coal and crude oil.

The Japanese people, however, remembered that in the 1930s the Great Depression spread over the capitalist countries, with a fierce trade war. The trade war gave way to World War II and destroyed a significant portion of the civilization which humanity had built up for centuries. Quite a few Japanese thought that something was wrong with the capitalist system and some corrections were needed to alleviate what are now called market failures. They thought that the market mechanism would no longer work efficiently because big businesses or monopolistic firms could wield their power in fixing market prices and act monopsonistically in labour markets. They believed that the tremendous productivity of capitalism would not be met with sufficient demand in the world market let alone the domestic market, and therefore trade wars were inevitable and would lead to another bloody war. Moreover, they were worried about the gap between the rich and the poor in Japan which resulted from market competition. Free competition was often equated with the law of the jungle where 'the weak are victims of the strong'.

It is not very surprising that during the occupation period (1945–52) following the conclusion of World War II, Marxian economists, including communists, enjoyed a favourable reputation, because they were the only political group who had opposed the old regime (see Ikeo 1996c). Many of them were kept in prison during the wars against China and the Allies, and were subsequently released and rehabilitated in Japanese society and at national universities such as the University of Tokyo and Kyoto University. The professors openly resumed their study of Karl Marx's writings and other socialist literature, and enthusiastically lectured on the historical development of Japanese capitalism and its transition to the socialist regime. They confidently predicted that capitalism was just a necessary preparation for socialism and that the capitalist economies had been in general crisis since the Socialist Revolution had succeeded in Russia in 1917. It seems that the wars, the establishment of socialist economies by newly independent colonies, and the confrontation between the East and the West intensified Japanese Marxists' belief in socialism. Yet Japanese Marxian scholars were a very diverse group and had separated into several sects since the interwar period. They included both revolutionary and nonrevolutionary elements: economists, economic historians, philosophers, and leaders of the labour movements (see Ikeo 1996a).

The discussion and debate among the Japanese economists depended heavily on the environment brought about by the Allied occupation during 1945–52, the onset of the Cold War in 1947, and by the formation of an international economic society through the establishment of economic organizations such as the International Bank for Reconstruction and Development (World Bank), the International Monetary Fund (IMF), and later the General Agreement on Tariffs and Trade (GATT) and the Organization for Economic Cooperation and Development (OECD). On one hand, the Japanese government and civil servants had to represent the nation and rehabilitate it in the international community after the defeat in World War II; they had to represent the nation's interests in negotiations first with the Allied Occupation Force, and then with these international economic organizations and member countries. On the other hand, the government had to play the leading role in the economic recovery and reconstruction of the nation's ruined economy during the immediate postwar period in Japan. This was the case in the United States and Europe as well. Gerhard Colm's *The American Economy in 1960* (1952) was taken as a model in making Japan's long-term Plan for Economic Self-Support (1955). Jan Tinbergen's *The Design of Development* (1958) and *Central Planning* (1964) were important sources for Japan's basic policies for economic development. It is noteworthy that the United Nations also supported development policies by publishing the *Manual on Economic Development Projects* (1958) and *Planning for Economic Development* (1965).

Until around 1970, many non-Marxian economists agreed that the primary targets of government economic policies were economic development and economic stability including full employment. 'Economic growth' was a nice catchword for Japanese politicians to attract their electorates. 'Economic planning' was first needed for economic recovery, and then used mainly for a political purpose after the conclusion of the occupation policy. Government officials, who had worked for the wartime mobilization planning and the economic recovery planning, had no doubt about their strong position over private business and their superior ability to coordinate economic activities compared with the market mechanism. In fact, it is found in the documents of the day, published only recently, that Japanese economists challenged the officials' traditional prejudice and tried to persuade them of the importance of creativity and entrepreneurship in the market economy.[2]

3. THE FLYING-GEESE-PATTERN THEORY OF DEVELOPMENT

The relationship between Japan's economic development and international trade was probably the most often discussed topic in Japan in the 1930s and 1940s. Many Japanese economists studied the role of trade in development and the interdependence of trade and development. This is probably the reason why several Japanese economists have made important contributions to the theory of trade in the post-1945 period.[3]

Kaname Akamatsu (1896–1974) became well known to non-Japanese audiences thanks to his flying-geese-pattern theory (Ganko Keitai Ron). His papers entitled 'A theory of unbalanced growth in the world economy' (1961) and 'A historical pattern of economic growth in developing countries' (1962) were published in English. However, it is relatively unknown that already by the 1930s Akamatsu had started to create the theory based on his empirical studies of Japan's cotton yarn, cotton cloth, spinning, weaving machinery and general machinery industries over the period from around 1870 to 1940 in his 'Waga kuni yomo kogyohin no boeki susei' (The trend of foreign trade in manufactured woollen goods in Japan, 1935) and 'Waga kuni keizai hatten no sogo benshoho' (Synthetic dialectics of industrial development in Japan, 1937). Originally it was the flying-geese-pattern theory of industrial development, or the catching-up product cycle theory of development as phrased more accurately in English by Ippei Yamazawa in his *Economic Development and International Trade* (1990, p. 69). As several authors have misinterpreted the theory, it is useful to examine Akamatsu's academic career and research environment, and to see how he invented this 'historical' theory.

Kaname Akamatsu was born to a son of a rice merchant in Fukuoka in 1896 and studied at Kobe High School of Commerce from 1915–19. From 1919–21 at the Tokyo Higher Commercial School (now Hitotsubashi University), he made a critical study of Marxian economics under Tokuzo Fukuda (1874–1930), who was never a Marxist at all but was interested in various types of economic thought and theories. Fukuda served as a mentor to the leading economists of the next generation.[4] Akamatsu was appointed lecturer at Nagoya High School of Commerce (now Nagoya University) in 1921 and promoted to full professor in 1922. Although he was formally ordered by the Japanese government to study commerce and economics in Britain, Germany and the United States for two years in 1924, he studied Hegelian philosophy at the University of Heidelberg for most of the time and spent two months at the Business School of Harvard University. Although his stay at Harvard was short, he was deeply impressed by Harvard's empirical work such as the studies of the variation of management cost depending on the size of retailers, the optimal size of retailers in each industry, business barometers and the case method.

Returning to Japan in July 1926, Akamatsu proposed the establishment of the Industrial Research Room to the President of Nagoya Commercial College (formerly Nagoya High School of Commerce) and his proposal was immediately accepted. Ernest Francis Penrose (1895–1984) arrived in Nagoya from England and began to teach commerce and business English in 1925, and then started to work at the newly established Industrial Research Room.[5] He made the price and quantity indices of agricultural products and stimulated Akamatsu to embark on a 'cliometric' study of Japan's industrial goods industry. He friendlily asked why Akamatsu was using a calculator because Akamatsu was a Hegelian philosopher (as well). Akamatsu advocated 'synthetic dialectics', that is the theory of 'those which are generated from experiences and rule experiences'. He was taking a synthetic approach to economics by combining Hegelian dialectics and American empirical studies.[6]

Akamatsu drew three time-series curves denoting the import, the domestic production and the export of manufactured goods in a plane with time on the horizontal axis and the yen value on the vertical axis. He realized that the import curve usually increases until it reaches some peak and declines with the increase of domestic production at which time the exports increase. This means that many import curves had a mountain-shape with one peak. The industry of cotton yarn had a mountain shape on the export curve and showed a sign of decline in the domestic production curve towards World War II. The industry of cotton cloth showed a little decline in both the domestic production and the export curves in the late 1930s. Both curves continued to increase in the industries of spinning and weaving machinery as well as machines and tools. This pattern might sound like what is suggested in a Hecksher–Ohlin trade model with many goods. As capital accumulates, there is shifting comparative advantage over time.[7]

Akamatsu believed that his findings for Japan could be generalized into a theory for many countries and called his findings the wild-geese-flying pattern of industrial development in developing countries, or more exactly, late-developers. Akamatsu explained that the name referred to the three time-series curves and said, 'Wild geese fly in orderly ranks forming an inverse V, just as airplanes fly in formation. The flying pattern of wild geese is meta-phorically applied to the... three time-series curves' (1962: p. 9). Akamatsu said, '[I]n various parts of Asia clothing had been produced by the handicraft industry, which was destroyed as a result of the import of cotton cloth from abroad, particularly from England' (1962: p. 3). Moreover Akamatsu applied this theory to the growth of Japan's transistor radio industry after 1945, in which 'the wild-geese-flying development completed its course from import to domestic production and, further, to export in the short period of several years' (1962: p. 23). Akamatsu believed that this 'historical theory' should depict the development of the less-advanced countries (like several Asian countries) which entered into extensive trade relations with advanced (European and American) countries after the age of a closed self-sufficient economy.

Akamatsu's explanation of his theory may be confusing because its name had little to do with the shapes and positions of the three curves in the diagram. It is hard for me to find the evidence for Akamatsu's suggestion that the goose flying at the front corresponded to an advanced country, like Britain, with the remaining geese following the front being less-advanced, developing countries. There was some room for interpretation in his flying-geese-pattern theory. Akamatsu's development theory has been applied to a picturesque description of a group of developing countries and led to the discussion of which country is the front flyer.[8]

Akamatsu and his student Kiyoshi Kojima (1920–) in their *Sekai Keizai to Gijutsu* (The World Economy and Technology, 1943) discussed the importance of innovation and the realization of 'increasing returns' or the economies of scope for the increase in productivity. It could be traced back to the government campaign for the enhancement of productivity in the last half of the 1920s. Japan copied the German campaign which had been initiated to increase international competitiveness following the introduction of the Taylor system in the United States. The Japanese economists were more interested in dynamic comparative advantage rather than static Ricardian analysis.

Hiroshi Kitamura (1909–) was also critical of the Ricardian theory of free trade and the international division of labour. He left Japan for Europe in 1931, studied economics at the University of Berlin, and made a special research of international economics and foreign investment at the University of Basel. He published his *Zur Theorie des internationalen Handels: Ein kritischer Beitrag* (On the Theory of International Trade: A Critical Contribution) in 1941. He developed an early macrodynamic theory, which was considered to be more appropriate for developing countries than advanced countries and supplied the theoretical support for protectionist policy like Friedrich List's *Das Nationale System der Politischen Oekonomie* (The National System of Political Economy,

1930). He brought German development and trade theory back to Japan in January 1948 and became active in Japan as well.

Three leading international economists including Akamatsu established the Japanese Society of International Economics in 1950, in order to bring together academics and other experts in the field of international economics with its related subjects, and to encourage further research (see Ikeo 1998). Not only non-Marxian economists like Kojima and Kitamura but also Marxian economists joined the society and discussed issues related to trade and development in the 1950s.

4. PRO-TRADE VERSUS PRO-DEVELOPMENT STRATEGIES?

The economic issues debated around 1950 were the differing views of international trade and the questions of how to increase exports and which industries to promote in order to secure the necessary imports. Therefore we have to look carefully at the situation evolving over time. We focus on a leading non-Marxian economist, Ichiro Nakayama (1898–1980), while referring to the discussion conducted by members of the Japanese Economic Policy Association (JEPA) in Section 5. It is because Nakayama was one of those best informed of international and domestic economic situations at the time, and JEPA had been discussing Japan's economic policies seriously since its establishment in 1940.

Ichiro Nakayama was born in 1898. He studied under two economists, Tokuzo Fukuda at Tokyo University of Commerce in the early 1920s and J.A. Schumpeter (1883–1950) at the University of Bonn during 1928–29. Nakayama and the agricultural economist Seiichi Tobata (1899–1983), devoted themselves to Schumpeter, translated many of his works into Japanese, and formed a close intellectual relationship with their mentor. Following Schumpeter's *Das Wesen und der Hauptinhalt der theoretischen Nationalökonomie* (1908) and *Theorie der wirtshaftlichen Entwicklung* (1912) and borrowing the title from Walras's *Elements d'économie politique pure* (1874–77), Nakayama published his *Junsui Keizaigaku* (Pure Economics, 1933). He explained the methodology of pure economics or general equilibrium theory, the theories of marginal utility and production, equilibrium and economic circulation, the variation in data such as population, demand, and technology and the economic adaptations to them, and the theory of economic development. He argued that entrepreneurs seeking profits should make new investments and give impetus to economic development. With the addition of the 'Memorandum on Keynesian Theory', Nakayama's *Pure Economics* was still widely read by economics students in the 1950s.

Nakayama also wrote many articles and essays on the current conditions of the Japanese economy for various journals and magazines, and later had them published in book form. He was the target of criticism by the majority Marxian economists. Nonetheless, it can be said that he was always calm and his writings were objective and encouraging. During the period immediately following the establishment of the People's Republic of China in October 1949 to the early 1950s, there was a controversy over international trade, which was initiated by one of Nakayama's articles and was followed by a series of critical reviews in several magazines. China was one of the most important trade partners for Japan prior to 1937, when the Sino–Japanese War broke out. Marxian economists were worried about the conspicuous decline in trade with China, while the United States became Japan's largest trading partner by far from the occupation period.

In December 1949, Nakayama published an article entitled 'Nihon keizai no kao' (The face of the Japanese economy) in a monthly magazine *Hyoron* (Review in explicit English).[9] What he had in mind was Schumpeter's memorial lecture 'The face of the German economy' (c1930) on the day of the establishment of the University of Bonn. Nakayama argued that the Japanese economy must frown, beset with deflation under the so-called Dodge Line or the Nine-Part Directive on Stabilization. The Dodge Line was implemented by the Allied Occupation Force in order to achieve fiscal, monetary, price and wage stability and to maximize production for exports.[10] The Japanese government was directed to adopt measures designed to:[11]

a. Achieve a true balance in the consolidated budget at the earliest possible...
b. Accelerate and strengthen the programme of tax collection...
c. Assure rigorous limitation of credit expansion...
d. Establish an effective programme to achieve wage stability.
e. Strengthen and, if necessary, expand the coverage of existing price control programmes.
f. Improve the operation of foreign trade controls and tighten existing foreign exchange controls, to the extent that such measures can appropriately be delegated to Japanese agencies.
g. Improve the legal effectiveness of the present allocation and rationing system, particularly to the end of maximizing exports.
h. Increase production of all essential indigenous raw material and manufactured products.
i. Improve efficiency of the food collection programme.

After the implementation of the plan, commodity prices began to decline in the black markets and finally the price level was stabilized, but this was accompanied by formidable social instability, including massive unemployment.

In his 1949 paper, Nakayama utilized three statistical data; population, international trade, and national income. First, Nakayama called attention to the fact that Japan had 80 million people and its population was increasing at two per cent per year. This fact was important and surprised the world. Italy had 48 million people and its population was increasing at one per cent per year, which was the fastest pace among European countries. Criticizing Malthus's pessimistic, biological viewpoint on population, Nakayama argued that an occupational, industrial viewpoint was more relevant and that the increase in population was a positive result of social and economic phenomena such as the increases in productivity. Second, calling attention to Adam Smith's absolute advantage theory of trade and idea of international division of labour, Nakayama confirmed that the benefit of international trade was common sense. Japan lacked iron ore, cotton, and crude oil, which were to be brought to Japan by international trade. He argued that the imports and the exports which were needed to secure the imports were the basis for Japan's industrialization and the increase in its population. Third, Nakayama regarded the level of national income as the best measure to describe the face of a national economy. He examined the historical changes in Japan's real income per hour and compared it to other countries. Japan's real income per hour had increased more than sixfold from 0.03 in 1900 to 0.19 in 1937. In 1944, Japan's figure was 0.18, USA 0.96, UK 0.61, and France 0.21. Nakayama said that national income was already found in textbooks such as Hicks's *The Social Framework of the American Economy* (Hicks and Hart, 1945) and Samuelson's *Economics* (1948).

Several economists including Hiromi Arisawa (1896–1988) and Shigeto Tsuru (1912–) attacked Nakayama's description of the Japanese economy immediately and questioned why Nakayama had chosen these three data. The focal point of their discussion gradually moved toward international trade. Arisawa's 'Nihon shihonshugi no unmei' (The destiny of Japanese capitalism, February 1950) and Tsuru's 'Keizaigaku no hitori aruki wa abunai' (It is dangerous for economics to walk alone, March 1950) appeared in the same magazine, *Hyoron*.

Nakayama defended his points in his 'Boeki-shugi to kokunai kaihatsu-shugi' (Pro-trade and pro-domestic development, March 1950), which appeared in *Keizai Hyoron* (Economic Review). He misnamed his position as pro-trade (boeki-shugi) and the critics as pro-domestic development (kokunai kaihatsu-shugi), because he knew that both sides agreed that it was necessary to develop the domestic economy even though there was disagreement on the future prospect and importance of international trade. He argued as follows. It was easy to understand that Japan needed to engage in international trade,

when one looked at the long sheet of international balance in *Industrialization in Japan and Manchuria* (1940) edited by E.B. Schumpeter[12] and the
Nine-Part Directive's policy of promoting exports first for the purpose of
securing imports. This reflected Japan's economic conditions. Japan had a
large population compared with its territory and so could not supply enough
food for its people to live in isolation. It had few natural resources. Its living
standards were still low. The world economic conditions should determine
whether one country would import food or produce more food on its own.

Nakayama continued. There were two groups. One considered the future of
the Japanese economy to stand on international trade, while others put more
weight on domestic economic development with a supposition of a limit on
international trade. Nakayama argued that Japan did not have capital accumula-
tions large enough to promote either trade or domestic development as of yet.
He rebutted the critics point by point. First, the exportable goods had been
changed compared with the pre-World War II period because of technological
development. Silk was replaced by nylon, rubber goods by artificial materials.
Second, GATT was signed by a number of countries because the expansion of
multilateral trade was expected to maintain high employment and enhance
national income, and to contribute to the development of productive resources
in each country. Nakayama understood the critics' points. Japan was not allowed to join the GATT group as yet (because of the British government's
strong opposition) and its exports to the sterling bloc were strictly limited.[13] Its
exports to China and the Soviet Union would not expand substantially because
Japan had joined the Western bloc led by the USA and the cold war would
continue. He agreed that Japan could learn a way of economic planning for
domestic development from the experiment of the Tennessee Valley Authority
based on the New Deal Policy in the USA of the 1930s. Nonetheless, he
concluded that the future course of the Japanese economy must be found in the
expansion of international trade. He pointed out that the prosperity of the
British economy, whose mainland was smaller than Japan's, depended on
international trade and the import of food, and that no country had prospered in
isolation. Referring to the 1949 annual report of the World Bank, he suggested
that Japan needed capital imports as well, although everyone knew that no one
was willing to lend money to Japan at the time.

The entire May 1950 issue of *Keizai Hyoron* featured a round table on the
destiny of the Japanese economy with participation by Nakayama, Arisawa,
Tobata, Yuzo Morita (1901–94) and Tsuru. Referring to Morita's latest economic data, they discussed the current economic conditions in both the world
and the Japanese economy. Nakayama repeated his arguments and there were
no big differences among the participants, although Arisawa and Tsuru were
pessimistic about the future of a capitalist country. Their round table spawned
a series of reviews and discussion among other economists and businessmen.

The question of trade was shifted to the political arena, and the issue became whether Japan should sign the San Francisco Peace Treaty with Western liberal or capitalist countries, including the United States and Western Europe, or whether it should wait for an overall treaty including China and the Soviet Union. Non-Marxians, including Kaname Akamatsu and Nakayama, supported Japan's prompt return to the international society by the treaty in order for Japan to secure the natural resources which it lacked, because they did not attach so much economic importance to China (and Korea), which did not have many of these resources (Akamatsu et al. 1951, p. 123). The Japanese government signed the treaty in September 1951.

In 1953, the series of Nakayama's articles related to trade and development were collected and published as *Nihon Keizai no Kao* (The Face of the Japanese Economy), and Arisawa's as *Saigunbi no Keizaigaku* (The Economics of Rearmament). Arisawa was worried about capitalism's connections with militarism, in the face of the establishment of Japan's Self Defence Force and the Korean War (1950–52). He studied economics at the University of Tokyo in the mid 1920s and learned the standard economic principles of the day from Emile Lederer (1882–1939). Although he was a Marxist-oriented economist and doubted the market mechanism, he joined numerous government committees after 1945 and played an important role on those committees relating to industrial rationalization and industrial policy.

5. CRITERIA FOR WHICH INDUSTRIES TO PROMOTE

When we look at the discussion by the Japanese Economic Policy Association (JEPA) members, it was unanimously confirmed by non-Marxian economists that there were two basic facts to take into consideration in making government policies for development and international trade in the 1950s. First of all, Japan was overpopulated, or had massive unemployment, because many Japanese soldiers and civilians returned home barely alive from the battlefields and the former colonies such as the northeast region of China (Manchuria), Taiwan and Korea when Japan lost World War II. The second point was that Japan did not have enough natural resources such as crude oil, coal, iron ore, bauxite, and other mineral materials, which would supply the basis of an industrial economy. It was impossible for Japan to raise its standard of living if it kept its economy isolated from the rest of the world. Japan had to trade with the rest of the world to import what it lacked. Moreover, the Japanese economy suffered from the severe shortage of food and other consumer goods, which had been reduced to subsistence level during the war.

Therefore the second economic issue which was discussed in the 1940s and 1950s was which industries to promote. It was natural to believe that the government should do something to secure imports in exchange for exports and then to protect Japanese lives. The Ministry of International Trade and Industry (MITI) was established from the former Ministry of Trade and Industry in 1949, for the primary purpose of promoting exports to acquire foreign currency in order to pay for essential imports in the short run (MITI 1990, vol. 4, 422–30). Based on the Nine-Part Directive, even the Occupation Force maintained that Japan should make exports its first priority in 1949. In the longer run MITI targeted the strengthening of international competitiveness of various modern industries (Shinohara 1982, p. 21). No Japanese industry was efficient enough to sell their goods abroad without governmental support. MITI's basic policy was to pay attention to an industry as a whole rather to an individual company. MITI searched for the industries which were expected to become exporters in the presence of subsidies.

There were a couple of criteria in judging which industry could earn foreign currency most efficiently, as was summarized by Shigeru Fujii (1908–) in his 'Keizai jiritsu to boeki kozo' (Economic self-support and the trade structure, 1955; JEPA 1988). The criterion used most often was the ratio of foreign currency earnings per industry, which was obtained by dividing domestic value-added by the export price. In reality, the ratio was modified by taking marketability, the turnover ratio of fixed capital and labour productivity into consideration. The higher the ratio of foreign currency earnings, the bigger the national income which was acquired from the same amount of exports. The modified ratio was the highest in the machinery industry, followed by the metalworking, food, textile, chemical and ceramic industries. The textile industry was declining in rank compared with the pre-1937 period, but it was still placed fourth. Fujii concluded that the light and traditional industries were still very important exporter industries, whereas it was urged that it was necessary to make the heavy and chemical industries competitive enough to export their products (1955; JEPA 1988, 212–13).

Thus the Japanese government promoted the heavy and chemical industries based on 'more sophisticated' criteria in order to strengthen international competitiveness of the Japanese economy until around 1970. There were two criteria which were proposed by Miyohei Shinohara (1919–) and adopted by MITI. One was the income elasticity criterion and the other the comparative technical progress criterion. Shinohara discussed these criteria first in the 1950s ('Sangyo kozo to toshi haibun', The industrial structure and the allocation of finance, 1957) and discussed them in retrospect in his conference paper entitled 'Japanese-type Industrial Policy'[14] as follows (Shinohara 1982, p. 25):

> The 'income elasticity criterion' provides a suggestion that an industry whose elasticity of export with respect to world real income as a whole is comparatively

high should be developed as an export industry. Under this criterion, as long as the income elasticity of textile products is higher than that of agricultural commodities, and the elasticities of automobiles and electronic products are higher than those of textile goods, automobiles are obviously preferable to textiles as export products, and textiles are more advantageous than agricultural products.

The 'comparative technical progress criterion' pays more attention to the possibility of placing a particular industry in a more advantageous position in the future through a comparatively greater degree of technical progress, even if the cost of the products is relatively high at this stage. This could be 'dynamized comparative cost doctrine'.

Shinohara concluded that 'the industrial policy concept adopted by MITI, which tried to take into account potential intertemporal dynamic developments rather than automatically applying the ready-made static theory of international economics, proved to be a wise choice' (Shinohara 1982, p. 25). However this kind of policy and Shinohara's arguments were sometimes criticized as Stalinist by economists like Martin Bronfenbrenner (1914–97) and later Chalmers Johnson (*Japan: Who Governs?*, 1995). In his *Keizaigakusha no Hatsugen* (The Statements made by an Economist, 1967), Shinohara was critical of the critics and maintained that they did not read his paper carefully (p. 81).

6. 'CENTRAL PLANNING' AND THE ECONOMIC COUNCIL

In April 1952, Japan returned to the international community on the basis of the San Francisco Peace Treaty, which marked the end of 15 years of central control over the Japanese economy. As mentioned, MITI was established in 1949 in order to de-control the Japanese economy and increase its international competitiveness, and reorganize for a regulated economy in 1952. The Economic Stabilization Board, which had wielded the strong controlling power in reconstructing Japan's war-torn economy, was replaced by the Economic Council Board (Keizai Shingi Cho) from July to August 1952. The agency was reorganized into the Economic Planning Agency (EPA) in May 1955. The main task of the agency since its establishment has been the drafting of long-term economic plans. Also in 1952, the Economic Council and the Japanese Development Bank (JDB) were established by the government. The Economic Council had been an auxiliary organ of the Economic Council Board and the EPA and was to 'conduct surveys and to deliberate on important economic policies and plans in response to inquiries by the Prime Minister'. Moreover JDB became the most important pro-growth factor in Japan.

Economic development became the priority target in Japan's public policy in the late 1940s, and remained so until the late 1960s. It was urgent for the government to construct an adequate infrastructure such as electric power plants, ports, and arterial roads, and to encourage other large-scale industries such as iron and steel, machinery, and airline service by financing them under favourable conditions. The government had to raise funds for further development to avoid financial constraints and infrastructural bottlenecks including a shortage of energy. JDB played crucial roles such as being the guarantor in borrowing funds from the World Bank and foreign private banks for national projects and huge capital projects by private companies (see Ikeo 1996c). In September 1957, the finance minister visited Washington DC to propose a new loan programme for the electric companies directly to the World Bank. Japan's government and civil servants were eager to set the Japanese economy on the growth track. Around this time, the importance of public assistance for economic development had next to unanimous consent among Japanese economists, politicians and government officials. Japanese economists regarded economic growth as the primary purpose of government economic policy.[15]

The Income Doubling Plan of 1960, namely the economic plan of doubling real national income in a decade (regardless of the increase in population), was the most conspicuous episode in Japan's economic history since 1945 from the viewpoint of political economy. It also caught the attention of several international scholars on the Japanese economy including the American economist Martin Bronfenbrenner. It was the mixed product of the three complementary elements, namely the economic optimism expressed by JDB members such as Osamu Shimomura (1910–89), the political strategy promoted by the ruling Liberal Democratic Party (LDP), and the strong will for central planning and industrial policy by brilliant government officials such as Saburo Okita (1914–93) of EPA and by members of MITI.[16]

In the last half of the 1950s, thanks to vital entrepreneurs and avid workers, Japan's economy was already growing more rapidly than had been expected in the Five Year Plan for Economic Self-Support (1955) and the New Long-Term Economic Plan (1957), which were the first and second official long-term (five-year) economic plans and were drafted by EPA members including Okita. While the 1955 plan's main targets were economic independence (of the aid from the United States and special procurement) and full employment, the 1957 plan's were maximum growth, the enhancement of living standards, and full employment. The problem was that neither plan survived to maturity, namely the end of the planning period, and therefore were replaced by new economic plans. In the late 1950s, there was a big debate regarding economic plans among Shimomura, Okita and other policy-oriented economists and econometricians (Kushida, 1960). Using hindsight, most of their discussion was confusing to some degree, although Shimomura made the most optimistic but correct economic forecast and relevant points in criticizing EPA's method for central planning.

Shimomura in his 'Nihon niokeru seichoryoku no ginmi' (The examination of Japan's growth potential, 1959) and elsewhere criticized the New Long Term Economic Plan (1957) in many ways but we focus on the following two points. First, he maintained that the expected growth rate, 6.5 per cent, was too low compared to both the actual rate, 8–12 per cent in the 1950s, and the potential growth rate (which was forecast by him) of 10 per cent. Meanwhile many economists and economic journalists maintained that EPA had set the rate too high. Second, the period of five years was too long a period for central planning, because it was difficult to predict what private economic business people were doing and were planning to do.

However LDP politicians liked the sound of 'income doubling', which was probably hinted at by the economist Ichiro Nakayama's new year's message that 'wage doubling' was first necessary to improve economic life in Japan. Prime Minister Shinsuke Kishi asked the question 'Is it possible to make a long term economic plan to double national income?' of the Economic Council in November 1959. The Council organized many subcommittees and task forces by utilizing many non-Marxian economists and other learned scholars in order to process the necessary information, and build up the plan. 'Ten years' was selected for the period of the Income Doubling Plan, because no one believed it possible to double income in five years (Okita 1981, p. 19). The draft for the economic plan was written by Okita and EPA members.[17] It was calculated that a growth rate of 7.2 per cent was necessary for doubling income in a decade. The Economic Council reported back the draft of the plan to Prime Minister Hayato Ikeda in November 1960. The draft was slightly modified by the politicians in the Cabinet in December 1960. However soon after 1960, it was found that this plan had inconsistencies between the macroeconomic level and the level of industrial sectors.

Then the Midterm Economic Plan of 1965 was created as a supplement to the Income Doubling Plan, and became more important than the master plan from the viewpoint of the history of economic thought. The econometric method, connecting with the inter-industry table, was used seriously for the first time in Japan's economic planning and it impressed observers that the new economic plan was finally built up on a really scientific basis. Incidentally around this time in Japan, those who had mastered neoclassical and Keynesian economics outnumbered Marxian economists or those who used the Marxian economic language in discussing economic problems (see Ikeo 1996a, c). However the plan had to be replaced by another in a year because the actual inflation rate turned out to be higher than the planned rate, and the Eisaku Sato cabinet decided to implement fiscal policy through deficit financing to alleviate economic recession in 1965. This was done in spite of the fact that the plan recommended against issuing this kind of national deficit bond.

The Japanese government's economic 'plans' did not serve as real plans. Therefore from late 1968 to early 1969, the Economic Council and its General Subcommittee decided to form the Committee to Study Basic Issues in Economic Planning. The committee had Kazushi Ohkawa (1908–94) serving as the chair and six other members including Okita. Their report became available in June 1969. They argued that central planning had three important functions. Later Okita summarized them as follows:

> First is the educational and informative role centering on economic forecasting. With economic plans providing an overview of the outlook for the economy, private-sector companies are then able to formulate their own long-term plans with this in mind. Second is the statement of long-term commitments centering on practical planning. Every plan includes policy programs to be carried out by the government, including the distribution of investment in the major public sectors. As such, the plan is a statement of the administration's long-range policy directions. And third is its role in mediating among different interests. The Economic Council, which deliberates on these plans, includes industrialists, labor leaders, journalists, academic economists and other people representing a broad range of interests. As a result, the Council's deliberations serve to mold compromises among these conflicting interest and to forge popular consensuses on what kind of a society and economy Japan should strive to be. (Okita 1989, p. 180)

As noted by the Study Committee, the process of making economic plans was very political in the sense that the Economic Council's deliberation was important for an industry to reach a consensus usually on output by the curtailment of operations and for Japan's economy to grow in 'harmony'. Harmony in a group such as a company, an industry or a nation is a lofty Japanese value. People in a group were supposed to maintain a harmonious balance rather than rocking the boat. They did groundwork before moving ahead and avoided conflicts in advance. The Economic Council might serve well to protect this Japanese value (Ikeo 1990).

7. AFTER THE GROWTH ERA

In the period of economic growth, the Japanese government negotiated with the international economic organizations for capital imports, and protected Japanese infant industries and agriculture. It made major public investments in infrastructure to set its economy on a smooth growth path, and set up a financial network reaching every corner of the country to collect savings for industrial investment. As noted, it suggested that fast-growing companies cooperate with other companies to avoid major changes and to maintain harmony in the industry. This alleviated the harsh workings of the market mechanism.

The Japanese enjoyed their new life equipped with an increasing number of durable consumer goods, which were the fruits of the economic development after 1950. However by 1970, when Japan had become one of the advanced countries, they found several negative external effects on the environment, such as mercury poisoning caused by sewage drainage, and air pollution and traffic jams in large cities. They also realized that they did not have a welfare system extensive enough for them to enjoy their retirement lives. Economic development was finally questioned as the policy priority and put behind a welfare programme. Nonetheless the Japanese socioeconomic system did not change immediately. Finally after around 1990, the system which had supported economic growth became really fatigued, while the internationalization of economic activities demanded a global standard instead of the Japanese standard. Some Japanese economists began to discuss seriously the role of the government and the market for the first time in the history of Japanese economic thought (see Ikeo 1997). The discussion will continue until the current major administrative reform is completed in the early twenty-first century.

NOTES

I thank Young Back Choi, Takenori Inoki, Takatoshi Ito, Asahi Noguchi, Kaoru Sugihara, and Shiro Sugihara for their valuable information, and Paul Pecorino for his comments on a draft of this chapter.

1. Probably Patrick and Rosovsky's *Asia's New Giant* (1976) is the best book in English on the post-World War II Japanese economy.
2. Kosuke Oyama in his *Gyoseishido no Seijikeizaigaku* (Political Economy of Administrative Guidance) (1996) clarified part of the battle between government officials and economists toward the introduction of more market mechanisms into the Japanese economy based on unpublished government documents.
3. For example, Takashi Negishi's *General Equilibrium Theory and International Trade* (1972) and its references.
4. Fukuda advised his students to make special studies of modern economists and translate them into Japanese. See Ikeo (1993).
5. Penrose's 'Memoirs of Japan, 1925–30' in Dore and Sinha (eds) (1987), pp. 6–7.
6. See Akamatsu's 'Jigazo: gakumon henro' (Self-portrait: my academic path) in Akamatsu's Students (eds) (1975), especially pp. 35–6.
7. This point was suggested by Paul Pecorino.
8. For example, see Korhonen's *Japan and the Pacific Free Trade Area* (1994), Hatch and Yamamura's *Asia in Japan's Embrace* (1996), and Ito's 'Japanese economic development' (1996).
9. The *Hyoron* was published by Kawade Shobo only in the period from February 1946 till April 1950.
10. Joseph Morrell Dodge (1890–1964) was sent by the US government to Japan in February 1949, and found the Japanese economy supported by American aid and that the Japanese

government subsidies covered the differential between the producer and consumer prices. He compared Japan to an economy walking on stilts high off the ground. See Bronfenbrenner's 'Four positions on Japanese finance' (1950) and Hein's *Fueling Growth* (1990) chapter 6.

11. The Nine-Part Interim Directive on Stabilization (11 December 1948) in the Ministry of Finance's *The Financial History of Japan*, Vol. 20 (1972), pp. 740–41.
12. Other contributors were G.C. Allen (1900–1982), M.S. Gordon and E.F. Penrose. Allen taught at Nagoya for three years in the 1920s. See Ikeo (1996b).
13. Japan became a member of GATT in September 1955 and of the United Nations in December 1956.
14. This paper was presented at the International Symposium on Industrial Policies for the 1980s.
15. See JEPA (1961) and Tachi and Komiya (1964).
16. Japanese economists such as Ryutaro Komiya and Hiromi Arisawa were critical of EPA's long-term central planning and MITI's initiative over private enterprise. See Komiya (c1959) and Oyama (1996).
17. Isamu Miyazaki of EPA gave a paper on the methodology of the Income Doubling Plan to the annual joint meeting of the Association of Theoretical Economics and the Japanese Econometric Society in October 1960. Yet his paper was not published because his message was included in Okita (1960). Sometimes the treatment of authorship in Japanese government agencies is really mysterious. See the first footnote to Shimomura (1961, p. 1).

REFERENCES

Akamatsu, Kaname (1935), 'Waga kuni yomo kogyohin no boeki susei' (The trend of foreign trade in manufactured woollen goods in Japan), *Sangyo Keizai Ronso*, Nagoya College of Commerce.

Akamatsu, Kaname (1937), 'Waga kuni keizai hatten no sogo benshoho' (Synthetic dialectics of industrial development in Japan), *Sangyo Keizai Ronso*, Nagoya College of Commerce.

Akamatsu, Kaname (1961), 'A theory of unbalanced growth in the world economy', *Weltwirtshaftliches Archiv*, Band 86, Heft 2. Also in Akamatsu's Students (1975).

Akamatsu, Kaname (1962), 'A historical pattern of economic growth in developing countries', *The Developing Economies*, Preliminary Issue, (1), March–August. Also in Akamatsu's Students (1975).

Akamatsu, Kaname and Kiyoshi Kojima (1943), *Sekai Keizai to Gijutsu* (The World Economy and Technology), Tokyo: Shoko Gyosei-sha.

Akamatsu, Kaname, Yoshio Nakano, Toichi Nawa and Sadaharu Yabe (1951), 'Zadankai: Zenmen kowa to tandoku kowa no taiketsu' (Round table: the peace treaty with all the nations or only with the western bloc), *Chuo Koron*, supplement issue, (753), 114–28.

Akamatsu's Students (eds) (1975), *Gakumon Henro* (Academic Path: The Memorial for Doctor Kaname Akamatsu), edited by Kiyoshi Kojima, Tokyo: Sekai Keizai Kenkyu Kyokai.

Arisawa, Hiromi (1950), 'Nihon shihon-shugi no unmei' (The destiny of Japanese capitalism), *Hyoron*, (40), 5–14.

Arisawa, Hiromi (1953), *Sai-gunbi no Keizaigaku* (The Economics of Rearmament), Tokyo: Tokyo Daigaku Shuppan-kai.

Bronfenbrenner, Martin (1950), 'Four positions on Japanese finance', *Journal of Political Economy*, **58**(4), 281–8. Also in Bronfenbrenner (1988).

Bronfenbrenner, Martin (1988), *Keizaigaku Tokoro-Dokoro* (Here and There in Economics) Tokyo: Aoyama Gakuin University.

Colm, Gerhard (1952), *The American Economy in 1960: Economic Progress in a World of Tension*, Washington DC: National Planning Association.

Dore, R. and R. Sinha (eds) (1987), *Japan and World Depression: Then and Now: Essays in Memory of E.F. Penrose*, London: Macmillan.

Economic Council (1960), *Shotoku Baizo Keikaku* (Income-Doubling Plan), in Okita (1960).

Economic Council's General Subcommittee and the Committee to Study Basic Issues in Economic Planning (1969), *Nihon no Keizai Keikaku* (Japan's Economic Plan) Tokyo: Ministry of Finance Printing Bureau.

Economic Planning Agency (ed.) (1965), *Chuki Keizai Keikaku* (Midterm Economic Plan), Tokyo: Ministry of Finance Printing Bureau.

Hatch, Walter and Kozo Yamamura (1996), *Asia in Japan's Embrace: Building a Regional Production Alliance*, Cambridge: University of Cambridge Press.

Hein, Laura E. (1990), *Fueling Growth: The Energy Revolution and Economic Policy in Postwar Japan*, Boston, MA: The Council of East Asian Studies at Harvard University.

Hicks, John Richard and Albert Gailord Hart (1945), *The Social Framework of the American Economy: An Introduction to Economics*, New York: Oxford University Press.

Ikeo, Aiko (1990), 'Japanese economics from another sociological perspective', *Kokugakuin Keizaigaku* (Kokugakuin University), **39**(1), 112–28.

Ikeo, Aiko (1996a), 'Marxist economics in Japan', *Kokugakuin Keizaigaku* (Kokugakuin University), **44**(3/4), 425–51.

Ikeo, Aiko (1996b), 'The advent of marginalism in Japan', *The Research in the History of Economic Thought and Methodology*, **14**, 217–45.

Ikeo, Aiko (1996c), 'The internationalization of economics in Japan', in A.W. Coats (ed.), *The Post-1945 Internationalization of Economics*, (Annual Supplement to Volume 28 of the *History of Political Economy*), Durham, NC: Duke University Press, pp. 121–39.

Ikeo, Aiko (1997), 'Nihon no keizaigakusha to keizai seisaku' (Japanese economists and economic policy), paper for the annual meeting of the Society for the History of Economic Thought, Fukui: Fukui Prefectural University, 8–9 November 1997.

Ikeo, Aiko (1998), 'Sengo nihon no keizaigakusha-tachi to gakkai katsudo' (Japanese economists and learned societies in the post-1945 period), *Kokugakuin Keizaigaku* (Kokugakuin University), **46**(1), 1–45.

Ito, Takatoshi (1996), 'Japanese economic development: idiosyncratic or universal?', to be included in J.Y. Lin (ed.), *Regional Experiences and System Reform*, volume 1 of Proceedings of the International Economic Association, 11th World Congress, Tunis, December 1995.

Japanese Economic Policy Association (eds) (1961), *Gendai Nihon niokeru Kokka no Yakuwari* (Role of the Government in the Present-day Economy of Japan), *The Annual of the Japanese Economic Policy Association*, (9), Tokyo: Keiso Shobo.

Japanese Economic Policy Association (eds) (1988), *Keizaiseisakugaku no Tanjo* (The Birth of the Science of Economic Policy), Tokyo: Keiso Shobo.

Johnson, Chalmers (1995), *Japan: Who Governs?: The Rise of the Developmental State*, New York: Norton & Company.

Kitamura, Hiroshi (1941), *Zur Theorie des internationalen Handels: Ein Kritischer*

Beitrag (On the Theory of International Trade: A Critical Contribution), Japanese publication, Tokyo: Aoya Shoten, 1949.

Komiya, Ryutaro (c1959), *Shin-choki Keizai Keikaku no Post-Mortem* (The Post-Mortem of the New Long-Term Economic Plan), Tokyo: Tokei Kenkyukai.

Komiya, Ryutaro (1990), *The Japanese Economy: Trade, Industry, and Government*, Tokyo: University of Tokyo Press.

Korhonen, Pekka (1994), *Japan and the Pacific Free Trade Area*, London: Routledge.

List, Friedrich (1922), *Das nationale System der politischen Oekonomie* (The National System of Political Economy), Gesamtwerke Bd. 6, Berlin: Akademie-Verlag.

Ministry of International Trade and Industry, The Committee for the History of International Trade and Industry (1989–94), *Tsusho Sangyo Seisaku Shi* (The History of International Trade and Industry), 17 volumes, Tokyo: Ministry of Finance Printing Bureau.

Ministry of Finance, Financial History Section (1972), *The Financial History of Japan: The Allied Occupation Period, 1945–1952*, Vol. 20, English Documents, Tokyo: Toyo Keizai Shinpo-sha.

Nakayama, Ichiro (1933), *Junsui Keizaigaku* (Pure Economics), Tokyo: Iwanami Shoten. In Nakayama (1972–73) vol. 1.

Nakayama, Ichiro (1949), 'Nihon keizai no kao' (The face of the Japanese economy), *Hyoron*, 38, 1–9. In Nakayama (1953) and Nakayama (1972–73) vol. 12.

Nakayama, Ichiro (1950), 'Boeki-shugi to kokunai kaihatsu-shugi' (Pro-trade and pro-domestic development), *Keizai Hyoron*. In Nakayama (1953) and Nakayama (1972–73) vol. 12.

Nakayama, Ichiro (1953), *Nihon Keizai no Kao* (The Face of the Japanese Economy), Tokyo: Nihon Hyoronsha. In Nakayama (1972–73) vol. 12.

Nakayama, Ichiro (1972–73), *Nakayama Ichiro Zenshu* (Complete Works of Ichiro Nakayama), 18 volumes and a supplement, Tokyo: Kodan-sha.

Nakayama, Ichiro, Hiromi Arisawa, Seiichi Tobata, Yuzo Morita and Shigeto Tsuru (1950), 'Toronkai: Nihon shihonshugi no unmei' (Round table: The destiny of the Japanese capitalism), *Keizai Hyoron*, May, 2–108.

Negishi, Takashi (1972), *General Equilibrium Theory and International Trade*, Amsterdam: North-Holland.

Okita, Saburo (1960), *Shotoku Baizo Keikaku no Kaisetsu* (Outline of the Income Doubling Plan), Tokyo: Nihon Keizai Shimbun-sha.

Okita, Saburo (1981), *Tohon Seiso: Watashi no Rirekisho* (Constantly On the Move: My Personal History), Tokyo: Nihon Keizai Shimbun-sha.

Okita, Saburo (1989), 'Japan', in Joseph A. Pechman (ed.), *The Role of the Economist in Government: An International Perspective*, New York: New York University Press.

Oyama, Kosuke (1996), *Gyoseishido no Seijikeizaigaku* (Political Economy of Administrative Guidance), Tokyo: Yuhikaku.

Patrick, Hugh and Henry Rosovsky (eds) (1976), *Asia's New Giant*, Washington DC: The Brookings Institution.

Samuelson, Paul (1948), *Economics: An Introductory Analysis*, New York: McGraw-Hill.

Schumpeter, Elizabeth Boody (ed.) (1940), *The Industrialization of Japan and Machukuo, 1930–1940: Population, Raw Material and Industry*, New York: Macmillan.

Schumpeter, Joseph Alois (1908), *Das Wesen und der Hauptinhalt der theoretischen*

Nationalökonomie (The Essence and Main Contents of Theoretical Economics), Leipzig: Duncker & Humblot.

Schumpeter, Joseph Alois (1912), *Theorie der wirtshaftlichen Entwicklung* (Theory of Economic Development), Leipzig: Duncker & Humblot.

Shimomura, Osamu (1959), 'Nihon niokeru seichoryoku no ginmi' (The examination of Japan's growth potential), *Kinyu Zaisei Jijo*, **10**(9). Also in Kushida (ed.) (1960), 3–30.

Shimomura, Osamu (1961), 'Seicho seisaku no kihon mondai' , *Kikan Riron Keizaigaku* **11**(3/4), 1–15. 'Basic problems in economic growth policy', *Translation Series*, no. 37, Calcutta: Indian Statistical Institute, 1963.

Shinohara, Miyohei (1957), 'Sangyo kozo to toshi haibun' (Industrial structure and investment allocation), *Keizai Kenkyu* (Hitotsubashi University), **8**(4), 314–21.

Shinohara, Miyohei (1967), *Keizaigakusha no Hatsugen* (The Statements made by an Economist), Tokyo: Nikkei.

Shinohara, Miyohei (1982), *Industrial Growth, Trade, and Dynamic Patterns in the Japanese Economy*, Tokyo: University of Tokyo Press.

Tachi, Ryuichiro and Ryutaro Komiya (1964), *Keizai Seisaku no Riron (Theory of Economic Policy)*, Tokyo: Keiso Shobo.

Tinbergen, Jan (1958), *The Design of Development*, Baltimore: The Johns Hopkins Press.

Tinbergen, Jan (1964), *Central Planning*, New Haven: Yale University Press.

Tsuru, Shigeto (1950), 'Keizaigaku no hitori aruki wa abunai' (It is dangerous for economics to walk alone), *Hyoron* (41), 13–23.

United Nations (1958), *Manual on Economic Development Projects*, New York: United Nations.

United Nations (1965), *Planning for Economic Development*, New York: United Nations.

Yamazawa, Ippei (1990), *Economic Development and International Trade: The Japanese Model*, Hawaii: East-West Center. (The Japanese original version, 1984.)

9. Economic development and economic thought after World War II: economic development and Marxian political economy

Toshio Yamada

INTRODUCTION

In this chapter we examine how Marxian political economy envisaged economic development in the postwar era. As is well known, postwar Japan, emerging from the military defeat of World War II, realized an astonishing economic development and became an 'economic power'. From today's point of view, this is obviously one of the major events in world history. But, for the economists present during these historical events, what were the main issues in Japanese economic development, in which direction did they want to guide the Japanese economy, and how did they develop their own economic thoughts and theories? Here we examine these questions in the case of Marxian political economists.

We use the term 'Marxian political economy'; indeed, Marxism had greater influence in the field of economics in Japan than in Western countries until at least the 1960s. We may count as the reasons for its strong influence, first, its demonstration of high analytical power through the Japanese Capitalism Debate in the 1930s; second, the high prestige it accrued as a science which confronted directly and bravely poverty and war; and third, the great distance between the realities of Japanese society and the theoretical world of American neoclassical economics.

However the success of Marxian economics was confined to universities and labour movements; its historical view was not necessarily supported by the general public. On the contrary, as early as the 1950s, Japanese Marxian economics had begun to lose its capacity for scientific analysis and its popular support due to various conflicts and splits in the international communist movements and in the Japanese Communist Party (JCP). This meant naturally that Marxian economists had begun to lose the will and ability to participate in planning economic policies. In this way Marxian political economy, which entirely lost track of actual political concerns in some cases, became an abstract discourse of criticism against capitalism in general. Marxian political economy defended itself, as it were, by running away from realities.

Japanese Marxist economists ran away from the international academic societies also. The Japanese are of course very sensitive to the world's newest academic trends; they have translated into Japanese many Marxist texts such as those of P.M. Sweezy, M.H. Dobb, E.S. Varga, and so on. But these 'international exchanges' were only occasions of scientific import, and not of reciprocal contributions and controversies at all. Consequently, until the 1970s, Japanese Marxian political economy formed in isolation from trends in the rest of the world. And, as a result of this isolated development, '(rather like some fragment of a biological species which is cut off from others by geographical circumstances) their theories began to evolve in a number of distinctive directions' (Morris-Suzuki, 1989, p. 104). The most 'distinctive directions' were a systematization into grand theories and a flourishing of exegetical studies of Marx's texts.

We can summarize the last half century of Japanese Marxian political economy as a period in which the discipline, despite enjoying the high-level heritage of the Japanese Capitalism Debate of prewar Japan, failed to adjust to the conditions of postwar Japan. However we cannot grasp the full import of Japanese postwar Marxism by noting only this general trend. Because of the historical and critical point of view which the Marxian perspective alone could provide, Marxian economists proposed a number of insightful ideas concerning the issues of postwar economic development. Here we consider these ideas by dividing these 50 years into three periods: the economic reconstruction period, the high economic growth period and the post-oil shock period.

DIRECTIONS OF ECONOMIC RECONSTRUCTION IN JAPAN

The main issue of 'economic development' in the period of recovery just after the war (1945–55) centred around the fundamental directions of economic reconstruction. The Japanese economy and the citizens' livelihoods were utterly destroyed by the war. But, under the direction of the American Occupation Force, democratic reforms of the Japanese economy were carried out: land reform, dissolution of the *zaibatsu* financial cliques, and the emancipation of trade unions. From 1950, aided by the special procurements of the US military during the Korean War (1950–53), the Japanese economy started its recovery.

However no one believed that the purpose of reconstruction should be to reproduce the prewar era Japan. What form, then, should the new Japanese economy take? Marxists joined the debates of the new era. And what was better, Marxists alone enjoyed the benefit of having succeeded to the heritage of the prewar Capitalism Debate. Japanese Marxian political economy was at the height of its influence in the period of economic recovery, during which some prototypes of the representative Marxian schools of postwar Japan were formed.

State Monopoly Capitalism

An orthodox and typical viewpoint of postwar Japanese Marxism is presented by Inoue and Usami (1951). Taking up the definition of Japanese capitalism as a 'militarist and semi-feudalistic imperialism' as proposed by the prewar *Koza-ha* school, they point out its insufficiency and introduce a new concept of 'state monopoly capitalism' (SMC) first conceived by V.I. Lenin. With the establishment of the Soviet Union in 1917 capitalism entered, they argue, an era of 'general crisis', in addition to the crises of the world wars and the Great Depression. Under such intense pressure, monopoly capitalism became unable to sustain itself without transforming itself into SMC. Thus SMC reveals 'the last aspect' of capitalism, and implies a 'high commanding position' for the establishment of socialism.

Here we observe an erroneous schema of history: general crisis → SMC → collapse of capitalism → socialism. This is, however, just the schema of economic development on which orthodox Marxism has long insisted in postwar Japan. According to orthodox Marxism, capitalism will collapse before long, and therefore there will be no room for economic development under a capitalist system. Today we can easily point out Marxism's errors, but we must not forget that it was very persuasive at that time. First, capitalism in the 1930s and 1940s was in a crisis seemingly equivalent to its final crisis, and second, the notion of SMC correctly posited the growing role of the state in the advanced capitalist countries during and after the war. This is why, in postwar Japan, Marxist theories on contemporary capitalism or economic development have most often been constructed upon the concept of SMC. Indeed, 'this ... is quite crucial to an understanding of the controversies of the postwar Japanese left' (Morris-Suzuki, 1989, p. 122).

Based on these general conceptions of history, Inoue and Usami (1951) argue that Japanese capitalism was an SMC which constituted the last phase of capitalism, and at the same time a capitalism which was structurally articulated with semi-feudal elements. The wartime economy had deepened these structural contradictions, objectively creating the necessity of land reform through dissolution of the semi-feudal system of landholding and the liberation of tenant farmers. However, the land reform carried out from 1946 under the control of the Occupation Force, according to Inoue, only 'reorganized' the feudal system, allowing the semi-feudal system of landholding to survive as before. Consequently what was needed was a struggle for 'the complete overthrow of the semi-feudal system' (Inoue et al., 1953).

In short, there was no possibility of economic development not only because Japan was in the historical phase of SMC in general, but also because Japanese capitalism in particular preserved semi-feudal elements from the prewar era. According to this orthodox Marxist view, Japanese capitalism still retained its structural contradictions in spite of the postwar reforms, and existed as an extremely weak capitalism compared with Western models. So, Inoue suggested, the reconstruction of Japanese economy could not be performed without transforming it into socialism; only socialist revolution could lead to economic development.

Modernization Theory

There was, however, another group which, succeeding the same *Koza-ha* school, established a different theory. This was named 'modernization theory', though not in the Rostowian sense. This group was not necessarily composed of Marxists alone. Even those members who were near to Marxism treated Marx in relation to Adam Smith or Max Weber, and they did not privilege Marx exclusively. Among them we examine here Hisao Otsuka (1907–96) who was remarkably active in this period.

His point of view on the development of Japanese economy can be summarized as follows (Otsuka, 1946). What is most important for the reconstruction of the Japanese economy is the creation of a 'modernized human type'. Its objective conditions consist of a liberation of the peasantry through a way 'from below' (general formation of an independent and self-sustaining peasantry), and the creation of a domestic market. In other words, it is only on these two conditions that the modernized human type can be formed in Japan, and this human type will constitute one of the most powerful 'productive forces' in the reconstructed Japanese economy.

Otsuka's conception is based upon his studies from the prewar period of European economic history, and its result is an original and influential doctrine called 'Otsuka historiography'. That is to say, Otsuka (1951, 1964), calling into question the driving forces which had brought modern capitalism into existence, sharply criticizes the accepted theory of the historical school that had located these forces in the 'development of commerce', and proposes a new theory that located them in the formation of 'mediocrity of fortune' (intermediate producers' stratum) and its later polarization. According to Otsuka, while the 'path from above', or the progression from commercial capital (early capital) to industrial capital, was seen primarily in Prussia, the 'path from below', or the progression from yeoman capital (intermediate producers' stratum) to industrial capital, was evident in Britain and America. The 'path from above', could not be truly revolutionary in the birth of capitalism. On the contrary it was the 'path from below' that constituted a pure and civilized capitalism which was sustained by a modernized human type and modern productive forces.

From Otsuka's perspective, the direction of development for postwar Japan should have been one in which the peasants became landed farmers by liberating themselves from semi-feudal relations and in which a broad domestic market was built up on the bases of both the public wealth (*Volksreichtum*) in the hands of farmers and the division of national labour between agriculture and industry. What was definitively important at that moment was that working people would be modelled into a 'modernized human type' and so would become bearers of 'modern productive forces'. While orthodox Marxism insisted on the impossibilities of capitalist development and on the possibilities of socialist development, Otsuka, despite having inherited the same *Koza-ha* theory, emphasized that the authentic path of economic development consisted in the way 'from below' supported by the modernized human type, regardless of whether the Japanese were in a capitalist or a socialist system.

The 'Uno Theory'

We have so far followed two theories stemming from the *Koza-ha*'s tradition, but postwar Japan also had an excellent political economy framework developed from *Rono-ha*, the other prewar school. The political economic thought of Kozo Uno (1897–1977) was named 'Uno Theory', and it brought together many followers to form the influential 'Uno School'. Uno's works are, we can surely say, among the greatest achievements in postwar Japanese economics. His political economy is constructed in a very systematic way from a pure and abstract theory into a concrete analysis of the real world. Though the domains which Uno himself researched are centred on the level of pure theory ('general principles'), his methodology not only originates from his own reflection on the Japanese Capitalism Debate in the interwar period, but also is deeply related to debates on the reconstructive direction of Japan. So before we examine his system of political economy, we will first review briefly what he wrote about economic reconstruction.

The reconstruction of postwar Japan, Uno (1946) argues, should be based mainly on the establishment of capitalist agriculture and large enterprises, rather than on landed farmers and industrial capital, so that farm and factory workers will have the organizational basis to develop democracy. In short,

Uno stressed that economic democratization had to be founded on industrial socialization, and he predicted the emergence of socialism in Japan based upon industrial socialization and a widening economic democratization.

Uno Theory, which emphasizes capitalist management of agriculture and the socialization of industries, contrasts sharply with Otsuka historiography, which stresses a broad formation of small commodity producers. Uno presents the new conception that economic democratization in contemporary Japan should be achieved, in contrast to the case of England, for instance, on the basis of industrial socialization. Uno's new insight lies, in short, in the recognition that a backward country does not simply imitate and repeat the historical processes of advanced countries, but that its capitalist development must take a distorted form according to the historical stage of world capitalism in which it starts its development. Hence his own methodology and system of political economy.

Any system of Marxian political economy, Uno (1962) argues, has to be divided into three progressive levels: the general principles, the stage theories and the analyses of real conditions. The first level, that of the general principles, is a field in which, supposing methodologically a pure capitalist society, we define the most fundamental economic laws of capitalism. The second level, that of the stage theories, is a field of research on the particular contents of different stages of capitalist development, such as a stage of commercial capitalism (represented by the mercantilist policies in the sixteenth and seventeenth centuries), a stage of industrial capitalism (represented by liberal policies after the Industrial Revolution), and lastly a stage of finance capitalism (represented by the rise of imperialism since the late nineteenth century). And it is only on these foundations and criteria of general principles and stage theories that we can undertake analyses of the real conditions of any particular country in any particular period, for example postwar Japanese capitalism. Analysis of real conditions constitutes the third and last level, and also the ultimate goal of all economic studies.

Certainly the pure capitalism which was presupposed in the general principles has never existed. But a methodological supposition of pure capitalism is, Uno says, neither arbitrary nor unreasonable because capitalist societies, especially that of England, have manifested, from the seventeenth century to the middle of the nineteenth century, a tendency to evolve toward a pure capitalism. It is on this real and historical basis that one can construct the general principles of political economy. From Uno's point of view, Marx's *Das Kapital* is no doubt a text of pure theory or general principles on capitalism, but a text absolutely insufficient and incomplete as such. This is because one finds there a careless mixture of pure theories with a number of propositions which should not belong to the level of general principles, for example those of the pauperization of the working class, primitive accumulation, and so on. According to Uno, the thesis of pauperization, for example, is a characteristic particular only to English capitalism, especially during the first half of the nineteenth century, and a phenomenon whose study ought to belong to the level of stage theory or of the analysis of real conditions.

Now, if all the capitalist countries had moved toward pure capitalism, it would be enough for us to have, as disciplines of political economy, merely the general principles and the analyses of real conditions. However, in reality, the self-purifying tendency of capitalism was reversed with the historical appearance of finance capital at the end of the nineteenth century. This is why the general principles, by themselves, are not sufficient and a stage theory is required. Uno extracts these reflections from the debate between *Koza-ha* and *Rono-ha*. Both schools, he claims, made the same mistake, a mistake that would have applied *Das Kapital* directly to the actualities of Japanese society at that time. Hence the *Koza-ha* school overestimated the distance between *Das Kapital* and Japanese society while the *Rono-ha* school underestimated it. The necessary task for both schools was to construct a theory of the imperialist stage as an analytical criterion of Japanese capitalism at that time.

Even as he devised the above methodology of political economy, Uno devoted himself to the completion and perfection of the general principles (Uno, 1950–52). Uno Theory is very characteristic of postwar Japan in having a grand theoretical system, and is a great achievement of which postwar Japanese Marxian political economy deserves to be proud. Furthermore, in advocating 'the separation of science from ideology', Uno criticized Stalinism from an early time, and also the disturbance of academic studies by particular political parties or sects. Uno's main book has been translated into English (Uno, 1980), his ideas are often introduced in English (Mawatari, 1985), and today we can also find English works making use of his ideas (Albritton, 1986, 1991). Although the historical limitations and defects of Uno Theory are obvious when we consider it from the viewpoint of the end of the twentieth century, it still shines, side by side with Otsuka historiography, as a representative achievement of the social sciences in postwar Japan.

THE EMERGENCE OF HIGH ECONOMIC GROWTH AND ITS SIGNIFICANCE

In the 1950s and 1960s, the capitalist world experienced a long period of prosperity called the 'Golden Age of Capitalism' or the 'Fordist Era'. In Japan also, in 1956, just one decade after the military defeat, the White Paper on the Economy pointed out: 'We are no longer in the postwar'. In fact in the previous year, 1955, the GNP of the Japanese economy had recovered to the highest level of the prewar era. By 1956, the period of economic growth through postwar reconstruction ended. The new expectation was for growth through the modernization of technology and the economy. Although a pessimistic view prevailed inside and outside Marxism, the Japanese economy thereafter enjoyed, contrary to all forecasts, an average annual real growth rate of around 10 per cent for some 20 years, an exceptionally high sustained rate. This period (1956–73) is often called the era of high economic growth. During that time, the rural population decreased sharply, the real wages of workers increased, new consumer goods became popular, and people's lifestyles and values changed drastically.

The Marxian political economists were in general critical toward high economic growth or viewed it impassively. But high growth raised serious questions for Marxism. The first was how to explain the very emergence of high economic growth, not only in Japan but also in advanced capitalist economies in the age of the so-called general crisis of capitalism, and the second was how to understand why the mechanism of rapid growth existed in Japan and nowhere else. Now we trace the bitter struggles of Marxian economists *vis-à-vis* these questions.

The Socialization Theory of SMC

As we saw above, the postwar Japanese Marxists consecrated the term 'State Monopoly Capitalism' (SMC) as a paradigmatic concept for the analysis of contemporary capitalism. In this conception of economic development, two suppositions are implied: first, that SMC is a product of the general crisis of capitalism (crisis theory of SMC); and second, that economic stagnation lasts for a long time under SMC (stagnation theory). These theoretical suppositions necessarily result in treating the fact of high economic growth as an 'exception' to the basic tendency to stagnation of twentieth century capitalism. In brief, according to the dogmatic view of postwar Japanese Marxism, high economic growth was, after all, something exceptional.

However a new group began to confront the fact of high growth, finding that structural changes had altered the nature of capitalism from what it had been in the prewar period. One member was T. Ikumi. Utilizing many suggestions from K. Zieschang (1957) of East Germany, this group intended to explain SMC not in terms of the general crisis of capitalism, but the 'socialization of productive relations'. That is, as the 'socialization of productive forces' develops in a capitalist system, the productive relations also must necessarily become socialized. This socialization is expressed in the formation of joint-stock companies and monopoly corporations, and SMC constitutes the ultimate development. So SMC is not a product of the crisis of capitalism, but a product of a certain degree of capitalist development (Ikumi (ed.), 1958).

This view is often called the socialization theory of SMC. However, the basic explanatory conception is nothing but historical materialism, according to which the productive relations must develop (socialize) themselves in proportion to the development (socialization) of the productive forces. The explanation is a product of the direct and immediate application of the abstract formulae of historical materialism to contemporary economies, and has no relevance as a theory of economic development. However, it is precisely to the facts of development in productive forces within contemporary capitalism and its long-term prosperity that this group paid the utmost attention behind their erroneous theorization.

Although this group perceived clearly the fact of high economic growth, their new theory of SMC failed. Based on these reflections, the advocates of the socialization theory of SMC realized in the course of time that the true roots of their failure consisted in the very concept of SMC itself. 'SMC' is inseparable, by virtue of its origin in the thought of V.I. Lenin, from a historical schema of 'more and more contradictions and final collapse of capitalism'. The sustainable growth of 1960s capitalism cannot be well grasped by the old concept of SMC. For this reason, before long they declared that they would cease using the term SMC (Tamagaki, 1976). The paradigmatic concept of the postwar Marxists started to be brought into question.

The Crisis Theory Approach of SMC

Alongside the trend toward abandoning the theory of SMC, there appeared another movement intended to revise and restructure it: the theory of SMC by Tsutomu Ouchi (1918–). As one of the leading followers of Uno, his objective consisted in building up a base for the analyses of real conditions which Uno had left incomplete. Hence Ouchi's approach to the theory of SMC. The essence of SMC is explained by Ouchi (1970) as control of the economy by the state through the fiscal policies based on a managed currency system. As Ouchi indicates by naming his doctrine 'the crisis theory approach', the ultimate objective of the state under SMC consists in escaping from crises, and the principal method for doing so is reducing real wages through inflationary measures. Ouchi thus explains SMC not simply by resorting to the general crisis alone, but by paying attention to the modifications in capital–labour relations in capitalist countries caused by the general crisis.

In spite of these positive contributions, Ouchi's theory has a decisive weak point: it is incapable of explaining high economic growth because it accepts the theories of general crisis and chronic stagnation. For him Japanese high growth was, after all, an abnormal phenomenon (Ouchi, 1962). And the reason for rapid growth was explained exclusively by the 'backwardness' of the Japanese economy and the 'postwar factor'. 'Backwardness' he considered in particular to be 'an abundant existence of low-wage labour', and the 'postwar factor' as new possibilities for the expansion of investment and the domestic market owing to the end of the war. However 'backwardness' and the 'postwar factor' of Japanese capitalism were only temporary phenomena which would disappear before long, and rapid growth based upon these particular conditions was nothing but an 'abnormal', 'particular', 'temporary' and exceptional phenomenon. From today's point of view, we can judge his opinion to be quite mistaken.

We have examined two new versions of SMC theory. These are a precious record concerning how the theory of SMC, which was born in the difficult conditions of capitalism, has faced the fact of high economic growth and endeavoured to change itself. One approach rejected the crisis-oriented character of the theory so as to start from the fact of rapid growth and prosperity, but failed to establish a positive economic theory. The other was successful in building a refined economic explanation based on Uno Theory, but was unable to explain rapid growth, retaining the crisis-oriented character of the theoretical framework. Indeed both are unsuccessful theories. But the two played an important role of 'negative intermediate' in bringing postwar Japanese Marxian political economy to finally abandon the paradigmatic concept of SMC.

The Civil Society Theory

There appeared, however, in Japanese Marxian political economy, a view of economic development which did not adopt any position on SMC: this was Yoshihiko Uchida's civil society theory. Since the early postwar period, Uchida (1913–89) had continued, through reflection on the Japanese Capitalism Debate, to deal with the questions of the particularity of Japanese economic development as well as of the direction of social reform. He had learned much from Otsuka historiography from which he took, for example, the conceptions of 'modernized human type' and 'mediocrity of fortune', which he elaborated into a concept of 'civil society'.

Here 'civil society' implied an abstract and trans-historical sense like 'a system of equivalent exchange and productive forces' or 'a society with freedom and human rights'. Based on this concept of civil society, he pointed out the problems of capitalist development in Japan and criticized the Japanese form of high economic growth (Uchida, 1967, 1981). According to Uchida, the establishment of capitalism in Japan was achieved not through the creation of liberated and equal individuals, but rather through the incorporation of feudal and pre-modern elements. These facts, advanced by the *Koza-ha* school in the prewar period, led Uchida to posit 'the distinction of civil society from capitalism', and finally to characterize Japan as 'capitalism without civil society'. Of course, prewar and postwar conditions are different. In the postwar era, especially in the era of high economic growth, we cannot deny a certain degree of development of civil elements. But can we really say that the unprecedentedly high economic growth solved the question of civil society in Japan? Or was it through the very weakness of the civil or modern elements that she could develop so rapidly?

Uchida (1967) blames the weakness of the civil elements *vis-à-vis* the power of capital on the fact that people's lives and collective consciousness are still organized around the logic of capital; the latter is robust, in contrast to the weakness of human rights, as demonstrated in the problems of education or pollution. In the 1960s, he criticized the Japanese form of high economic growth by citing Hajime Kawakami's old comparison between Japan and Europe: 'In Europe, God created human rights, and afterwards man created the rights of the state. Conversely in Japan, God first created the rights of the state, and then the state created human rights' (Kawakami [1911] 1982, p. 119). In the Japanese way of economic development, only the powers of capital and the state manifested themselves, while human rights and civil society remained immature. This is just the reason why Japan has developed so rapidly.

His conception bears, beyond a mere criticism of Japan in the period of high growth, a critical perspective on Japan as an 'economic power', that is, of the post-1970s Japan in the vanguard of ultra-modernization, boasting the catchphrases 'information-oriented society' and 'high tech society'. In this way, Uchida's view of Japanese capitalism becomes crystallized into a proposition of the 'articulation of the pre-modern with the super-modern'. It means that 'something pre-modern that underlies the Japanese economy or society does not work in the direction to prevent Japan from developing, but to realize excessively high growth or to create the super-modern without the modern' (Uchida, 1981, p. 11). However paradoxical it may seem, says Uchida, Japanese capitalism develops through the weakness of civil society.

It is obvious that the question of a country's economic development must not be reduced to a mere realization of industrialization or a high growth rate. High economic growth may indeed resolve unemployment and material poverty. In Japan, however, growth was realized not by strengthening human rights and civil society, but by suppressing them. In this sense Japanese economic development goes together with a new discrimination and poverty. So Japan is never a model to be followed, for example, by other Asian countries.

UNIVERSALITIES AND PARTICULARITIES OF JAPANESE-STYLE CAPITALISM

With the outbreak of the first oil shock in 1973, Japanese high economic growth ended. Not only in Japan but in all the advanced countries, economic growth stopped; afterwards, all economic indices continued to worsen for a long time. Advanced countries were afflicted by stagnation, which brought on an era of long-term world depression. However Japan's economy, the most severely damaged by the oil price shock, recovered relatively quickly, contrary to most predictions. In fact Japan rapidly introduced microelectronic technologies, transformed her industrial structure, and above all benefited from the cooperation of the working class in this transformation. By the early 1980s, the Japanese economy was again relying on export demands as it developed into a global power. At the end of the decade, Japan experienced the speculation-driven 'bubble' economy, as well as its burst and a subsequent depression in the early 1990s.

In the post-oil shock period (1974–), the traditional theories of general crisis and SMC completely lost their validity and were abandoned by almost all the Marxian economists. Marxian political economy found itself marginalized within the economic world. On the other hand, however, new theorizations appeared which were not predetermined by the traditional views. In this period there were two major economic development issues to which economics was expected to provide answers: first, what were the causes and mechanisms of the long-term world depression; and second, stemming from the desire to understand the secrets of Japan's economic success, what were the universalities and particularities of the Japanese economic system?

Long-Term World Depression

The transformation from sustainable growth to long-term depression in the early 1970s was a great challenge to the entire economic world. How could one explain the change from growth to crisis, and show the way out of the depression? Makoto Itoh (1936–) wrestled squarely with the questions.

Itoh (1990) points out first of all four major factors or conditions for the sustained economic growth of the postwar capitalist world: the economic hegemony of the USA and her dollar expenditures, a long wave of technological innovation, relatively cheap primary products (especially crude oil) from Third World countries, and the availability of relatively cheap-wage workers. The background of the crisis since the 1970s lies, according to Itoh, in the fact that these conditions began to erode during the continuous process of high economic growth. In particular, this erosion 'simultaneously contained the more fundamental difficulty of overaccumulation of capital in relation to the inelastic supply of both the labouring population and primary products from Third World countries, so squeezing the rate of profit throughout the capitalist world' (Itoh, 1990, p. 45). That is to say, the cause of crisis lay in the fact that capital accumulation, which had greatly advanced in the advanced countries throughout the sustained growth period, became excessive with regard not only to the supply of domestic labour but also to that of primary products in the Third World. In brief, says Itoh, it is the over-accumulation of capital that constitutes the cause of the crisis. For Itoh, a successor to Uno Theory, this indicates the direct validity of Uno's crisis theory (excessive capital theory), which was proposed at the level of general principles, for explaining the current depression, which must be analysed in terms of real conditions. In other words, it means that the process generating the current world depression is very similar to those of classical crises in the nineteenth century.

It means further, for Itoh, that capitalism is now revealing its own difficulties at the level of general principles, or that capitalism today is, to a surprising degree, once again approaching the theoretical world of general principles. While Uno confirmed a historical reversal of the self-purifying tendency of capitalism at the end of the nineteenth century, Itoh verifies, at the end of the twentieth century, a new reversal of capitalist development over the century and a 'flowing backwards' of capitalism. It is typically manifested in three facts: a shift of capital investment from heavy and large-scale to lighter and smaller-scale industrial plant and equipment, a weakening of the roles of trade unions, and a reduction of the economic role of the state (critique to the theory of SMC). The current recomposition of Fordism into post-Fordism and the rise of neo-liberalism are rooted, says Itoh, in this flowing backwards of capitalism.

What about Japan? In this period one has heard all over the world a chorus of 'Learn from Japan'. But Japanese capitalism can not be a model for the workers in the world to study and follow. In fact though the Japanese trade surplus has increased enormously in the period after the oil shock, we have seen behind it a degradation of the workers' position: a stagnation of real wages, an escalation of precarious employment, increasingly severe conditions of labour, and so on. Japanese capitalism leads in this sense, argues Itoh, to a flowing backwards *à la* post-Fordism.

The Japanese-Style Economic System

In the post-oil shock period, there was a great deal of discussion about the 'Japanese-style economic system'. The main reason was the desire to elucidate the secrets of Japanese 'success' in the 1970s and 1980s. This was followed by a series of debates over issues like the closed nature of the

Japanese economy and its failure to observe rules, as reflected in trade friction and frequent corporate scandals, and doubts about the relevance of the postwar economic system in the midst of the long depression in the 1990s. Marxian political economy also began to move beyond its traditional focuses on capitalist or socialist systems, to devote more attention to comparative institutional analysis. Many hypotheses on Japanese capitalism were proposed. Among these the 'companyism' hypothesis of Hiroji Baba (1933–) stirred the greatest interest.

According to Baba (1991, 1997a, 1997b), we can enumerate as characteristics of Japanese companies: the weakness of stockholders' control, the small gaps between various classes and ranks in a company, the active participation of employees in their jobs, and the strong consciousness of employees of being members of their companies. Baba terms this company-centred attitude or consciousness 'companyism'. These facts themselves were already often pointed out in discussions of Japanese-style management; Baba's originality lies in reconsidering companyism from a historical point of view.

First, he argues, companyism was formed in the high-growth era, and strongly led the Japanese economy in the period after the oil shock, giving rise to the strong performance of the postwar Japanese economy.

Second, companyism is 'the most suitable organizational form that one can think of for elevating the productive forces'. 'Effective' companyism has helped make Japan the world's most productive country. Moreover, companyism, being 'the greatest mechanism for the development of productive forces', possesses a worldwide universality. While thus emphasizing the historical efficiency and universality of companyism, Baba also points out that its excessive elevation of productive forces has brought forth many negative phenomena.

Third, as a theorist of the Uno school, Baba aims at a critical reconstruction of Uno's stage theory. Reexamining Uno's definition of the stage of finance capital, Baba confirms in it a development from managerial capitalism *à l' américaine* (the postwar period) to companyism *à la japonaise* (the post-oil shock period). Companyism is not only an extreme form of finance capital, but also, says Baba, the participation of workers in management means that it is the most advanced capitalism, and a form going beyond managerial capitalism. And finally he finds in companyism 'a penetration of socialism into production centres' or 'a creeping socialism'.

In brief, Baba provides the historical context of companyism, acknowledging its efficiency, universality and advanced character, and furthermore finds in it 'socialist' elements. To be sure there exist in his discourses some exaggerations and errors. But his principal intention does not lie in boasting about efficiency, universality and the advanced character of Japanese capitalism. His true message is that it is very important for humankind to seriously consider what awaits us beyond the current 'economic development' under capitalism, a system able to engender even something as extreme as companyism. Baba shows this through a concept termed 'mass overenrichment' (Baba, 1986, 1997a, 1997b).

Evidence of overenrichment is not only evident in the fashionableness of dieting and jogging in advanced countries, but also suggested by the well-known calculation that the earth would at once become an unlivable planet if its entire population attained living standards or income levels equal to those of the advanced countries. The index of mass overenrichment is, according to Baba, $5000 (in 1982 dollars) in per capita GDP, corresponding to a living level shown by the popularity of cars, a declining increase in caloric intake, and 30 per cent of Engel's coefficient. The so-called advanced countries had already attained this level by 1970.

And the ultimate outcome of this capitalist development is the destruction of environments and communities. These two aspects of destruction imply of course a crisis of humankind's existence. And it is only and above all by reversing economic growth and reducing living standards in advanced countries that humankind will be able to escape the crisis. This means escape, argues Baba, from capitalism. Thus he gives a warning on capitalist 'economic development' by using his own concepts: companyism and mass overenrichment.

Baba's argument provoked a grand debate, and many of the criticisms made of him were quite emotional. Some rejected him on an emotional basis (Lie, 1987). But it must be admitted that his question is very suggestive, whether his answer is correct or not. First, he has questioned 'economic development' from a historical point of view. Is it not a task appropriate to Marxian economists like Baba to bring up questions with a long time-frame? Second, he has overturned almost all the debates and viewpoints of postwar Marxian economics: turning from the state to the company (critique of the SMC theory), from stagnation theory to growth theory (critique of general crisis theory), from pauperization theory to mass enrichment theory (critique of the theoretical model based in the nineteenth century), and from a theoretical approach to Japanese capitalism emphasizing its particularities and backwardness to an approach emphasizing its universalities and advanced character (critique of the Japanese Capitalism Debate). Whether or not they agree with Baba, Marxian political economists will have to seriously consider this change of economic perspective if the discipline is to remain relevant in the twenty-first century.

CONCLUDING REMARKS

We summarize here the outstanding features of Japanese Marxism as a whole with regard to postwar economic development in Japan.

1. In general there have existed, within postwar Japanese Marxian political economy, three schools: the orthodox school, the Uno school and the civil society school. While the Uno school is a descendant of the prewar *Rono-ha* school, the other two constitute two types of successors to the *Koza-ha* school. The differences between the two schools originate in their evaluations of the importance of civil and modern elements. Generally speaking, postwar Japanese Marxism has tended to decline in the long run, in particular because it has remained wedded to the theory of general crisis in the midst of the high growth era. One can properly say: 'While modern economics was shown to be in error by the end of high growth, Marxian political economy had already collapsed as a result of high growth itself' (Furihata, 1983, p. 6). So most of the Marxian economists fled from the analysis of actual economies, turning to textual critiques of Marxian manuscripts, the study of which expanded abnormally after the high growth era (Takasuka, 1985). Thus Japanese Marxian economics became autistic and fell into crisis. The crisis was further amplified by the successive collapses of the socialist countries from the end of the 1980s. But it is also true that, out of the crisis, we can observe the birth of a fruitful new approach making more flexible use of Marxian approaches.

2. In so far as economic development matters, the history of postwar Japanese Marxism has been one of conflict over the theory of SMC based on the general crisis theory, and at the same time one of a disengagement from it. As we saw above, the theory of SMC was proposed in the early postwar period, and followed by many Marxian economists in the high growth period. On the other hand, an effort to free themselves of it was started early on with the socialization version of the SMC theory, and in the period after the oil shock, almost all first-rate analyses in fact criticized SMC theory, which completely collapsed. This means that the Marxists began to accept the fact of the growth and development of the Japanese economy.

3. The issue to which Japanese Marxism has continuously adhered with regard to economic development is that of 'universalities and particularities of Japanese capitalism'. This also, of course, constituted the central issue of the Japanese Capitalism Debate in the interwar period. The *Koza-ha* school found in Japan a 'type' of the militarist imperialism based on the semi-feudalistic system of landholding, and emphasized its particularities and weakness as a form of capitalism. On the other hand, the *Rono-ha* school considered the so-called semi-feudalism as a backwardness generally seen in capitalist late developers; according to the *Rono-ha*, Japanese capitalism

would have to acquire the universalities of capitalism with its further development. The same confrontation continued for a long time in the postwar period as well. Both camps were agreed, however, on recognizing the backwardness (and specificities) of Japanese capitalism. After the 1970s, with the rise of Japan as an 'economic power', Marxists began to propose different arguments, and to emphasize the advanced character and the universality of Japan. This is a major change of position on the Japanese economic development for the Marxists.

4.   The other change of position on economic development is represented in a shift from theorizing about grand systems to theorizing about institutions. Until the 1970s, Marxian political economy often operated in the broad framework of system choice (capitalism or socialism); it has shifted gradually to a more elaborate framework centred on institutions and organizations. If we reflect from this point of view, it is easy to understand that 'institutions' are better studied in the framework of Marx's theory than in the neoclassical one which is fundamentally based upon market equilibrium theory (Yagi, 1993).

5.   Marxian political economic studies in postwar Japan have so often adhered to theoretical consistency, methodological strictness, and exegetic exactness that they have neglected the creative analysis of real economies and bold theoretical development. The *raison d'être* of Marxian political economy today has to consist, not in adherence to exegetic studies and so forth, but in explaining, from a long-term historical point of view, the objective outcomes of current economic development.

REFERENCES AND FURTHER READING

Albritton, Robert (1986), *A Japanese Reconstruction of Marxist Theory*, London: Macmillan.

Albritton, Robert (1991), *A Japanese Approach to Stages of Capitalist Development*, London: Macmillan; Japanese Translation by Kiyoshi Nagatani et al., *Shihon-shugi Hatten no Dankai-ron*, Tokyo: Shakai Hyoron-sha, 1995.

Baba, Hiroji (1986), *Huyuka to Kin'yu Shihon* (Mass Enrichment and Finance Capital), Kyoto: Mineruva Shobo.

Baba, Hiroji (1991), 'Gendai Sekai to Nihon Kaisha-shugi' (Contemporary World and Japanese Companyism), in Tokyo Daigaku Shakai-kagaku Kenkyujo (ed.), *Gendai Nihon Shakai* (Contemporary Japanese Society), vol. 1, Tokyo: Tokyo Daigaku Shuppan-kai, 29–83.

Baba, Hiroji (1997a), *Shin Shihon-shugi-ron* (A New Theory of Capitalism), Nagoya: Nagoya Daigaku Shuppan-kai.

Baba, Hiroji (1997b), 'Japanese Companyism and the End of Cold War', in Junji Banno (ed.), *The Political Economy of Japanese Society*, vol. 1: *The State or the Market?*, Oxford: Oxford University Press, 162–89.

Furihata, Setsuo (1983), *Kaitai-suru Uno Gakuha* (The Uno School in Collapse), Tokyo: Ronso-sha.

Ikeo, Aiko (1996), 'Marxist Economics in Japan', *The Kokugakuin University Economic Review*, **44**(3/4), 13–39.

Ikumi, Takuichi (ed.) (1958), *Kokka Dokusen Shihon-shugi* (State Monopoly Capitalism), Tokyo: Otsuki Shoten.

Inoue, Harumaru et al. (1953), 'Nochi Kaikaku to Han-hokensei' (Farmland Reform and Semi-feudalism), in Iwanami Shoten Publishers (eds), *Nihon Shihon-shugi Koza* (Symposium on the Japanese Capitalism), Tokyo: Iwanami Shoten, vol. 5, 1–116.

Inoue, Harumaru and Usami, Seijiro (1951), *Kiki niokeru Nihon Shihon-shugi no Kozo* (Structure of Japanese Capitalism in the Crisis), Tokyo: Iwanami Shoten.

Itoh, Makoto (1988), *The Basic Theory of Capitalism: The Forms and Substance of the Capitalist Economy*, London: Macmillan.

Itoh, Makoto (1990), *The World Economic Crisis and Japanese Capitalism*, London: Macmillan.

Kawakami, Hajime (1911), 'Nihon Dokutoku no Kokka-shugi' (An Etatism peculiar to Japan), *Chuo-Koron*, March; in *Kawakami Hajime Zenshu* (Completed Works of Hajime Kawakami), vol. 6, Tokyo: Iwanami Shoten, 1982.

Lie, John (1987), 'Reactionary Marxism: The End of Ideology in Japan?', *Monthly Review*, **38**(11), 45–51.

Mawatari, Shohken (1985), 'The Uno School: A Marxian Approach in Japan', *History of Political Economy*, **17**(3), 403–18.

Morris-Suzuki, Tessa (1989), *A History of Japanese Economic Thought*, London: Routledge; Japanese Translation by Takashi Fujii, *Nihon no Keizai Shiso*, Tokyo: Iwanami Shoten, 1991.

Otsuka, Hisao (1946), 'Kindaiteki Ningen-ruikei no Soshutsu' (Creation of Modernised Human Type), *Daigaku Shinbun* (University Journal), 11 April; in *Otsuka Hisao Chosaku-shu* (Collected Works of Hisao Otsuka: *CWHO*), vol. 8, Tokyo: Iwa nami Shoten, 1969.

Otsuka, Hisao (1951), *Kindai Shihon-shugi no Keifu* (Genealogy of Modern Capitalism), vol. 1, Tokyo: Kobundo; in *CWHO*, vol. 3, Tokyo: Iwanami Shoten, 1969.

Otsuka, Hisao (1964), 'The Market Structure of Rural Industry in the Early Stages of Capitalism', *Second International Conference of Economic History in Aix-en-Provence* 1962, 2, Paris.

Ouchi, Tsutomu (1962), *Nihon Keizai-ron* (On Japanese Economy), vol. 1, Tokyo: Tokyo Daigaku Shuppan-kai.

Ouchi, Tsutomu (1970), *Kokka Dokusen Shihon-shugi* (State Monopoly Capitalism), Tokyo: Tokyo Daigaku Shuppan-kai.

Sugihara, Kaoru (1992), 'The Japanese Capitalism Debate, 1927–1937', *Occasional Papers in Third World Economic History*, **4**, 24–33.

Takasuka, Yoshihiro (1985), *Marukusu Keizaigaku no Kaitai to Saisei* (Collapse and Renaissance of Marxian Economics), Tokyo: Ochanomizu Shobo.

Tamagaki, Yoshinori (1976), 'Kokka Dokusen Shihon-shugi-ron no Konponteki Hansei' (Fundamental Reflections on the Theory of State Monopoly Capitalism), *Gendai no Riron* (Contemporary Theories), **144**, 59–72.

Uchida, Yoshihiko (1967), *Nihon Shihon-shugi no Shiso-zo* (Japanese Capitalism reflected into the Social Thoughts), Tokyo: Iwanami Shoten; in *Uchida Yoshihiko Chosaku-shu* (Collected Works of Yoshihiko Uchida: *CWYU*), vol. 5, Tokyo: Iwanami Shoten, 1988.

Uchida, Yoshihiko (1981), *Sakuhin toshiteno Shakai-kagaku* (A Social Science for Common People), Tokyo: Iwanami Shoten; in *CWYU*, vol. 8, Tokyo: Iwanami Shoten, 1989.

Uno, Kozo (1946), 'Keizai Minshuka to Sangyo Shakaika' (Economic Democratization and Industrial Socialization), *Shinsei*, December; in *Uno Kozo Chosaku-shu* (Collected Works of Kozo Uno: *CWKU*), vol. 8, Tokyo: Iwanami Shoten, 1974.

Uno, Kozo (1950–52), *Keizai Genron* (Principles of Political Economy) 2 vols, Tokyo: Iwanami Shoten; in *CWKU*, vol. 1, Tokyo: Iwanami Shoten, 1973.

Uno, Kozo (1962), *Keizaigaku Hoho-ron* (Methodology of Political Economy), Tokyo: Tokyo Daigaku Shuppan-kai; in *CWKU*, vol. 9, Tokyo: Iwanami Shoten, 1974.

Uno, Kozo (1980), *Principles of Political Economy: Theory of a Purely Capitalist Society*, translated by Thomas T. Sekine, Sussex: Harvester Press & New Jersey: Humanities Press.

Yagi, Kiichiro (1993), 'Seido no Keizaigaku toshiteno Marukusu Keizaigaku' (Marxian Economics seen as an Economics of Institution), *Keizai Riron Gakkai Nenpo* (The Bulletin of Japan Society of Political Economy), **30**, 189–208.

Yamada, Toshio (1987), 'Les tendances du marxisme japonais contemporain', *Actuel Marx*, **2**, 34–44.

Zieschang, Kurt (1957), 'Zu einigen theoretischen Problemen des staatmonopolistischen Kapitalismus im West Deutschland', *Jahrbuch des Instituts für Wirtschaftwissenschaften*, **1**.

General bibliography

This general bibliography was prepared by Shiro Sugihara with the cooperation of the contributors, especially Aiko Ikeo. It is limited to the basic literature and is a complement to the chapter references and further reading suggestions. Most of the publications included are books, but there also are a few articles.

I GENERAL

Borton, Hugh (1961), 'Modern Japanese Economic Historian', in W.G. Beasley and E.G. Pulleybank (eds), *Historians of China and Japan*, London: Oxford University Press.

Chou, Yukio and Sumiya, Kazuhiko (eds) (1969–1971), *Kindai Nihon Keizai Shisoshi* (History of Economic Thought in Modern Japan), vols 1 and 2, Tokyo: Yuhikaku.

Honjo, Eijiro (1946), *Nihon Keizai Shisoshi Gaisetsu* (An Outline of Economic Thought in Japan), Tokyo: Yuhikaku.

Honjo, Eijiro (1957), 'The Development of Economics in Japan', *Bulletin of University of Osaka Prefecture*, Series D, vol. 1, 1–14.

Keizai Gakushi Gakkai (The Society for the History of Economic Thought, Japan) (ed.) (1984), *Nihon no Keizaigaku: Nihonjin no Keizaiteki Shii no Kiseki* (Economics in Japan: The Track of the Economic Thinking of the Japanese), Tokyo: Toyo Keizai Shinpo-sha.

Nomura, Kanetaro (1939), *Gaikan Nihon Keizai Shisoshi* (A Historical Survey of Economic Thought in Japan), Tokyo: Keio Shuppan-sha.

Sugihara, Shiro and Yukio Chou (eds) (1979), *Nihon Keizai Shisoshi Tokuhon* (Readings in History of Economic Thought in Japan), Tokyo: Toyo Keizai Shinpo-sha.

Sugihara, Shiro (1984), *Nihon no Ekonomisuto* (Economists in Japan), Tokyo: Nihon Hyoron-sha.

Sugihara, Shiro (1990), *Nihon no Keizai Shisoka-tachi* (History of Economic Thought in Japan: Men and Times of Theirs), Tokyo: Nihon Keizai Hyoron-sha.

Sugihara, Shiro et al. (eds) (1990), *Nihon no Keizai Shiso 400-nen* (Economic Though in Japan, 1600–1990), Tokyo: Nihon Keizai Hyoron-sha.

II   THE TOKUGAWA ERA

Honjo, Eijiro (1935), *Economic Thought and History of Japan in the Tokugawa Period*, Koyoto: Institute for Research in Economic History of Japan, new edn (1965), New York: Russell and Russell.
Honjo, Eijiro (1963), 'The Anti-Feudalistic Thought in Tokugawa Period', *Bulletin of University of Osaka Prefecture*, Series D, vol. vii, 1–13.
Najita, Tetsuo and Scheiner, Irwin (eds) (1978), *Japanese Thought in the Tokugawa Period, 1600–1868: Methods and Metaphors*, Chicago and London: University of Chicago Press.
Nishikawa, Shunsaku (1979), *Edojidai no Poritikaru Ekonomi* (Political Economy in the Edo Era), Tokyo: Nihon Hyoron-sha.
Nomura, Kanetaro (1935), *Nihon Keizai Gakusetsusi Shiryo* (Materials for History of Economic Doctrine in Japan: the Tokugawa Era), Tokyo: Keio Gijuku Shuppan-kyoku.

III   THE MEIJI ERA

Hori, Tsuneo (1935), 'Liberalist and Protectionist Controversies in the Early Meiji Era', *Journal of the Osaka University of Commerce*, no. iii, December, 1–46.
Hori, Tsuneo (1935), *Meiji Keizai Shisoshi* (History of Economic Thought in the Meiji Era), enlarged edn (1975), Tokyo: Meiji Bunken, and reprinted and enlarged edn by Toshihiro Tanaka (1991), Tokyo: Nihon Keizai Hyoron-sha.
Honjo, Eijiro (1962), 'Introduction of Western Economics into Japan', *Bulletin of University of Osaka Prefecture*, series D, vol. vi, 1–19.
Kosaka, Masaaki (ed.) (1958), *Japanese Thought in the Meiji Era*, Tokyo: Pan-Pacific Press.
Nishizawa, Tamotsu (1996), 'Business Studies and Management Education in Japan's Economic Development: An International Perspective', in Rolve Petter Amdam (ed.), *Management, Education and Competitiveness: Europe, Japan and the United States*, London and New York: Routledge, 96–110.
Sugiyama, Chuhei and Mizuta, Hiroshi (eds) (1988), *Enlightenment and Beyond: Political Economy Comes to Japan*, Tokyo: University of Tokyo Press.

IV THE TAISHO ERA

Garon, Sheldon (1987), *The State and Labor in Modern Japan*, Berkeley: University of California Press.

Hitotsubashi Daigaku Gakuenshi Hensan linkai (ed.) (1985), *Hitotsubashi no Gakufu to sono Keihu* (The School Tradition of Hitotsubashi University and its Academic Genealogy), no. I (Economics), Tokyo: Hitotsubashi Daigaku Gakuenshi Hensan linkai.

Kawada, Minoru (1993), *The Origin of Ethnography in Japan: Yanagita Kunio and His Times*, Kegan Paul International.

V THE SHOWA ERA

Masamura, Kimihiro and Hayasaka, Tadashi (1974), *Sengo Nihon no Keizaigaku* (Economics in Post-War Japan), Tokyo: Nihon Keizai Shimbunsha.

Tsuru, Shigeto (1964), 'Survey of Economic Research in Post-War Japan', *American Economic Review*, **54**(4), part 2, supplement, 79–101.

Tsuru, Shigeto (1984), 'A Survey of Economic Research in Japan, 1960–1983', *Keizai Kenkyu* (The Economic Review), Hitotsubashi University, **35**(4), October, 289–306.

Union of the National Economic Association in Japan (ed.) (1977), *Bibliography of Japanese Publications on Economics*, 1946–1975, Tokyo: University of Tokyo Press.

Yasuba, Yasukichi (1972–73), 'Modern Economist's views on the Japanese Economy: A Survey', *Japanese Economic Studies*, **1**(2), winter, 3–46.

Yamanouchi, Yasushi (1979), 'Japan', in George G. Oggers and Harrold T. Parker (eds), *International Handbook of Historical Studies, Contemporary Research and Theory*, Westport: Greenwood Press, 253–76.

Name index

Abe, Isoo xvi, 47, 54
Akamatsu, Kaname xxi, 134–7, 141
Amano, Tameyuki 45, 63
Arahata, Kanson 80
Arisawa, Hiromi xx–xxi, 139–41
Aristotle 71
Aso, Hisashi 52

Baba, Hiroji xxii, 165–6
Bastiat, C.F. 32
Böhm-Bawerk, E. 66, 102, 107, 118
Brentano, L. 52, 54, 60–61, 64–5
Bright, J. 32
Bronfenbrenner, M. 99, 143–4
Bücher, K. 60
Buckle, H.T. 23, 32, 34, 41

Cannan, E. 70–71
Carey, H.C. 45
Cassel, G. 99, 101, 106
Chu Hsi 2, 4–5, 7–9, 14–15, 18, 33, 37
Clark, J.B. 61, 101
Cobden, R. 32
Colm, G. 133
Confucius 26, 41
Cournot, A.A. 65
Cunynghame, H.H. 99

Dazai, Shundai 7
Dobb, M.H. xx, 153
Dodge, J.M. 147

Edgeworth, F.Y. 70, 99

Fawcett, M.G. xiv, xxiv
Fenollosa, E.F. xxiv, 44–5
Fetter, F.A. 61
Fisher, I. 61, 70
Fujii, Shigeru 142
Fukuda, Tokuzo xvi–xix, xxiv–xxv, 49–
50, 52, 54–8, 60–66, 70–74, 118,
134–5, 137
Fukuzawa, Yukichi xiv–xv, xxiii, 2, 4,
23–32, 34, 37, 39–40, 45

Gompers, S xxiv
Gossen, H.H. 65
Gottle-Ottlilienfeld, F. 119
Guizot, F.P.G. 23

Hani, Goro 80, 95
Hasegawa, Nyozekan 86, 94
Hattori, Shiso 80, 86, 91
Hegel, G.W. 119–20, 135
Hicks, J.R. 139
Hirano, Yoshitaro 80, 87, 91
Hirata, Atsutane 12
Hobbes, T. 119–20, 127
Hobson, J.A. 70–71
Honda, Toshiaki 10–13
Honjo, Eijiro xxiv, 56

Ihara, Saikaku 5
Ikumi, Takuichi 159
Inomata, Tsunao 80–81, 83, 90–91
Inoue, Harumaru 154–5
Inukai, Tsuyoshi xv, 36
Ishida, Baigan 13, 19
Ito, Jinsai 13–14, 18–19
Itoh, Makoto xxii, 163–4

Jevons, W.S. xiv, xxv, 65
Johnson, C. 143

Kaiho, Seiryo 7–9
Kaldor, N. 107
Kanai, Noburu xv–xvi, 44–5, 47–50, 52,
54, 63, 65
Katayama, Sen 47, 54
Kawai, Eijiro xviii

Kawakami, Hajime xvi–xix, xxiii–xxv, 49, 52, 55–7, 60–64, 66–70, 74–5, 79, 98, 105, 162
Kawashima, Takeyoshi 94
Kazahaya, Yasoji 93, 125
Keynes, J.M. 98, 104–5, 112, 119, 123–4, 137
Kimura, Takeyasu 101, 103
Kinoshita, Naoe 61
Kitamura, Hiroshi 136–7
Koizumi, Shinzo xix, xxv
Kojima, Kiyoshi 136–7
Komiya, Ryutaro 148
Kotoku, Shusui 47, 66
Kushida, Tamizo xviii, xxv, 67, 79, 83–4
Kuwata, Kumazo xvi, 47, 49–51, 63

Lange, O. xx, 106
Lederer, E. 141
Leibenstein, H. 99
List, F. xxiv, 47, 94, 118–9, 122, 136
Locke, J. 120

Macleod, H.D. xxiv, 32, 38
Malthus, T.R. 11, 139
Mandeville, B. 69–70
Marshall, A. xiii–xiv, xxv, 61, 65–6, 70, 72, 99–100
Maruyama, Masao 41, 94
Marx, K. xxi, xxv, 66, 69–72, 74, 87–8, 93–4, 98, 101, 106–7, 117–18, 123–4, 127–8, 133, 155 , 157, 168
Matsuzaki, Kuranosuke xv, 68
Mill, J.S. xiv, xviii, xxiii, xxv, 23, 45, 69, 100
Miura, Baien xvii, 7, 16, 19
Miyamoto, Kenichi xxii
Miyazaki, Isamu 148
Miyazaki, Yasusada 5
Morishima, Michio 97, 107, 111
Morita, Yuzo 140
Morito, Tatsuo xvi
Morris-Suzuki, T. xxiv–xxv, 48
Motoori, Norinaga 16–19

Nakayama, Ichiro xix–xxi, xxv, 101, 137–41, 145
Ninomiya, Sontoku 13
Nitta, Masanori 112
Noritake, Kotaro 63

Noro, Eitaro xix, 80–88, 90–92, 94

Ogyu, Sorai 5–9, 11, 15–16, 18
Ohkawa, Kazushi 146
Okada, Soji 90
Okishio, Nobuo 97, 107, 113
Okita, Saburo 144–6
Okouchi, Kazuo 93, 117–18, 121–6
Onozuka, Kiheiji 50
Oshima, Sadamasu xv, xxiv, 47–8
Otsuka, Hisao 94, 155–8
Otsuka, Kinnosuke xix, xxv, 66, 118
Ouchi, Hyoe 54–5, 67, 86, 91
Ouchi, Tsutomu 160
Oyama, Ikuo 79
Oyama, Kosuke 147

Pareto, V.F.D. 70, 103
Penrose, E.F. 135
Perry, A.L. 32
Pigou, A.C. 61, 70
Pyle, K.B. 48

Rae, J. 99
Ricardo, D. xxiv–xxv, 107–8
Roscher, W.G.F. xiv
Rousseau, J.J. 94, 127

Sakai, Toshihiko 62, 66, 74, 80
Sakisaka, Itsuro 80, 90–91
Samuelson, P. 139
Sato, Issai 32
Sato, Nobuhiro xvii, xxiv, 10–13, 18
Schmoller, G. xxiv, 44
Schumpeter, E.B. 140
Schumpeter, J.A. 98, 101, 118–19, 137–8
Seligman, E.R.A. 61
Shibata, Kei xix–xx, xxv, 97–8, 101, 105–8, 111–13
Shibusawa, Eiichi xvi, xxiv, 50
Shimomura, Osamu xxi, 144–5
Shinohara, Miyohei xxi, 142–3
Smiles, S. 23
Smith, A. xviii, xx–xxi, xxiii–xxv, 32–3, 68–70, 72, 94, 99, 117–19, 121–8, 139, 155
Soeda, Juichi xiii–xvii, xxiv, 50–51
Sombart, W. 119
Spencer, H. 23, 32, 34, 37, 41

Stackelberg, H. 106
Stigler, G.J. 107
Sugihara, Shiro 75
Sugiyama, Chuhei 41
Sumiya, Etsuji 48, 55
Sweezy, P.M. 153

Taguchi, Ukichi xiv–xvi, xxi, xxiv, 23–
    4, 28, 32–41, 45, 48
Tajima, Kinji 50
Tajiri, Inejiro xiii, xxiv
Takabatake, Motoyuki 58, 66, 95
Takahashi, Kamekichi xix, xxv, 81
Takano, Fusataro xxiv
Takano, Iwasaburo xvi–xviii, xxiv–xxv,
    49–51, 54–8
Takashima, Zenya 117–21, 125–7
Takata, Yasuma xix, xxv, 97–107, 113
Takimoto, Seiichi 56
Tamanoi, Yoshiro xxii
Tanaka, Kyugu 14–15, 19
Tanuma, Okitsugu 8
Tinbergen, J. 133
Tobata, Seiichi 137, 140
Tsuchiya, Takao 56, 80, 86, 91, 94
Tsuru, Shigeto xxii, 139–40
Tugan-Baranovsky, M. 100, 108

Uchida, Ginzo xxiv, 55–7
Uchida, Yoshihiko 94, 117–18, 123–8,
    161–2
Uchimura, Kanzo 61
Uno, Kozo xxii, 156–8, 160–61, 164–5,
    167
Usami, Seijiro 154
Uzawa, Hirobumi xxii

Wadagaki, Kenzo xvi, xxiv, 45
Wagner, A. 44, 54, 66
Walker, F.A. xiv, xxiv
Walras, L. 65, 70, 101, 110, 113, 137
Wayland, F. 29
Weber.M. 94, 118–19, 155
Wicksell, J.G.K. 101–2, 107, 113
Withers, H. 67

Yamada, Katsujiro 86
Yamada, Moritaro 80, 87–91, 93–4
Yamagata, Banto 7, 9–10, 18
Yamakawa, Hitoshi 66, 80
Yamazawa, Ippei 134
Yanagita, Kunio 3, 54–8
Yasui, Takuma 111
Yokoi, Tokiyoshi 63
Yoshino, Sakuzo xxv, 61

Subject index

Absolute monarchy 88, 120, 125–8
Adam Smith problem 122
Adamu Sumisu no Kai (Adam Smith Society) xxv
anarcho-syndicalism xviii
Austrian School xxiv

Binbo Monogatari (A Tale of Poverty) xxv, 62, 67–9, 79
Bolshevik revolution xii, xvi–xviii
Britain xv, xvii, 25, 30–32, 39–40, 44–5, 49, 73, 75, 119–20, 124–6, 135–6, 156
British Economic Association xiii

cameralist xiv
catching-up product cycle theory of development 134
China xii, xvii, 4, 6, 13, 27, 29, 36, 39, 46, 78, 90, 118, 133, 138, 140–41
Christianity 12, 28, 61, 71
civil society xxi–xxii, 117–23, 126, 128, 161–2
  school 167
class struggle 53, 67, 73–4
classical school 23, 45, 47–9, 53
Club of Rome xxii–xxiii
Comintern xviii, 80, 84, 86, 92
  see also Third International
commercial society 5, 121, 124
Committee to Study Basic Issues in Economic Planning 146
companyism 165–6
comparative technical progress criterion 142–3
Confucianism 1–2, 5–6, 8, 15, 17, 19–20, 23–4, 26, 33, 37, 46
Constitution (1889) xii–xiii, 45, 53–4
crisis theory 159–60, 164, 166–7
  see also general crisis of capitalism

democratic revolution 80, 86, 90, 95, 125–6, 128
democratization xii, xxii, 126, 157,
Dodge Line (1949) 138
domestic market 13, 63, 82, 86, 89, 118, 123–4, 126–8, 132, 155–6, 161
Dutch learning 2, 9, 11–12
dynamic comparative advantage 136

Economic Council 131, 143, 145–6
economic growth xiii, xxi–xxii, 131, 133–4, 144, 146–8, 153, 158–63, 166
economic interpretation of history 61
Economic Journal xiii, xxvi
economic law 29, 39, 91, 157
economic man 65, 69, 74, 123
Economic Planning Agency (EPA) 143–5
economic reconstruction 153, 156
economic sociology 118–19, 126–7
Economic Stabilization Board 143
Emperor system 80, 82, 85–6
entrepreneur 40, 50, 103, 109–11, 123, 137, 144
entrepreneurship 132, 134
equilibrium 15–16, 19, 36, 41, 72–3

Fabian socialism xviii
Factory Law (Legislation) xvi–xvii, 37, 49–52, 54, 57, 64
feudalism 23–5, 78, 83, 88–92, 120, 125–8
  semi- 167
flying-geese-pattern theory of development 134
foreign trade 11–13, 31–2, 35, 40, 124, 134, 138
free competition 23, 30, 53, 65, 72, 123, 132

free trade xiv–xv, xxi, 15, 23, 30–31, 33–9, 41, 136
free trader xiv–xv, 39, 63

general crisis of capitalism 159
  see also crisis theory
general equilibrium theory xix, xxv–xxvi, 97–101, 103, 105–8, 137
German historical school xv, 38, 61, 74, 119, 122, 155
German social policy school xv, 44–7, 52, 57
  see also social policy
German Studies Association xv
Great Depression xii, 132, 154

harmony 19, 50, 53–4, 146–7
Hecksher–Ohlin trade model 135
historical materialism 160
Hitotsubashi University 60, 98, 134
  see also Tokyo Higher Commercial School; Tokyo University of Commerce
human nature 14, 17, 34–5, 38, 40

imperialism 28, 55, 78, 81, 83, 85, 88–9, 91–2, 94, 127, 154, 157, 167
Income Doubling Plan (1960) 131, 144–5, 148
India 13, 27, 30–31, 90
industrial policy 124, 141, 143–4
  see also Japanese-type industrial policy
industrialization xv, xxii, 1–2, 45–6, 55, 57, 78, 93, 132, 139, 162
Industry and Labour Research Institute xix
Institute of Japanese Economic History xxiv
international division of labour 35, 136, 139
international trade 30, 47, 132, 134, 137–42
invisible hand 123, 128
irreplaceable resources 98, 112

Japanese Association for the Study of Social Policy xiv–xviii, xxiv, 44, 49, 52–4, 64, 57
  see also Japanese social policy school

Japanese capitalism xix, xxi, 78, 80–86, 88–95, 117–18, 120–23, 126, 133, 154–5, 157–8, 161–2, 164–8
  backwardness of 160–61, 166–8
  debate on xix, 78, 81, 86–7, 92, 95, 152–3, 156, 161, 166–7
Japanese civilization 25, 34
Japanese Communist Party xviii, 62, 79–80, 84, 86, 95, 152
Japanese Development Bank (JDB) 143–4
Japanese Economic Policy Association (JEPA) 137, 141–2
Japanese historical school 55–6
Japanese miracle xii
Japanese social policy school 37, 44, 48, 55
  see also Japanese Association for the Study of Social Policy
Japanese-style economic system 164
Japanese-type industrial policy 142
  see also industrial policy

Kaitokudo 9
(*Das*) *Kapital* xix, xxii, xxv, 66, 68, 87–8, 124, 157–8
Keio Gijuku (school) 29, 41, 65
Keio University xvii, 45, 56
Keizaigaku Kyokai (Economic Society) 33
Keynesian economics xxi, 112, 145
Kokka Gakkai (National Studies Association) xv
Kokka Keizaikai (National Economy Society) xv
Korea xvii, 13, 29, 39, 90, 141
Korean War (1950–52) 141, 153
Koza-ha (school/faction) xix, xxi–xxii, 78, 80–81, 83–7, 90–95, 117–18, 120–21, 123, 125, 154–6, 158, 161, 167
Kyochokai (Society for Harmony and Cooperation) xvi
Kyoto (Imperial) University xviii–xix, xxiv–xxv, 49–50, 55–6, 60–62, 66, 97–9, 105, 115, 133
Kyoto University Economic Review xix, 105

labour dispute xvi–xvii

labour movement xxiv, 47, 55, 121, 133, 152
labour problems 46–9, 51, 53, 56, 78
laissez-faire xvi, 23–4, 28, 32–3, 37, 39, 41, 47–9, 53
land reform 125, 153–5
landowner 15–16, 63, 78, 80–82, 84, 86, 90–91, 94, 125
  –tenant disputes 63
  –tenant relationship 17
landownership 80, 83–4, 88–90, 92–3
Lectures on the History of the Development of Japanese Capitalism xix, xxv, 80, 84, 95
li 4–5, 7, 9–10, 25, 30, 37
  dai- 37, 39
Liberal Democratic Party (LDP) 144–5
liberalism xvii, xxiii, 32, 40, 64, 78–9, 164

Manchester school 32
market economy xiii, xxv, 9–10, 46, 67, 134
market mechanism 29–30, 132, 134, 141, 147
Marxian economics (political economy) xix–xxii, xxv, 48, 62, 66–7, 70, 97–8, 105, 119, 134, 152–4, 157–8, 161–3, 165–8
Marxism xii, xvii–xviii, xxi, xxiv, 55–8, 61–2, 65–6, 69–70, 74, 79–80, 86, 92, 95, 117–18, 120–21, 128, 152–6, 159, 167
  Euro- xxii
  Russian 79
Meiji Restoration xi–xiv, xix, 1, 27, 44–6, 49, 81–2, 84, 86, 89, 92
mercantilism 8, 41, 123, 125–8
mercantilist xiv, 123, 127
Mid-Term Economic Plan (1965) 145
Ministry of International Trade and Industry (MITI) 142–4

national independence 23–5, 27, 32
national learning 2, 12, 16, 18
nationalism xv, 35, 40, 78
natural law 4, 7, 9, 24, 29, 33, 37, 39
natural order 6–7, 25
natural way of administration 12

neo-classical economics (school) xxi, 48, 52, 55, 57, 145, 152
New Left xxii
New Long-Term Economic Plan (1957) 144–5
Nine-Part Directive on Stabilization (1948) 138, 140, 142

Occupation Force 133, 138, 142, 153, 155
Ohara Institute for Social Research xvi, xviii–xix, 56
oil shock 153, 163–5, 167
Otsuka historiography 155, 157–8, 161

Peace Preservation Law (1925) xxiv, 124
physiocrat xiv
physiocratic view 9
Plan for Economic Self-Support (1955) 133, 144
poverty xxv, 11, 13, 44, 46, 57, 62, 67–8, 82, 152, 162
power theory 98, 101, 103–4
pro-trade and/versus pro-development strategy 131, 137
productive forces 117–20, 122–5, 155–6, 160–61, 165
  mobilization of xxi
  national 119
  socialization of 159
  theory of 117, 122, 125
protectionism xiv, 31, 36, 63
protectionist xiv–xv, 33, 63, 136
public utility 127–8
pure capitalism 157–8

quantity theory of money 16, 100

Reimei-kai 61
rice problem 62
Rice Riot (1918) 67, 78
Rono-ha (school/faction) xix, xxi–xxii, 80–81, 83–4, 86–7, 90–95, 156, 158, 167
Russian menace 11
Russo–Japanese War (1904–5) xvii, 24, 46–7, 62, 78, 89

San Francisco Peace Treaty (1951) 141, 143
self-interest 29–30, 34, 38, 41, 53, 64, 69, 123
self-love 122–4
Shakai Mondai Kenkyu (Studies on Social Problems) 62, 69
Shakai Seisaku Jiho (Journal of Social Policy) xvi
Sino–Japanese War (1894–95) xiv, xvii, 24, 29, 39–41, 46, 49, 78, 89, 138
Six Classics 5–7, 16
Social Democratic Party 47
social policy xvi, 48–9, 51–5, 57, 64, 66, 68, 69, 73, 93, 121–3
see also Japanese social policy school
social power 98–104, 107
social problems xv, 46, 48–9, 51–2, 54, 57–8, 67, 69, 74, 122
socialism xvi, xviii, xxii–xxiii, xxv, 47, 52–5, 57, 61, 68, 83, 92–5, 128, 133, 154–5, 157, 165, 168
socialist revolution 80, 90, 128, 133, 155
Sodomei 62
Sorai school 7, 9, 11, 16
stage theory 157–8, 165
state monopoly capitalism (SMC) xxi, 154–5, 159–64, 166–7
state socialism xviii
state socialist xiv, xx
stationary state xviii, xxiii, 101, 106, 111
non- 97

Taisho Democracy xii, xvii–xviii, xxiii, 54, 61–2, 78
Taylor system 136
tenant farmer xix, 51, 82, 89, 91, 155
Tenmei famine 11

Third International xii
see also Comintern
third school of economics 32, 38, 41
Tokai Keizai Shinpo (Tokai New Economic Review) 36
Tokugawa period xiii, xv, 1–5, 7, 10, 13, 17–20
Tokugawa shogunate xi, 32, 41, 84
Tokyo Higher Commercial School xvii, 60, 98, 134
see also Hitotsubashi University; Tokyo University of Commerce
Tokyo Keizai Zasshi (Tokyo Economist) 24, 33, 36, 45
Tokyo (Imperial) University xvii, 44–5, 49–50, 55–8, 60–61, 78, 87, 133
Tokyo University of Commerce xvii, 49, 118, 137
see also Tokyo Higher Commercial School; Hitotsubashi University
transformation problem 106
two-stage revolution 80, 91–2, 95

unemployment 73, 98, 100, 103–4, 112, 139, 141, 162
Uno Theory 156–8, 161, 164
utilitarian economics 103–4
utilitarianism xxiii, 68

Walras's law 110
Waseda University xxv, 45, 55
Wealth of Nations xx, 33, 68, 115, 119, 121, 123
welfare economics 61, 66, 70–74
Western civilization 23–7, 30, 32, 35, Wicksell's missing equation 101
World War I xxiv–xxv, 55, 58, 61, 67, 78, 82, 90, 121
World War II xii–xiii, xvii, xx, 117, 128, 131–3, 135, 140–41, 152